# THE
# CHINA
# DREAM

# THE
# CHINA
# DREAM

## GREAT POWER THINKING & STRATEGIC
## POSTURE IN THE POST-AMERICAN ERA

## LIU MINGFU
### FOREWORD BY LIU YAZHOU

BEIJING MEDIATIME BOOKS CO., LTD.
CN Times Books, Inc.
501 Fifth Avenue
New York, NY 10017
www.cntimesbooks.com

ORDERING INFORMATION: Quantity sales. Special discounts are available on quantity purchases by corporations, associations, and others. For details, contact the publisher at the address above. Orders by U.S. trade bookstores and wholesalers. Please contact Ingram Publisher Services: Tel: (866) 400-5351; Fax: (800) 838-1149; or customer.service@ingrampublisherservices.com.

COPYEDITED by Jon Gartner and Dix!
DESIGN AND COMPOSITION by Heather McAdams

ISBN 978-162774-140-8

Printed in the United States of America

# CONTENTS

# FOREWORD

# THE DUEL OF THE 21ST CENTURY

# BY LIU YAZHOU

One of President Obama's most important advisors on China, the famous "China hand" David Lampton, once asserted that China and the United States of America are involuntarily engaged in a "double gamble" with history. While the United States seeks to maintain its political and economic status, China will rise to challenge the United States as another leading world power in the 21st century. China is required to bet that America will provide support and cooperation during its rise. America is required to bet that the rise of a strong China in the decades to come will provide America a strong, active partner with which it can shares its responsibilities in the international arena and which doesn't threaten its interests. Lampton has asserted that China and America have laid their bets, and that the stakes, at present, are rational. But when you bet, you run the risk of losing. The deciding factors will be the effort and insight of these two countries' politicians and citizens.

In my opinion, the Sino-American competition in the 21st century seems more a game than gamble. Whoever can create more appealing fruits of development, and whoever becomes stronger faster, will win the influence necessary to lead and direct the progress of the world.

Whether game or gamble, the competition between China and the United States in the 21st century represents a new era in human history. America—tough but young—and

China —a strong and ancient nation—separated by the vast distance of the Pacific Ocean, are playing the largest game of global power in human history. If this is a gamble, these are two grand gamblers; if this is a game, these are two immensely powerful players. With their dominant roles on the Asian and North American continents, these two nations occupy leading roles on the 21st century's global stage, and their competition will be a power game unlike any the world has ever seen. No matter the outcome, both countries will develop and progress in the struggle, human society will find new motivation and vigor, and the face and shape of the world as we know it will be irrevocably changed.

While America and China are indeed competitors, they are far from enemies or antagonists. China's dream is not America's nightmare. The *National Journal* wrote in their article "After America: Chinese Century," published on June 3, 2009: "Does a Chinese Century mean doom and gloom for America? This is a widespread anxiety among Americans, but the case can be made that a Chinese ascension could be a useful spur to America. If America were to wake up one day and find that it was no longer number one, that the Chinese were now on top, then Americans might finally feel compelled to undertake the necessary changes that the country has so long resisted . . . [T]here is nothing in the logic of China being the number-one economy that suggests that the American economy cannot continue to grow at a healthy pace, too."[1] Sino-American competition will be the defining game of the century, and for both sides, the process will be magnificent, the outcomes brilliant, and the effects lasting and far-reaching. China and America are playing to win the lead of the 21st century. The outcome will certainly set the world down a path to a new age.

# CHAPTER 1

# CHINA'S DREAM FOR A CENTURY

It has been China's dream for a century to become the world's leading nation. It's a dream that combines the ideals of three of China's greatest leaders: Sun Yat-sen, the architect of China's republican revolution, Mao Zedong, the founder of the New China, and Deng Xiaoping, the designer of the Reform and Opening Up of China. The commonality of their struggles is that each aimed to build the Chinese nation into the world's leading nation.

But what does it mean for China to become the world's leading nation? First, it means that China's economy will lead the world. On that basis, it will make China the strongest country in the world. As China rises to the status of a great power in the 21st century, its aim is nothing less than the top—to be the leader of the modern global economy.

## I. China Strives to Be the World's Most Prosperous Nation

Sun Yat-sen lived in an era when China was one of the weakest nations in the world. He demanded that China become a nation of "determined gentlemen," determined to ensure that China become the world's most prosperous nation, a call he issued to each of China's 400 million citizens. His pioneering spirit inspires and surprises Chinese people even today.

## Rebuilding China

Sun Yat-sen's ideal for China was to do more than just keep pace with the United States and United Kingdom; he challenged China to surpass them. In 1894, in his petition to Qing viceroy Li Hongzhi, he put forward his national reform agenda. He called for China to become a nation where the people's talents are put to best use, where land is put to best use, where material assets are put to best use, and where goods can be easily distributed to where they are needed most. He thought these were the most important tenets on a path to prosperity; these were the most important tools with which to heal the country. With these four elements in place, China would outpace and exceed Europe. Sun Yat-sen repeatedly stated that by implementing the *Three Principles of the People*, China would create a nation that could race past Europe and America to become the world's most prosperous country.

Turning China into a country of the "Six Utmosts" and "Four Mosts" was the goal he spent his life fighting for. The "Four Mosts" included the most strength, the most wealth, the most uncorrupt and just government, and the happiest citizens in the world. The "Six Utmosts" included the utmost size, the utmost excellence, the utmost progress, the utmost dignity, the utmost wealth, and the utmost security and happiness. To Sun Yat-sen, China was a nation where these two groups of superlatives would one day become a reality.

Ensuring that mankind's most glorious feats would be the achievements of the Chinese people was Sun Yat-sen's most important mission in life. He also said that advocating peace and harmony while ensuring the greatest possible happiness for everyone on earth was up to China to guarantee. This meant more to him than simply looking out for the interests of one people or one nation; it meant supporting the needs of humanity.

In 1895, after the failure of the First Guangdong Uprising and his escape abroad, Sun Yat-sen traveled extensively, learning about the advantages and disadvantages of the world's political systems and the strengths and weaknesses of the world's countries while he laid the groundwork for a revolution. By the time of the Wuchang uprising, he had traveled around the world seven times, roughly once every two years. He lived for fifty-eight years and eight months, of which over a decade was spent in Europe and America. His belief that China could become the most prosperous nation on earth was founded on a rich reservoir of experience with the world at large.

## The Finest People on Earth

In *The Three Principles of the People*, Sun Yat-sen said that the people of China are the most ancient people, the most numerous people on earth, the most civilized, and the most harmonious. They have existed for at least 5,000–6,000 years and outnumber all other populations. Through the generations the Chinese people have persisted and continue to be the finest people on earth.

Owing to the fact that Chinese students almost always outperformed US students at American schools, he once said that China's youth should have the humility to learn from America, and the determination, courage, and confidence to surpass America. On December 21, 1923, Sun Yat-sen welcomed students back to school in Guangzhou's Linnan with a speech, in which he praised the inherent intelligence and wisdom of the Chinese people. All across the US, he continued, no matter the school, class or student, when the semester's final grades come out, the Chinese-American students always do a little better than the rest, and this is something Americans openly acknowledge. Sun Yat-sen used history as proof, pointing out that China has had more periods of strength and prosperity than weakness and poverty. He used the character of the Chinese people as proof as well, pointing out that China's people were better than foreigners.

Sun Yat-sen believed that the Chinese represent the best people on earth and would inevitably surpass Japan and the West. He said, "In terms of the size of our land, the number of our people, and our inherent intelligence, we exceed the West in each. When our nation is ready, when China is strong, we will outpace them. The happiness our people enjoy will naturally surpass that of the West and Japan. Fighting for our country, to make ours the best country on earth, that is true courage and ambition. I hope that from today, you will all find the will to do so."

## Adopting an Open Policy

Sun Yat-sen believed that the only way China would become the world's leading nation would be to opens its doors to foreign ideas and policies and learn from the mistakes of other nations. China would need to open up in order to revive the nation and to catch up. On October 23, 1912, at a meeting in Dudu Prefecture, Anhui, he shared this sentiment in a speech: that if China strived to industrialize, opening up to the West was the only choice. In Beijing, his grueling meetings with President Yuan and the heads of various ministries focused on policies of opening up. What did "being open" mean to Sun Yat-sen, specifically? He called for foreign industries to enter China to set up businesses, along with the associated affairs that accompany such policies. There was certainly precedence for the liberalism toward foreign involvement in China's ancient history. During the Tang Dynasty, tens of thousands of students from Italy, Turkey, Persia, Japan, and other countries came to China seeking education. China didn't oppose their presence then, because Chinese civilization was at its height, and everyone from royalty to peasantry seemed to understand that this openness could only benefit the country.

Sun Yat-sen also pointed out that Japan, a nation with a territory and population no larger than two of China's provinces, was one of the smallest, poorest, weakest nations on earth in the mid-19th century. Forty years later, however, after the Meiji Restoration, it was considered a great power, on par with the elite Western powers of the time. Japan accomplished this through liberalism and openness. The Republic of China's territory was twenty times that of Japan and had twenty times as many people. By using Japan's methods of liberalism and openness, Sun Yat-sen believed that within three to five years, China could be ten times stronger than Japan. He argued that if China wanted to build up its industry yet lacked the proper capital or talent, it can be imported from abroad; if the methods aren't ideal, methods from abroad can be adopted. With hard work and determination China could easily rival any nation in the East or West.

## Innovative Spirit

Sun Yat-sen's hope for a Republic of the Chinese People was that it would be built on innovation. At a tea ceremony on July 15, 1916, he explained why he preferred the term "Republic of the Chinese People" and refused to use the term "Republic of China." His understanding of the term *min*, or "people," was one he spent more than ten years refining while visiting Europe and the Americas' varied and long-standing republics. The founders of a 20th century Chinese republic would need to do more than simply enshrine their principles in 18th and 19th century forms of law; they would need to innovate. If they could, he believed a mighty, glorious republic of the Chinese people would arise on the East Asian continent—a nation that would surpass all the republics of the West.

His "Five Branches of Government," in contrast with the West's traditional three branches, were a way in which he demonstrated the differences, and advantages, of a Chinese political system. In a speech on August 18, 1916, he argued that in most civilized countries, there are three pillars of government, and although the system is at times beneficial, it produces no small amount of harm as well. A decade earlier he proposed a five-tier separation of powers. What are the five powers? In addition to the usual three, legislative, executive, and judicial, he proposed impeachment and examinations. These two systems would not be innovations. In ancient times, this system enforced good rule, and provided the framework for modern nation-states.

Sun Yat-sen's unique *Three Principles of the People* was followed by Mao Zedong's Sinification of Marxism and Deng Xiaoping's doctrine of Chinese characteristics. These ideologies all share the idea that China needed to be revived through innovation in a uniquely Chinese fashion. From that perspective, for China to become the world's leading nation it would also have to be the world's only nation. When England dominated the world in the 19th century, it appeared to be the world's only significant nation. The same applies to the US throughout the 20th, or "American," century. China is equally unique and has the potential to become the uncontested global leader. Every nation that has been the world's leading nation has been unique; they have been innovative and founded new systems. They have not been simply the copy of systems of the past, and other nations have failed to surpass them when they have attempted to copy the global leader. Those who have been on top have studied those who came before them, but every nation that has been the world's leading nation was without exception a great nation built on pioneering ideas and impossible to duplicate.

## A Country Founded on Military Strength

On September 20, 1912, at a military meeting in Shanxi, Sun Yat-sen said that nations founded in the 20th century had to be globally involved and cooperative, yet able to be militarily dominant. If equal powers were scrambling for power, peace would be impossible. He said that if a country isn't founded on military strength, it can't be founded at all.

At a talk with world labor representatives in the Philippines on June 23, 1924, Sun Yat-sen argued that two thousand years ago, China not only dominated Asia, but also threatened Europe. Despite China's strength, it tried to teach other countries the lessons of peace,;it tried to lead by example to stop fighting and live in harmony. While China was spreading such ideals, other countries were building massive armies and navies. Other countries saw in China a nation rich in territory and natural resources with a massive commercial market, protected by a weak military and passive culture; as a result, they carved up China's territory and established spheres of influence. This warlord mentality in modern international relations provided ample evidence of the relationship between military strength and national security.

To build China into the strongest country in the world, Sun Yat-sen created a far-reaching military reform outline that today is still shocking in its scale. In it, he proposed training a national defense force of 30 million men and a national defense engineering corps of 10 million. In a speech at the Nanchang Military Institute on October 26, 1912, he said: "Today and in the future, we look forward to every one of you becoming fine soldiers, learning military affairs, and becoming the men who teach 40 million of your countrymen the art of war." China, at the time, had a population of 400 million. Sun Yat-sen's plan to train 40 million as a national defense force and army engineers would have covered one-tenth of the country's population, clearly making him a politician with a military spirit.

## Learn from the United States and Surpass It

Sun Yat-sen believe that to learn from the United States meant China had to start with its founding spirit; to surpass it, the will of China and its people must be harnessed. He praised America as the world's most civilized country and the world's first republic and saw much in America that China could learn from. While he said that that China should study America's experience, he was confident that China could one day surpass it, and when six US gunboats arrived in Guangzhou's White Swan Pond in late December 1923 in a show of power, he encouraged Guangzhou's university students to use America's founding experience as a model for how to sustain their own revolution. He also challenged them to have the ambition to surpass America. On December 21, 1923, in a speech to students in Linnan, Guangzhou, he emphasized the importance of studying the history of other nations. America's rise came about because of revolution, but when it separated from England, it had a population of 4 million and only thirteen colonies, most of which were wilderness. At the time of the American Revolution, the US population was only a hundredth of China's in the early 20th century. China has 400 million people, twenty-two provinces, and abundant resources. Given how little America started with and how it has risen, if China followed in the footstep of the US, success will naturally follow.

Sun Yat-sen believed there were many things about China that could give it an advantage over America. In his *Fundamentals for National Reconstruction* he wrote that China surpasses the US in its resources and cultural treasures, its citizen number 400 million and Chinese learning and talent have been unrivalled since ancient times. China's 5,000 years of cultural continuity is unprecedented anywhere else, and for hundreds, even thousands of years, it was the world's strongest country. Sun Yat-sen further argued that China is equal to the US in its territory and resources; however, with a labor force that is four times that of the US, China is more productive. What the nation lacked, according to Sun Yat-sen, was capital and talent. If China could obtain those elements, industry would develop and China would not only keep pace with the US, but would be four times as productive.

## II. Mao Zedong's Great Leap Forward to Surpass the West

Mao Zedong also believed in building a China that would be the world's leading nation. In his strategy and implementation there was exploration and innovation, but there were also severe limiting factors imposed by historical circumstances. There was brilliance and folly, there were successes and failures, but every turn went down in history as legend.

### *The Responsibility of a Nation*

To Mao Zedong, catching up to and surpassing the US was China's responsibility. On October 29, 1955, in a lecture at a forum on the transition of industry and commerce from capitalism to socialism, Mao Zedong argued that China's goal should be to catch up to and surpass the United States. The US only has 100 million people, while China has 600 million. Only on the day China catches up to and surpasses America can the Chinese people rest. "Today, we are an embarrassment. We have to take abuse. A country like ours, with thousands of years of history, with our vast territory and resources and giant population, we produce only a little over 2 million tons of steel a year. We've only just started producing cars, and not many at that. We are an embarrassment. That's why in every sector across the country, including the commercial sector, and including the members of every democratic political party, we need to work harder to establish our country as a prosperous one. This is a responsibility we owe to the entire world. One out of every four people on earth is ours, and it's unacceptable that we are so lacking. We need to get ourselves and nation into shape."

Mao Zedong believed China could only contribute to the cause of humanity by surpassing the United States. In 1956, in his *Memorial to Mr. Sun Yat-sen*, he wrote: "Things are always progressing. It has only been 25 years since the Revolution of 1911, but the face of China has entirely changed. In another 45 years, that is, by the year 2001, at the beginning of the 21st century, China will have undergone an even greater change. It will have become a powerful industrial socialist country. And that is as it should be. China is a land with an area of 9,600,000 square kilometers and a population of 600 million, and it ought to make a greater contribution to humanity. But for a long time in the past its contribution was far too small. For this we are regretful."[1] Mao said that surpassing America was not only possible; it was absolutely necessary. If China didn't do so, it meant that they owed the world an apology, because they were not contributing to their potential.

To Mao Zedong, if the Chinese people couldn't surpass the United States, they deserved to have their membership in humanity revoked. At the CCP's Eighth Party Congress Preparatory Meeting in 1956, when the subject of surpassing America came up, he said: "We are uniting all these resources inside and outside the party, and inside and outside the country, but for what purpose? For the establishment of a mighty socialist nation. For a country like ours, we can and should use the word mighty. Ours is a mighty party, a mighty people, a mighty revolution, and a mighty mission. There is only one nation on earth with 600 million inhabitants: ours. In the past, others had good reason not to respect us. We had contributed nothing to the world, our steel production was in the hundreds of thousands of tons, and that was in the hands of the Japanese. The Nationalist Party's Chiang Kai-shek held power for 22 years, and his China only managed to produce several tens of thousands of tons of steel per year. Our steel production this year will be 4 million tons and it will top 5 million tons next year; it will top 10 million tons during the second five-year plan, and could top 20 million tons during the third five-year plan. We have to work hard to reach these goals. Of about 100 nations on earth, only a few manage to top 20 million tons a year. In the founding of our mighty socialist nation, we must completely change 100 years of backwardness, of being looked down upon, of being unlucky. We are going to catch up to the strongest capitalist nation on Earth, America. America has 170 million people, we have several times that number, plentiful resources, and a similar climate; catching up is possible. Should we catch up? Of course we should, or else what are you 600 million people doing? Are you asleep? Should you be sleeping, or working? If America can produce 100 million tons of steel with 170 million people, why can't 600 million people produce 200 or 300 million tons? If you can't catch up, you don't deserve any glory, and you don't deserve to be called mighty. America was founded 180 years ago, and 60 years ago its steel production was also just 4 million tons a year; we are only 60 years behind. In another 50 or 60 years, we should be ahead of them. This is a responsibility, we have this many people, this much territory, this many resources, and a socialist society. If in 50 or 60 years you still can't catch up to America, what's the matter with you? You deserve to have your membership in the human race revoked!"

## Creating a Timetable to Surpass the US and UK

Mao Zedong made several adjustments to his timetable for surpassing the UK and US, and from these adjustments we can see how his attitudes on the subject changed. On November 18, 1957, at a meeting with the Communist and Workers' Party in Moscow, Mao Zedong said to Comrade Krushchev that although the Soviet Union promised to surpass the US in 15 years, China would undoubtedly do the same. Not long after coming back, he called a meeting with representatives of the democratic parties and non-party members, where he informed them of his plans to catch up with the UK and surpass America. His 1958 New Year's predictions in the People's Daily Mao included that China should prepare to surpass the United States economically within 20–30 years. On April 15, 1958, he updated those projections: within 10 years China would catch up to the UK; within another 10 years it would catch up to the US. His slogan "15 years to catch up to England" remained.

By May 1958 at the Second Session of the Eighth Party Congress, Li Fuchun predicted a timeframe of seven years to catch up to England and 15 to catch up to America. Mao Zedong changed this in his speech to seven years to catch up to England and another 8–10 years to catch up to the America. On June 22, 1958, he made edits to a report submitted by Bo Yibo: surpassing England wouldn't take 15 years, or even 7 years; it would only take 2–3 years it was even possible in less than 2 years. He also believed that, excluding ship production, car production, and electricity production, China could surpass England within a year.

On September 2, 1958, Mao Zedong announced a new slogan: Struggle for the goal of catching up to England within 5 years and surpassing America within 7 years! To ensure the success of his plans to surpass the UK and US, Mao Zedong launched the Great Leap Forward. In early 1958 at a conference in Nanning, he said that he refused to believe that construction could be more difficult than war. The Great Leap Forward did not realize the goal of surpassing the UK and US. It actually brought China's economy to a standstill and then recession. It caused a large number of unnatural deaths and pushed China's global share of GDP from 5.46% in 1957 to 4.01% in 1962, lower than its share of 4.59% in 1950. After this, Mao Zedong's passions were expressed more calmly and rationally in execution. On January 13, 1961, at the Central Worker's Conference, he said that China should not be so anxious to establish socialism. To adopt socialist policy too hastily would likely lead to failure. Rather, China should rest and proceed in waves. Just like the man who plans to walk a great distance, a growing nation, too, needs the occasional rest.

After that, on January 30, 1962, in a speech at the larger Central Worker's Conference, he explained his summary of the lessons learned from the Great Leap Forward: "As for the construction of a strong socialist economy, in China 50 years won't be enough; it may take a hundred years or even longer. In your country the development of capitalism took several hundred years [ . . . ] In our country, the construction of a great and mighty socialist economy I reckon will take more than one hundred years [ . . . ] Before this, in the seventeenth century, a number of European countries were already in the process of developing capitalism. It has taken over 300 years for capitalist productive forces to develop to their present pattern. Socialism is superior in many respects to capitalism, and the economic development of our country may be much faster than that of capitalist countries. But China has a large population, our resources are meager, and our economy backward so that in my opinion, it will be impossible to develop our productive power so rapidly as to catch up with, and overtake, the most advanced capitalist countries in less than one hundred years. If it requires only a few decades, for example only 50 years as some have conjectured, then that will be a splendid thing, for which heaven and earth be praised. But I would advise, comrades, that it is better to think more of the difficulties and so to envisage it as taking a longer period. It took from three to four hundred years to build a great and mighty capitalist economy; what would be wrong with building a great and mighty socialist economy in our country in about 50 or a hundred years? The next 50 or hundred years from now will be an epic period of fundamental change in the social system of the world, an earth-shaking period, with which no past era can be compared. Living in such a period, we must be prepared to carry out great struggles, differing in many respects from the forms of struggle of previous periods. In order to carry out this task, we must do our very best to combine the universal truth of Marxism-Leninism with the concrete reality of Chinese socialist construction and with the concrete reality of future world revolution and, through practice, gradually come to understand the objective laws of the struggle. We must be prepared to suffer many defeats and setbacks as a result of our blindness, thereby gaining experience and winning final victory. When we see things in this light, then there are many advantages in envisaging it as taking a long period; conversely, harm would result from envisaging a short period."[2]

## The Road Map of the Great Leap Forward

Mao Zedong strongly believed that China needed a Great Leap Forward in order to surpass America. In 1949 the average annual income of Chinese citizens was $27 USD, while the total average for Asia was $44 USD. In 1952 the average annual income of Chinese citizens was only 2.3% that of the average US citizen. To surpass the United States, a great leap of some sort was necessary.

The Great Leap of the late 1950s was a deeply painful lesson for China, but the failure of this Great Leap was not a deterrent. On December 13, 1964, Mao Zedong added lines to the draft of a government work report written by Zhou Enlai for the Third Session of the National People's Congress: "We cannot just follow the beaten track traversed by other countries in the development of technology and trail behind them at a snail's pace. We must break away from conventions and do our utmost to adopt advanced techniques in order to make China a powerful modern socialist country in not too long a historical period. This is what we mean by a giant stride forward. Is this impossible of attainment? Is this boasting or bragging? Certainly not. It can be done. It is neither boasting nor bragging. We need only review our history to understand this. In our country haven't we fundamentally overthrown imperialism, feudalism and capitalism, which were seemingly so strong? Starting as we did from 'poverty and blankness,' haven't we scored considerable successes in all fields of socialist revolution and socialist construction after 15 years of endeavor? Haven't we too exploded an atom bomb? Haven't we wiped out the stigma of 'the sick man of the East' imposed on us by westerners? Why can't the proletariat of the East accomplish what the bourgeoisie of the west has been able to? Early this century Dr. Sun Yat-sen, the great Chinese revolutionary and our precursor, said that China would take a giant stride forward. His prediction will certainly come true in the coming decades. This is an inevitable trend no reactionary force can stop."[3]

Mao Zedong's Great Leap was rooted in the belief that China would break through traditional models and find a new path to development. The Great Leap Forward, a three-year program begun in 1958, failed; however, the great leap that began in 1978 has been a resounding success for the economically backward China to quickly catch up to and surpass economically developed Western nations. In his *Plan for National Reconstruction* Sun Yat-sen drafted a plan for China's industrialization, which was itself a map for China's progress. Mao Zedong's Great Leap Forward was more than just his failed 1958 policy; it was the foundation for over 30 years of struggles and hard work toward modernization. Although Sun Yat-sen's and Mao Zedong's "great leaps" both had objective and subjective material limits, both suffered derailments and setbacks. The lessons and experience of their efforts, however, were the invaluable legacy they left China. In 1958 the Great Leap Forward brought hardship upon China.

Twenty years later, in 1978, China attempted another great leap, as Deng Xiaoping sifted through and summarized the lessons of his predecessors. Unlike his predecessors, he found a successful set of rules for China to proceed with and created the 30-year miracle known as China's Reform and Opening Up. Although modern China was formed in the wake of the Reform and Opening Up, it still needs to continue making great leaps along the path of scientific, pragmatic, and systematic development. After another 30 years of informed progress, China will lead the world.

## III. There Is Great Wisdom in Biding Time and Concealing Strength

In the new era of Reform and Opening Up, Deng Xiaoping's strategy for leading China toward becoming the world's leading nation was to lead the world through joining it. This would allow China to make the necessary changes while biding its time and concealing its strength. Deng Xiaoping spoke of establishing a new political and economic world order; these ideals demonstrated the global reach of his transformative vision of China leading the world.

### *Xiaoping's Exalted Ambition: The Design for China's Future*

In his public speeches and published works Deng Xiaoping never mentioned wanting China to surpass the US or become the world's leading nation. However, his desire to lead China's people toward such a goal was strong and lasting. China's strongest, fastest strides toward becoming the world's leading nation were made under his policy of Reform and Opening Up under which China closed more distance between itself and the other leading countries. Deng Xiaoping enabled more progress than any other modern Chinese leader.

As the architect of China's Reform and Opening Up, Deng Xiaoping's designs were centered on the demands of a strong, modernized socialist country. This meant making China the strongest nation in the world. He designed a complete system, rich in details, that included a goal to struggle toward—to establish a strong, modernized socialist nation; a basic map for how to get there by building the economy while upholding the Four Cardinal Principles and the principles of Reform and Opening Up; three stages of development to pass through—from basic sustenance for all, to healthy growth, and eventually to modernization and prosperity within the first 50 years of the 21st century; and a peaceful strategy for China's rise and development, in which it would bide its time and make the necessary changes quietly.

### *"We Should and Can Do Better"*

Japan's Meiji Restoration was China's model for rejuvenation. On May 24, 1977, Deng Xiaoping said, "The Meiji Restoration was a kind of modernization drive undertaken by the emerging Japanese bourgeoisie. As proletarians, we should and can do better."[4] On April 15, 1985, he again said, "We are doing something that China has never done before, not in thousands of years. The current reform will have an impact not only domestically but also internationally."[5]

"We're doing something today that China, in its thousands of years of history, has never accomplished. Reform and Opening Up influences more than just China; it influences the world." Deng Xiaoping's goal was just that: to influence the world. He believed, "Our reform is an experiment not only for China but also for the rest of the world. We believe the experiment will succeed. If it does, our experience may be useful to the cause of world socialism and to other developing countries."[6]

On April 7, 1990, in a keynote speech titled "Revitalizing the Chinese People," Deng Xiaoping said, "Since the Third Plenary Session of the Eleventh CPC Central Committee, we have been concentrating on modernizing the country so as to revitalize the Chinese nation [ . . . ] It will not be long before the People's Republic of China, which is already a political power, becomes an economic power as well. China's seat in the United Nations belongs to the People's Republic."[7] He went on to say, "We Chinese should bestir ourselves. The mainland has developed a solid economic foundation. Besides, we have tens of millions of overseas compatriots, and they want to see China grow strong and prosperous. We are unique in that respect. We shall seize every opportunity to develop. We do not interfere in the internal affairs of other countries, nor do we fear their sanctions. China opposes hegemony, and we shall never seek hegemony ourselves. China's prospects for the next century are excellent."[8] At Sun Yat-sen's Revitalization Meetings, Deng Xiaoping popularized the idea and vision of a revitalized China—a China that would surpass Europe and the US and once again lead the world. To Deng Xiaoping, a revitalized China would inevitably become the world's leader.

## Deng Xiaoping's Three Steps

What kind of process would it take for China to become the global leader? In the 1980s Deng Xiaoping promoted his Three Steps, a policy that he had introduced in the 1970s. He believed that these three steps could be achieved by the 100th anniversary of the country's founding. The first step would be to establish basic sustenance for all; this would likely take ten years. The second step, healthy growth, would take another ten years. The third and final step is the overall revitalization of the nation; this would be accomplished within the first 50 years of the 21st century. Deng Xiaoping was a realist, but he was also an idealist, and his last request of his nation was one of encouragement: "From today to the middle of the next century will be a critical time for China; we have to bury ourselves in the task at hand and work hard. The burden we bear is heavy, and the responsibility is immense!" Why did he consider the period from the end of the 20th century through the first half of the 21st century so important? Because this was the period when China would take its first steps toward becoming the world's leading nation.

## IV. Predictions About China's Future in the World

China's development will influence the future development of the world. Politicians, experts, and citizens of the world's great countries are busy making predictions about China's future, and in many countries they've reached a basic consensus regarding China.

## China's Size and Strength

"How do we get along with our gigantic neighbor?" is a question being discussed and debated at many levels of Japanese society. Naturally, the Japanese opinion of China is a hot topic. Kenichi Ohmae, the Japanese scholar and management consultant known around the world as the father of Japanese military strategy, is a prominent representative of a widely held view within Japan. Kenichi has repeatedly emphasized that by the year 2055, China's economy will be 10 times the size of Japan's; Japan will have to get used to a situation in which Japan's influence is only 10% that of China's. He believes Japan needs an appropriate sense of scale regarding its neighbor. He reminded Japan that in the past 2,000 years of history, Japan has typically been only 10% as powerful as China, a situation that only changed after the Meiji Restoration. Today, things are only returning back to normal. Japan needs to accept the fact that Japan is smaller than China, and has become a small but powerful country. The massive Chinese market represents a huge opportunity for Japan, and the key factor in whether Japanese enterprises can succeed is whether they can embrace China. Take road construction as an example: Japan has 9,000 km of highways, while China builds 8,000 km of highway a year. Kenichi has traveled extensively between China and Japan in the last decade; in 2009 alone, he made the trip eight times. He says you can't research the world without researching China. He believes that the US financial crisis illustrated that the United States is a country without any of the trappings or qualifications of a leader. In his book *Goodbye, America?* he listed three prescriptions for the US: first, apologize to the world for the mistakes of the past eight years, including attacking Afghanistan, occupying Iraq, and sparking the global financial crisis; second, become a global actor, and do things after discussion with other countries rather than acting like a lone tyrant; and third, say goodbye to war.

Japan's self-awareness and ability to adapt to changing world power structures was shown in its abandonment of Asia for Europe a century ago, and its shifting emphasis to American markets, and current return to Asian markets. The new generation of Japanese politicians think the world is developing toward two poles: the United States and China. They see Japan as a bridge, both politically and geographically, between these two poles of power. Japan is currently changing its foreign relations policy away from tailing America. In the first half of 2009, China's share of Japan's foreign trade was 20.4%, and the US share was 13.7%, while, comparatively, in 1990, the US share was 27.4%, and China's share was only 3.5%. This was the first time China's share of Japan's foreign trade had surpassed 20% since the Second World War, and Asia now makes up more than half of Japan's foreign trade. Japan has already adjusted to a China-centric, Asia-based foreign trade market.

## The Beijing Plan Will Replace the Washington Consensus

Americans are very sensitive about China's moves to become the world's leading nation, an attitude that was evident even 20 years ago. In 1987 American Paul Kennedy made three predictions about the future of global politics: First, in the near future, no other countries would be able to enter the five-headed power arrangement shared by the US, the Soviet Union, China, Japan, and the European Economic Community (Henry Kissinger believes that India ought to be included, making it a six-headed power arrangement), and that these would ultimately be the great powers. Second, he believed that the balance of productive strength, in some aspects, was moving away from the Soviet Union, US, and the EEC toward Japan and China, and even though China lagged far behind Japan in development, it was catching up quickly. The third prediction was that China's current leadership, after a long period of bitter, difficult struggle, was executing an ambitious, coherent, long-term strategy, and that in this regard it would overtake Moscow, Washington, and Tokyo, much less to say Western Europe.

Zbigniew Brzezinski, more than a decade ago, predicted that within twenty years China would become a global power, equal in strength to the United States and Europe. In the US National Intelligence Council's 2020 Project, prepared for the White House, they write that China's rise, like that of Germany in the 19th century, or America's emergence in the 20th century, is inevitable. Goldman Sachs has predicted that by the year 2027, China's economy will surpass the United States in size, and that by 2050, it will be twice the size of the US economy.

In "China Rising," which appeared in the autumn 2008 compilation of the US foreign affairs publication *World Policy Journal*, it was predicted that by 2033, China could unquestionably occupy the leading place in the world economic order, with America in second. They go on to say that America's government and its people should begin to think about what such a watershed change will signify and start thinking of ways to cope. As time passes and problems of economic growth and development begin to appear, we will be hearing more about the Beijing Plan and less about the Washington Consensus.[9]

## The Center of the World Will Move to the East

The book *When China Rules the World: The Rise of the Middle Kingdom and the End of the Western World* shocked the West. The book's author, British scholar and academic Martin Jacques, said that for the United States, China's transformation into a great power will be a painful process. The United States will have to learn to play by others' rules and adjust to its relative decline. The worst possible choice for the United States will be to try to resist or contain China, which will only drag the world into the mire of a new Cold War; a new Cold War will only hasten America's decline and China's rise will only deepen the universal sense of loss across the Western world. The West is entering a long period of painful self-adjustment. China's rise will change more than just the world's economic order: it will change the way we live and the way we think. China's rise signifies a new era. In the latter half of the 21st century, China could very well become the world's strongest nation, which will mean important changes in international relations. Beijing will become the world's capital, and Shanghai will take New York's place as the financial center of the world.

A *Guardian* columnist asserted that China's transformation is moving the center of the world eastward and that the 21st century will be completely different from the preceding two centuries, with power no longer in the hands of Europe and America.

Noted British economist and professor Angus Maddison, in his book *Chinese Economic Performance in the Long Run*, predicted that China could become the world's largest economy by 2015. In May 2008 a report published by UK think tank Centre for European Reform stated that the world's center of power was moving toward the east. By 2020, the US, Europe, and China would have equal shares of the world economy, with each holding about 20% of global GDP. In their report "2008 World Outlook," UK magazine *The Economist* called 2008 the first year that global politics and economic forces were pulling out of America and moving into China, and the year in which an American-led world order began its transition to a Chinese-led world order.

## Only a Matter of Time

In June 2009 the *Global Times* began to conduct a two-month-long study with interviews with 85 economists, 80 of whom also participated in the accompanying survey. The survey covered three important questions: How many years would it take for the world's financial markets to recover from pre-crisis levels? Which economic body or nation would lead the world's economic recovery? How many more years would it take for China's economy to catch up to the United States? The survey showed 51 of the economists believed it would take three to five years for a full global economic recovery; 19 believed it would take one to two years; and nine believed it would take at least five years. In response to the second question, 66 economists believed China would lead the world's economic recovery; ten believed America would; and four believed another upcoming economic body or nation would lead the recovery.

In response to the last question, 18 respondents believed the size of China's economy would surpass the US within 10 years; 37 believed it would happen within 20 years; 14 believed it would take 30 years; and six and two believed it would take longer or never happen at all, respectively. Seventeen American economists took the survey—the most of any single country. The American economists in the survey were the most certain of any country that China's economy would surpass the American economy at some point, with most believing it would take 30 years.

The results of the survey show us three important trends: first is that the fact that China's economy will overtake America's is already widely acknowledged by experts, with 78 out of 80 experts agreeing; second is that among experts, the most mainstream view is that China will overtake the US economy in about 20 years; and third is that most believe China's economy overtaking America's will completely reshape the world.

## V. Are the Chinese People Ready?

China is rising very fast; the scale of the rise is huge, the environment in which it is taking place is complex, the conditions of the rise are unique, and the effects of the rise are deep. It is not just the outside world that is surprised and astonished: Chinese people themselves aren't ready either. China's lack of preparation to be the world's leading nation became even more evident when China's economy overtook Japan's.

### Five Significant Outcomes if China Leads the World

What does it mean to be the world's leading nation? What would it mean for China to become the world's leading nation? Is becoming the world's leading nation even a goal worth struggling toward for China's citizens today? Opinion on these questions is far from unified. Before we can reach a public consensus on these questions, we first need to attempt to understand them. Some people question whether China, with all the problems it already faces, has the time or energy to fight for a global leadership position. Some people find the goal of becoming the world leader too grandiose and far removed from the lives of ordinary people. Some people think China should be more realistic in dealing with its own problems. And these issues sound reasonable. The key to all these views is the idea that if China becomes the world's leading nation, it will be able to deal with these problems from a better starting point, and be able to form better strategies for dealing with its numerous problems. When China becomes the global leader, we will see five significant outcomes in the broad competition between China and the US.

1. When China becomes the global leader, it will be the outcome of the struggle between the world's largest developing country and the world's largest developed country, and prove that developing countries can become developed countries, and even surpass established developed countries.

2. When China becomes the world's leading nation, it will be the outcome of the struggle between the world's largest socialist nation and the world's largest capitalist nation, and prove that socialism with Chinese characteristics is the superior system. It will be the first time a socialist nation has surpassed a capitalist nation in productive output and the first

time the advantages of a socialist political system built upon a socialist economy is proven in practice. When socialism with Chinese characteristics finally produces the world's largest economy, it will become the world's foremost economic model, and from there ascend to brilliant new heights. The wealthiest countries in recent history have been Western nations. The Soviet Union rose after the Second World War to become a country determined to surpass America. At the height of their power, however, Soviet production was still only 60% that of American production. In the century of American hegemony, Europe's powers have rotated in and out of regional leadership. For two centuries, Western nations have been the most prosperous nations in the world, but a historic change will take place when China, a developing nation, slowly overtakes the Western economies. By the year 2030, China's economic output will surpass that of America. By 2050, when the world's three largest economies are, in order, China, the US, and India, the aging powers of the West will be ready to step back from their position of leadership.

3. When China becomes the world's leading nation, competition between Eastern and Western civilization will take on new significance. We will see proof that not only Western civilization can give the world wealth and prosperity, and the world will see that Eastern civilization has more charm, more vitality, and more creativity than it is credited with. In recent history, English-speakers have led the world, but as China becomes the world's leading nation we will see a new era in which Chinese-speakers lead the world.

4. When China becomes the world's leading nation it will put an end to Western notions of racial superiority. In 1924, in *The Three Principles of the People*, Sun Yat-sen argued that comparing Asians and Westerners isn't fair. Westerners are always thought to be more intelligent and more talented; they have a monopoly on everything. "The rise of Japan has broken down the traditional belief on the part of the white people that only white nations can be strong and progressive, and has inspired other Oriental peoples with the confidence that they can also rise up to match the Europeans and Americans. Before her Reformation, Japan was as weak as Annam or Burmah. During the recent Washington Conference she was considered one of the 'Big Five,' and she practically had a monopolistic control over the settlement of Far Eastern questions."[10] Japan may be a developed country, but it's never become the global leader. All the nations in recent history that have become the world's leaders have been nations founded by Westerners. When China takes its leading position, it will prove that Asians can lead the world as well—that it isn't the exclusive purview of Westerners. Whatever Westerners can do, Asians can do just as well or better.

5. When China becomes the world's leading nation it will alter the West's long-held sense of geographical superiority. Every global leader in recent history has risen from Europe and North America; however, Asia is the largest continent, and by all rights it should host

the world's leading nation. When China takes the lead in the global economy it will be a glorious day for all of Asia.

It should be obvious that China surpassing America will be of tremendous significance. The influence will stretch far beyond economic issues to affect global politics and culture; it will bring China of the future untold political and moral clout. In almost every field and sphere of experience, changes will occur that benefit every Chinese citizen. One could say that all bear the burdens of a nation's rise and fall; when China leads, all will benefit.

## Great Nations Require National Unity

As China works toward becoming the world's leading nation there is another factor that we can't do without: national will. Great nations require the will to rise. This is one of the unique and necessary factors behind any great nation. Great nations become great because they have the ambition to do so. Any rising great nation is a nation with the dream and the will to compete with and beat the current leading nations. Struggling to become a global leader is the common desire and personality of all great nations. The will, the pursuit, the passion, the faith, and the confidence required for a people to declare that we will turn ours into the greatest country on earth is precisely what makes certain nations flourish, and the source of strength that drives a nation to greatness. Peoples and nations without the ambition to truly become world leaders will find it very difficult to do so. Those that lead the world are those who desire fighting for and taking on global leadership. As they strive to become global leaders, it is these people who produce outstanding achievements and bring civilization to new heights.

Portugal was a nation of only one million people— smaller than even a large Chinese county—when their rise to greatness began. Today, even though they remain just a small country in Europe, with territory of just over 92,000 square kilometers and a population just over 10 million, every large landmass on earth contains nations or regions where Portuguese is spoken as a first or second language. The Portuguese Empire stood like a giant over the globe, spanning 140 degrees of longitude and 70 degrees of latitude. The Indian Ocean, Arabian Sea, and South China Sea were Portugal's backyard pond. A proud Portuguese poet of the time declared, "I am Portugal, bigger than the world!" It was the determination to be "bigger than the world" that made Portugal the first global leader of the modern era.

In the Netherlands, a small nation that has done great things, there is a painting titled *Allegory on the Prosperity of Amsterdam*. In the painting, the guardian spirit of Amsterdam has her hand resting on a globe. The painting signifies that Holland, despite its geographical size, could envelope the whole world in its breast, and play with it in the palm of its hand. When the Netherlands became a great power, the country had a population of only 1.7

million, but they dominated the world stage in the 17th century and created a golden age of prosperity.

Famous Russian author Fyodor Dostoevsky once said, "Truly great peoples never take a secondary role in human affairs, nor do they play the top role; they are only content playing a unique role." Or consider Charles de Gaulle's famous quote: "If France is not great, it is not France." He believed that what made France unique was its heart as a great nation, that what France strove for was greatness, and that greatness was inherent to France's national faith and national will. The United States, for two hundred years, has operated under maxims like "global model," "leader of nations," and "American century."

Humans are competitive by nature; nations, being creations of man, are naturally just as competitive. However, it takes confidence before nations have the strength to compete. The strongest nations are all confident, and nations without adequate strength need even more confidence. In truth, when these great nations arose, none of them were larger than China. In terms of land, population, and wealth, they couldn't compare with China by any means. In recent history, most of these great nations have been small, some with less than 100,000 square kilometers of territory and populations of only a few million—microscopic nations that rose to dominate the globe.

A look back at the history of great nations proves that what makes them great isn't size or population; it's their will to achieve and their vision. A great nation without great ambitions and will is sure to fall; small nations, with enough will, can also rise to greatness. If we see the 20th century as a century of wars and conflict, then the 21st century is one of economic competition. The world stage in the new century is a crowded one. Americans say the 21st century will be another American Century. India's former prime minister Atal Bihari Vajpayee declared: "The 21st century will be India's century!" There are certainly more nations with the will to lead the world in the 21st century. If 21st century China doesn't become world's leading nation, if it doesn't become the world's strongest country, then it will have fallen behind in the competition for greatness.

## Strategic Opportunity Depends on Strategic Preparation

Opportunity favors the well prepared, and strategic opportunities only present themselves to nations with strategy. As a nation or a people develop and rise to greatness, they will be presented with rare and potentially valuable opportunities, but whether they can reap the rewards depends entirely on the quality and extent of their strategic preparation.

After the establishment of the People's Republic of China, China missed two critical opportunities to develop the nation. The first was in the 1950s after winning the war in Korea. China was recognized internationally as a military power, its national security saw a drastic improvement, and the time was ripe for the country to develop economically. This opportunity was only seized effectively for four years, after which it was disrupted by the anti-Rightist movement and the Great Leap Forward, people's communes, and the communist fervor that followed. That was when Japan took advantage of the favorable international climate. They saw the opportune moment, maintained their development policies, and quickly made their economic rise a reality. China's second opportunity was in the early 1970s, when the balance of power between China, the US, and the Soviet Union prompted the US to counter the threat from the Soviet Union and begin normalizing relations with China in 1971. This produced a titanic change for the better in China's international relations—between 1971 and 1976 China established diplomatic relations with 51 countries; to give perspective, in the 22 years from 1949 to 1970, China established diplomatic relations with 54 countries. That opportunity, thanks to the ongoing Cultural Revolution, was not used effectively. It was only after Reform and Opening Up, with its strategy correctly aligned, that it was prepared to meet the dissolution of the Soviet Union, the stagnation of the Japanese economy, America being bogged down in the quagmire of its wars, and the 2008 world financial crisis. China was able to face the world properly, use the opportunities presented to develop, and quickly establish itself as a major economic power.

China's experience proves that the value of strategic opportunities is decided by the quality of strategy and preparation. China today is not merely in a period where nations encounter opportunities on their rise to greatness, China is on a strategic sprint to become the world's global leader. In this race, China will need preparation, strategic innovation, strategic design, and strategic leadership to take advantage of these opportunities.

## *Staying Calm Is Required for Chinese Prosperity*

Becoming the strongest nation in the world is China's goal in the 21st century. It will take passion and enthusiasm to reach that goal. Historically, China has been the world's strongest nation. The advantages and traditions that kept this nation and people in a position of strength have been lost. The reason these strengths were lost is because China's people collectively fell asleep. In 1924 Sun Yat-sen described China's place in the world as having fallen a thousand miles. The biggest reason, he said, was that we have lost our national spirit, although the Chinese people had fallen asleep. The Chinese need to recover that spirit, and rise again. We need to waken the sleeping dragon, reestablish the will to make China the global leader, and again make sacrifices to make our will a reality. We need to take responsibility for making China the leading nation, and again fulfill the dream of leading the world.

While the mighty Chinese people awaken from their slumber, amid this outpouring of passion, China needs to remember to stay sober and calm. During both the Chinese revolution and the founding of the new Chinese nation, China suffered terribly when passions went unrestrained. In today's chaotic times, with the country in uproar and tempers boiling over, the need for calmness is more pressing than ever. In 2007 China's GDP surpassed Germany's, to make it the world's third-largest economy. But China has a population of 1.3 billion, versus Germany's 80 million. In 2007 per capita GDP was $2,604 USD in China while it was $40,162 USD in Germany, 15.4 times that of China's total; the gap is still massive. China needs the will to close this gap, but it also needs a high degree of reason and calmness.

# CHAPTER 2

# THE FIGHT FOR THE CENTURY

The champion among nations is the nation that, after the formation of the modern world order, within the global framework and within the competitive framework among nations, is the strongest, most prosperous nation. These are the nations that set the tone for their era and wield enormous influence all over the globe. In the 21st century China and the United States will square off and fight to become the champion among nations.

## I. Champions Last for a Century

The rise and fall of these champion nations have common peculiarities and regular rules. Different types of champion nations wear different faces. The position and uses of these champion nations is apparent in their value to the wider world. Of the champions that have arisen in the past 50 years of modern political history the classic examples are 16th century Portugal, 17th century Holland, the United Kingdom in the 18th and 19th centuries, and the United States in the 20th century. In the 21st century China will become the champion among nations.

## The Driving Force in the Rise of Large Countries

Global development and progress is primarily driven by competition among nations. Much like how a country's development is driven by competition between classes, organizations, and social strata within it, the competition between nations is what drives global development, and what drives great nations to rise.

Harvard Kennedy School professor Joseph Nye said: "Some historians think that in Europe, the competition between the continent's nations put them in a state of unconscious, uninterrupted development. In Asia, China's uncontested position as the regional power left it without effective competitors, and its problems with invaders from the north were always solved internally, leaving it without motivation to expand beyond its borders. 1,500 years ago, China was the unquestioned superpower in East Asia. While Europe was only beginning its forays into deep-sea navigation, China was actually scaling back its maritime journeys. It stands to reason that most of the great powers which expanded across multiple continents were European nations." To Joseph Nye, the West developed so quickly because of the intensity of competition between nations. The intensity of that competition gave the Western world its motivation and vitality. Meanwhile, development slowed and even came to a standstill in Asia because of the lack of competition between nations.

Today, there are far more nations competing with each other than there ever were in the past. The number of recognized, politically independent nations grew gradually over the course of the 20th century; in the 1930s, there were only about 60 countries, but by the end of the 20th century, there were roughly 190. In September 2002, the UN had 191 participating member states. In 2008, according to relevant materials, there were 225 independent nations and autonomous regions in the world—194 nations, and 31 autonomous regions. The world develops through competition between nations and finds progress in the contests between them. The vitality, drive, and creativity of the international community are powered by the competition between nations. And the competition between nations, especially strategic competition between the great nations, is the primary driver of global progress.

Nations compete among themselves to achieve minimum and maximum goals. Noted American international relations expert Kenneth Waltz thinks nations "are bodies that fight simultaneously for survival as a minimum goal, and for the power to lead the world as a maximum goal." The lowest goal that nations have when they compete is to ensure their own continued existence; their highest goal is to become the champion among nations. Becoming the world's leading nation or the champion among nations is the highest goal of any nation's competitive struggle, and the highest heights to which any nation's competitive ability can ascend.

## The Four Levels of Competition on the World Stage

1. **Safety:** Achieving safety is the most basic, and most important, strategic goal of any nation. Thanks to global progress, today the vast majority of peoples and nations have at least some guarantee of safety. Of the roughly 194 countries in the world today, most are free of the threat of conquest or extermination; their national sovereignty is essentially safe. Only a dozen or so countries are currently facing the threat of war.

2. **Development:** The world has been at peace and focused on development for many years now, but the number of nations that have truly made significant and speedy moves toward development is in the minority. If we add the number of developed and newly industrialized nations together, they number only a quarter of the world's nations.

3. **Great Powers:** Among the crowd of developing nations, "great powers" are nations that can influence the world in significant ways. These nations have always, by definition, been few in number. In the past 500 years, nations worthy of the title number in the dozens. Today, there are only a few countries with the conditions and the opportunity to be considered world powers.

4. **Champion Nations:** This is the highest level of competition. Champion nations only emerge once in a century although seven or eight nations have held this title in the past 500 years. This is a position that only a few will ever hold. A nation needs to be a great power before it can possibly elevate to the status of a champion among nations, and not every great power will have that honor. To go from a nation whose existence is guaranteed, to a developing nation, to a great power, to a champion nation is an epic, legendary process of struggle.

## The Changing of Champions

Where there is competition among nations, there will be winners and losers. The decline of old champion nations is heralded by the rise of new champion nations. The cyclical replacement of one with another is proof that the world continues to progress and develop. The birth of every new champion nation indicates a drastic, historic step forward for the world. Henry Kissinger, in the opening words of his book *Diplomacy*, said, "Almost as if according to some natural law, in every century there seems to emerge a country with the power, the will, and the intellectual and moral impetus to reshape the entire international system in accordance with its own values."[1]

In truth, more than 2,000 years ago ancient Greek historian Herodotus formulated a famous theory based on the rise and fall of Greek city-states: the death of flourishing cities and the rise of weak polities is eloquent proof of the fact that good things don't last long. It shows the unfair ways in which competition between nations often develops, but it's also simply a cycle of hegemony: conditions do not remain favorable forever. Champion nations must be replaced; no single nation can hold a monopoly on the position forever.

In the 1980s American political scientist George Modelski proposed the hegemonic stability theory, which argues a hundred-year "life cycle" for global hegemons.[2] The argument states that "global leadership" switches roughly once every hundred years. He carved 500 years of global politics (1495–2030) into five periods of roughly a century, and pointed to the rise of a new power roughly once every century. The global hegemons he proposed were as follows: 16th century Portugal, 17th century Holland, 18th and 19th century-Britain, and 20th century America.

No matter whether we call it a century-long lease on global hegemony or global leadership, it shows that in the never-ending history of struggle between nations, there is no champion among nations who holds the title forever. Those who hold the position hold it for roughly 100 years. People often speak of the Dutch Century, the British Century, or the American Century; for each, the term of power given in everyday speech is only a century. No matter whether a country is fighting to maintain, or steal, its position as champion, the struggle gives global development new life and new force. When a champion nation is replaced, it means that the world is transitioning to a better way of doing things. The UK's rise meant the world shared in the benefits brought on by industrialization; when America took the title, it brought about more changes to the world. The next champion nation after America will undoubtedly reshape the world once again.

## Three Attributes of Champions Among Nations

1. **Colonization:** Colonizers are champion nations that practice colonialism. They occupy a territory militarily and practice direct rule, turning weak nations into their own territory and building a colonial empire. All the early great powers were colonizers, including the first modern champion nations of Portugal, Holland, and the United Kingdom. With the logic of discovering and occupying, they took their territory with military force, and built gigantic colonial empires.

In 1549 Spain's empire in the America's stretched over 10,000 kilometers from north to south, crossing 67 degrees of latitude and covering more than 25 million square kilometers. Holland of the 17th century was a colonial power in addition to being a commercial power. Their colonial activities were run through the West and East India companies. The Dutch East India Company's colonies were in Asia, while the Dutch West India Company operated in Africa and the Americas. These two companies founded colonies abroad that together were over 60 times the size of Holland's territory.

Britain's colonial empire took form as British capital expanded to take over the world. The British Empire took over more than 30 million square kilometers of territory, 100 times the size of the UK's territory. Their colonies accounted for roughly a quarter of the world's surface and governed nearly 400 million people, nine times the population of the British Isles. In the 50 years between 1815 and 1865, the British Empire added an average of 100,000 square kilometers of new colonial territory a year, creating an empire on which the sun never set and building an international trade system to serve the giant empire. The empire provided Britain with access to a variety of valuable resources, but also provided British manufactured goods with a guaranteed market abroad. A trifecta of overseas colonies, international trade, and a strong navy gradually formed in Great Britain, and Britain became a nation of colonialism and trade. Britain used its navy to protect its ships and control the world. British economist William Stanley Jevons described what his empire had become in 1865: "The plains of North America and Russia grow our corn; Canada and the Baltic grow our timber; Australia raises our sheep; Peru sends silver, while South Africa and Australia send gold to London; the Indians and Chinese grow our tea; and our coffee, sugar cane, and spices are grown in the gardens of the East Indies. For a long time, our cotton was produced in the southern United States, but now that has been expanded to every warm area of the planet."

**2. "Hegemon" Champion Nations:** Hegemonic champion nations have no desire to conquer and absorb territory. Instead, they try to lead and control the world to benefit. If colonizers are brutal thieves, hegemons are gentle thieves. Although there certainly is a difference, both are forms of theft. The United States is the template for a hegemonic champion nation.

In the conclusion of his 1993 book *The Cambridge History of American Foreign Relations* Walter LeFeber wrote: "Ever since 1776, Americans had dedicated themselves to establishing their own system that was adapted to their own evolving needs. That they competed with Europeans for world power was true. That they ultimately proved to be as vulnerable to the demands, even corruption, of world power as the Europeans and Japanese also was true. That they appeared, with good reason, to Filipinos, Cubans, Chinese, and Centrals Americans as little different than other imperialists was true as well. Unlike the other major powers, however, the United States had a continent to populate and exploit; it did not desire colonies for surplus population or vast protectorates for raw materials, or (as in the case of Russia) extensive areas that served as passageways to vital new ports."[3] This essentially describes the non-colonial flavor of American hegemony.

In times of war and revolution, and in times of peace and development, the United States is a global hegemon that tries to control the entire world. Its hegemony shows in politics, economics, military affairs, culture, and other aspects. America emerged from the Second World War as the leader of the anti-Fascist alliance with enormous amounts of political capital, and used it to lead the design and founding of many international institutions to cement its position: it established the collective security apparatus of the UN, which ensures American primacy in international politics; it established the World Bank and the International Monetary Fund to secure the US dollar-led international financial system and American leadership in international economics and finance; it established the GATT-based international system of free trade; it presented the Truman Doctrine and the Marshall Plan and founded NATO. It was the most important proponent, architect, and sponsor of the United Nations, and its biggest beneficiary. America's hegemony relies on the application of power through systems it dominates, as well as through hard power dominance. The UN was once described as the tyranny of the majority, and by appealing to the principle of unanimous power; the US designed, founded, and controlled the most important international organization—the United Nations. In the early years of the UN's existence, the United States controlled and manipulated the UN through its voting machine, and used it to make its own will and desires a reality. Of the 800 resolutions voted on by the UN General Assembly from 1946 to 1953, US-sponsored bills passed with a 97% success rate, while any question that touched on key national security issues for the US failed to pass. America also organized and supported several regional organizations. The so-called principle of great power unanimity was in practice the principle of agreeing with the United States. After the Second World War, the United States produced more than half the value of the world's industrial output, and they established a military presence in more than 50 countries and territories. America led the international order according to its own values. The USA and the Soviet Union struggled for hegemony for over half a century during the Cold War. In the wake of the Cold War, America had finally established itself as world hegemon. It then switched to a more unilateral stance, launching several wars and demonstrating its military prowess.

One of the most important facets of American hegemony is how it tries to reshape the world according to the American model, promote American democracy, and Americanize the planet. This is the most undemocratic characteristic of America's hegemony in international relations. This is a unique brand of despotism called American hegemony.

**3. Guiding Nations:** Guiding nations are those that do not use conquest as a means to spread civilization; they do not use hegemony and conquering as means to attain their national interests. China is not yet a champion nation, but when it becomes one in the future, it is certain to be a guiding nation.

Nineteenth-century American historian Brooks Adams believed that every great civilization used conquest as a means to expand and establish itself. He said the center of world civilization was destined to be the United States. He advocated for the US to take the opportunity to spread abroad, especially in Asia and the Asia-Pacific region, to reap the benefits of a global economy. In reality, this was just theoretical justification for expansion, conquest, and hegemony of the world. The fact that Western capitalism used conquest as a means to establish itself is not proof that all great civilizations should establish themselves through conquest. Chinese civilization was not established through conquest. If conquest is a necessary tool for civilization to establish itself, as suggested by Adams, then conquest becomes something without which civilization cannot exist. If there is no civilization without conquest and if abandoning conquest means abandoning civilization, then conquest is a necessary part of civilization. This is little more than a criminal's logic. More importantly, even if today's great civilizations have established themselves through conquest, it does not mean conquest will be necessary for the great civilizations of the future.

The great civilizations of the future won't use conquest as a means to establish themselves. China's job is to create a civilization that grows without conquest—a non-conquering civilization. If human civilization requires conquest to exist, it's no different than a civilization of savages and can hardly be called an advanced civilization. To use non-conquering methods to create a non-conquering civilization is China's responsibility. It is the demand on China to create a new world order that prefers peace, development, freedom, and cooperative civilization. Chinese civilization's traditions and cultural heritage will be able to accomplish this important historical task.

The champion nations of the past have been creatures of a dual nature: while they were at the forefront of world development and the strongest nations of their time in almost all respects, they also took control of others through occupation and conquest. They were tyrants who suppressed nations with different political views. But the champion of nations that China strives to be is a completely new kind—one of peace and guidance.

Brzezinski said, "In the long run, global political power is destined to be concentrated more and more unequally in the hands of a single global hegemon. This is why America is not only the first and only truly global superpower, it may very well be the last." Based on trends of the history of human society and social development, Brzezinski believes the United States is the world's last global hegemon and that the appearance of a new global hegemon is impossible. However, America is not the last champion nation. In the never-ending cycle of competition between nations as they develop, new champions will always appear to lead the world. It's impossible for there not to be a champion nation, and it's impossible for one nation to hold that title forever. The end of global hegemons does not signify the end of champions among nations. China can become champion among nations without being a global hegemon. The colonizing champions died out long ago, and it's inevitable that the hegemonic champions will die out as well to make way for a third kind of champion, a Chinese-style guiding champion. This new type of champion will have no desire to conquer or dominate, but rather it will lead and guide the world through progress. No matter when, or what form the champion among nations takes, each offers historic contributions to its era. Their value is apparent in seven aspects.

## Promoting New Progress

In modern world history, the appearance and rise of each new champion nation has always brought with it new ways of doing things and pushed human history into a new era. They have all brought a period of change, openness, and evolution to global civilization, and made the world more prosperous. The colonizer and hegemon champion nations may have also brought misery and disaster with them as they dominated the globe; but their contributions to global society are undeniable. When a nation's contributions to the world are no longer the best of what humanity has to offer, it loses its place as the champion among nations, and passes the title to a new champion, even if that transition requires war.

## Creating a New Historical Era

In modern history, humanity has witnessed a string of soul-stirring eras, with names like the Age of Discovery, Age of Industrialization, and the Information Age. The beginning of these eras is intimately tied to the rise of champion nations, whose contributions to the world usher in these new eras. Portugal and Spain gave humanity an era of seafaring and discovery. It was an era when history truly became global, and when human activity and competition between nations expanded to a truly global scale, which contributed greatly to human progress.

The age of global industrialization began with Britain. On May 1, 1851, the first World Expo was held in the UK, and it allowed the world to see the new level of abundance and prosperity achieved by the UK. The world had seen strong nations, large nations, and prosperous nations before Britain, but it had never seen a nation like this. England's new industrial civilization had brought it to untold heights of prosperity, and its productive capacity was equal to that of the rest of the world combined. Britain led the world down a path of industrialization and into the Industrial Revolution. It was the first nation in human history to transition from an agricultural economy to an industrial economy, and the world's first industrial power. The industrial output of the UK alone was equivalent or superior to that of all other nations combined. In 1860 the UK had a mere 2% of the world's population, and 10% of the population of Europe, but produced 40–50% of the world's industrial products and 55–60% of Europe's total. Industrial Era Britain was the factory of the world, and this was a world the UK led and dominated as it provided humanity with the basis for a new material economy.

The United States became a champion among nations because of its pioneering, era-defining contributions as well. Marx had high praise for the United States as the place where the idea of the modern democratic republic was born. He called the Declaration of Independence, published in 1776 by the migrants to North America, the first declaration of human rights. In response to the Emancipation Proclamation of 1863, he issued passionate congratulations on behalf of the First International: "The workers of Europe believe that, just as the American war of independence opened a new era for the proletariat, America's war against slavery will open a new era for the working classes. They believe that the unprecedented war led by the loyal son of the working class, Abraham Lincoln, to liberate the enslaved race and reform the social system of his own country is the first sign of the era to come."

The United States was also the global forerunner of the Information Age, and made the first contributions toward bringing us into today's era. In 1992 US President Bill Clinton instituted an economic strategy that would later be called Clinton Era Economics, or Clintonomics. One of the most important pillars of it was support for the technology sector. It used the enormous American advantages in science and technology to lead the world in the development of electronics and information technology. This made American products more competitive globally and put the United States at the head of the 21st century IT revolution that swept the whole world into the Information Age.

## Establishing a New World Order

Champion nations are those that design the world. This design includes crafting the international power layout, establishing new codes of behavior for nation-states, new international institutions, a new world order, and new international systems.

US foreign relations expert Warren I. Cohen argued out that even at the beginning of World War II, Americans were designing the outlines of the postwar world. He believed that if the president himself was guilty of spending too much time on military affairs and tactics, and didn't give enough consideration to the shape of a post-victory world, there were certainly other people who had time to invest in its design. The most obvious were the efforts of the State Department. Virtually in lockstep with the war, they began organizing research task groups and commissions to look into the future world. They brought their own officials together with congressmen, journalists, academics, and military officials for wide-ranging research and discussion of the country's tasks after the war, including the occupation of enemy nations, territorial adjustments, and questions of international security and trade. Although, at the time, these commissions never went much further than the exchange of views and information, certain ideas had already taken shape, and the moment Washington began searching for specific guidance on the post-war world, these ideas became part of official American policy. These ideas were obviously Wilsonian—the vast majority of research task group members agreed that after the Axis nations were defeated, the key to maintaining peace and the international order was a return to the principle of international cooperation, and not the outdated balance of power principle. After World War II, America began building according to its blueprints, and tried to craft a world suited to US national interests.

Champion nations design the world by building world systems that work for them. There are four primary pillars that support these world systems: a global economic system, a global framework of thought, a global military system, and a global system of rules.

## Leading the New Trends of the World

Champion nations are the world's model nations. They are the world's example to be followed, and the ideal to be reached. Champion nations are powerful demonstrations—they are influential and infectious. They are nations with a unique attribute or circumstance that can't be imitated. They are the nations most worthy of imitation, studied and followed by nations of admirers. Champion nations cause the world to reform itself in their image.

At the height of Britain's industrialization, it was the center of world attention. All the world's nations were its paparazzi. Its rise kicked off a tide of countries around the world trying to Anglicize themselves through policy, as Britain's industrial might pushed "Anglicization" from the outside. Britain baptized the world with its modern material and intellectual culture, and the world happily bathed in the ablution of British civilization.

When America, the next champion nation, arose, the tide of Americanization began. It was apparent in politics, economics, culture, and many other aspects. As America rose, the world's material and popular cultures quickly reformed in America's image. The American Dream became the world's dream, and the American way of life became humanity's goal. As the 19th century became the 20th, foreign observers were already discussing the universal impact of American culture and the American way of life. Americans, who enjoyed the world's highest standard of living, were admired around the world for lifestyles that seemed abundant, comfortable, and removed from the messiness of the old world. In the interwar period, when modern products like appliances, automobiles, and telephones were still rarities in most of the world, they were commonplace in the United States. This was especially apparent after 1919, when this process sped and Europe's place in the world began to decline. Pronouncements of the fall of the West found their way into mainstream thought, thanks to devastation caused by First World War and the increasing industrial output and trade of non-European nations. Europe felt its place in the world under threat; it was no longer the fount of wisdom and the center of world civilization. Europe faced a world restructuring itself, and had nothing to offer. The task of demarcating peace (not only in geographical politics, but in cultural politics as well) had to be handed to other countries, and the United States was the natural heir. The United States, which had suffered none of the devastation of war, became the symbol of material prosperity and popular culture. Culture homogenized within the United States, and at the same time American culture homogenized the world. Cars, movies, and radio, the three inventions that were uniting Americans, were having the same effect all over the world, and because all three were essentially American inventions, they brought American culture with them wherever they went.

## Creating New Development Miracles

Champion nations are nations that create miracles for mankind, and only nations that create miracles for the world can become champions among nations. The 17th century was Holland's century. This tiny nation, with an area just 2.5 times the size of Beijing and a population of less than 2 million people, created miracles that outsized even great nations. On July 26, 1581, the seven northern provinces of the Netherlands announced the formation of a republic, declared independence from Spain, and because the county of Holland was the richest and most developed, they named themselves the Dutch Republic. The Dutch Republic was the first bourgeois republic in history, and led the world in many aspects. Agriculture was an important facet of Dutch contribution. It was known as the Mecca of farming at the time, and its dairy products, cash crops, fruits, vegetables, flowers, and gardening were known throughout Europe, making it a crucial stop for anyone on the continent hoping to learn advanced agricultural techniques. It was first in marine transport, and it was known as the world's oceanic coachman. In 1602 the Dutch established the world's first stock company, the Dutch East India Company, and established the world's first stock exchange, the Amsterdam Stock Exchange. They established the world's first modern bank—the Bank of Amsterdam was established in 1609, a century before the Bank of England. The Dutch Republic was the first nation to see sustained economic growth. The 1993 Nobel Prize–winning economist Douglass North has argued that the Netherlands—a country that industrialized quickly as a result of its weak guild system—was the leading economy in Europe in the early modern era. Holland was perhaps the first country to meet our limited definition of sustained economic growth. Even today, the Netherlands is a wealthy nation, and the models of trade they developed continue to influence the world.

In the first half of the 17th century the Netherlands owned a fleet of 16,000 trade ships, three-quarters of Europe's total tonnage—as much as the tonnage of the English, French, Portuguese, and Spanish shipping fleets combined. Compared to individual countries, the tonnage of the Dutch fleet was 4–5 times that of the English fleet, and 7 times that of the French fleet. The Dutch essentially monopolized global maritime shipping. It was said of their trade network: "The Dutch take their wealth from every nation . . . their forests are in Norway, the banks of the Rhine are their vineyard, Ireland is where they pasture their sheep, Prussia and Poland are their granaries, India and Arabia are their orchards." Amsterdam was the center of commerce and trade in 17th century Europe. At the height of Dutch industry, the capital accumulated there was more than the rest of Europe combined, Dutch investments abroad were 15 times that of England, and the crafts emerging from Dutch workshops were the finest in Europe.

In 1664 British mercantilist Thomas Mun said, "This is a miracle in our mortal realm: a nation so minuscule, not even the size of our two largest counties, utterly lacking in natural wealth, grain, timber, and other common provisions required for war or ordinary military maintenance, has these and all other things in abundance." French historian Fernand Braudel described the reaction of Europeans to the rise of the Dutch Republic: "At the time, people only saw the astounding symbols of progress. As is typical, they didn't take notice of Holland's long process of preparation. At the moment of Holland's success, they were given a sudden, rude awakening. Almost instantaneously, without anyone understanding why, this fledgling upstart among nations achieved everything. It developed at lightning speed, and became unfathomably rich. Everyone was debating the 'Dutch secret,' the 'Dutch miracle,' and the 'stunning' Dutch wealth." Karl Marx had equivalent praise for the American miracle. In *German Ideology* Marx called North America the most perfect example of a modern nation. In *Metaphysics of Political Economy* he noted that the North American progress was faster than the rest of the world.

## Constructing Superior New Models

The systems a nation uses to structure itself, run itself, and develop itself are directly related to its nature, vitality, and potential. In short, these systems are a nation's core competitive strength. Champion nations have always created innovative, groundbreaking systems. They are the nations with the most advanced political systems in the world.

England's 18th and 19th century political model was the most advanced of its time. Their innovations defined the form of the modern nation-state, including a cabinet system, a constitutional monarchy, a two-party system, and government accountability to legislature. These political innovations were the guarantee for England's peaceful, stable development. The British economic model also marked the beginning of a new era, and their industrial model had a deep, long-lasting impact on the world.

The American political model secured America's rise and hegemony and is unquestionably more influential than any other model in the world today. The United States is the youngest major country, but it hosts the world's oldest republican government. In just over two centuries since America's founding, one of every two governments founded in the world has been overturned, while the United States of America has remained stable. There has not been a single coup or revolution since the country was founded. After the United States won independence, it created a unique political system with features uncommon with any other government of the time. The United States Constitution, written in 1787, was the world's first bourgeoisie constitution. It was based on the principles of bourgeoisie democratic thought and democracy, and created the first complete set of institutions for a democratic republic in a bourgeoisie nation. These included a republican government, a presidential system, three branches of government, popularly elected government officials, limited terms of office, and other defining features. The American government has three branches: legislative, executive, and judicial. Congress is responsible for legislation, but congressional bills do not go into effect until passed by the president; the president is responsible for execution and administration, but his appointees for important political posts and treaties must be approved by Congress; Congress also has the power to impeach and remove the president; the Supreme Court is the judicial branch, and is responsible for deciding all questions of legality and constitutionality. America's separation of powers ensures that decision-making is democratic, and avoids the abuse of power. The American model, when compared to the world's other political models, especially the Soviet model during the Cold War, proved its durability and robustness. It is one of the fundamental reasons the United States has retained its advantages over time and has so widely influenced the world.

## Becoming the Richest Country in the World

Champion nations are the richest nations in the world, the world's financial champions. Great Britain, the industrial hegemon of the world during the Industrial Revolution, produced half of the world's metallic products, woven fabric, and iron, as well as two-thirds of the world's coal in 1850. They also led the world in shipbuilding and rail construction. In 1860 the United Kingdom produced 40-50% of the world's industrial output, and 55%–60% of Europe's. In 1850 Great Britain was responsible for 20% of global trade volume, a figure that doubled to 40% a mere 10 years later. The British pound became the world's currency. Great Britain's area was 0.2% of the world's land area, and its population was just over 10 million, just 2% of the world's total population and 10% of Europe's population. Despite that, Great Britain's industrial output was equivalent to 40–50% of the world's industrial output capacity, and the British pound dominated the world.

The United States that emerged from World War II was immensely powerful. Beijing University International Relations Professor Liu Jinzhi, in his *History of the Cold War*, says that the United States leads the world in global trade volume, and that its products, entertainment, and lifestyle can be found everywhere in the world. Although 410,000 Americans lost their lives in World War II, it was the only major nation involved to come out of the war without suffering any direct damage to its infrastructure. Furthermore, during the war, its per capita income doubled. From 1940 to 1945 the after-tax profits of United States corporations totaled $124.95 billion, 3.5 times the same total 6 years prior. After the war, the United States controlled three-fourths of the world's capital and two-thirds of its industrial production capacity. It controlled 59% of the world's gold reserves, and more than half of the world's ship tonnage. The United States exported one-third of the world's total exports, and became the world's largest investor and creditor nation.

## II. Readjusting Sino-American Relations

As we get further into the 21st century, Sino-American relations need to be readjusted. The United States is the world's current champion nation, and China is the clearest potential successor. This kind of relationship is one that requires cooperation to solve important world problems, and one that requires strategic competition for the title of champion among nations.

## The Relationship Between a Champion and Its Potential Successor

The competitive relationship between major nations is what defines international relations in any given era. The core problem between major nations is which of them is the champion among nations. Competition between champion nations and potential successors is decisive; it's the highest vantage point in international relations, the thread holding international relations together, and the fulcrum on which international relations are leveraged. By controlling the vantage point, pulling the thread, and pushing the lever, a nation can see farther, dictate terms, and be proactive in creating strategy. A look at relations between champion nations and potential champion nations has strategic significance.

## The Conflicts Between Champion Nations and Successors Are the Fundamental Conflicts in International Society

The conflicts between champion nations and potential champion nations are the fundamental conflicts in international society, and they do not sway according to the potential champion nations' will. Conflicts between champion nations and their challengers are the most influential, the strongest, and have the most potential for further development. Competition between them is more than simply a struggle for position; it decides the power structure, appearance, and future of the entire world. Conflicts between champions and challengers are conflicts that influence other international conflicts as well and are the most fundamental conflicts in the international sphere.

Both world wars were the intensification of existing international conflicts. What were the conflicts that set them off? Conflicts between champion nations and their challengers. All the nations that challenged Great Britain for the lead role in global hegemony were potential champion nations, including the US. The difference was that in the presence of multiple potential successors, there was also competition between the challengers, which made the overall competition more complex and intense. Germany and other challengers used direct competition with Great Britain, while the US used strategic competition. Germany tried to simply take power, while the US tried indirectly leveraging them out of power. Despite differing methods, the two world wars were about deciding conflicts between the champion nation and its potential successors, and ultimately passing on the title and transferring power and responsibilities. In both world wars, the primary narrative was in the conflicts, struggles, and fights between the champion nation and its potential successor. These relationships influence and decide the nature and direction of the entire international order.

The Cold War was also the product of a struggle between a champion nation and a potential successor that reshaped international politics. The central international conflict of the Cold War was not ideology, a struggle between socialism and capitalism, nor a conflict between developed and developing nations; it was a conflict between a champion and a challenger. The US was the champion of that era, and the Soviet Union was a nation that wished to replace it. The US victory in the Cold War was a champion nation defending its title; the Soviet Union's defeat was a challenger nation losing the race to become a champion among nations.

## To Rise and Contain Is the Basic Form of Strategic Competition

Champion nations, which have hegemonic power, also have a hegemon's selfishness. Their core concern is protecting their position as champion, and their biggest fear is that a challenger will replace them. Containment and suppression are instinctual for champion nations, and it's impossible for a hegemon to truly get over their selfishness. Potential champion nations, on the other hand, always try to rise, break out of their containment, and move toward the goal of becoming the world's global leader. As potential champion nations rise, current champions will try to contain them, thus forming the basic conflict between the two sides. In the struggles to rise and contain, each side's basic strategic interests, risks, and future are omnipresent.

The long-standing British policy of continental balance in Europe was to prevent the rise of any power capable of challenging it for the title of champion among nations. This strategy was also used by the United States during the Cold War to eventually restrain the Soviet Union's rise to champion status; both are classic examples of containment by a hegemonic power.

In the struggle to rise and contain, are rising nations all beacons of progress and civilization? Are all containing nations all conservative reactionaries? No. Each unique case calls for detailed analysis. The rise of the Fascist nations, for example, was reactionary; the efforts to contain them were significant steps toward progress. The Soviet-American struggle to rise, contain, and take global hegemony during the Cold War was a betrayal of the modern era's spirit of peace and progress. It is necessary to understand the nature of each specific rise and containment measure. It is not the case that all rising nations are good, and all efforts to contain them are bad.

In the 20th century, the most important rise and containment measures were Great Britain and the US's containment of a rising Germany and Japan, and the US containment of the Soviet Union. Some say that we should include a third phase: American containment of China. But the first two phases were clearly antagonistic; they were solved with World

War II and the Cold War. This third phase of conflict is a civilized competition in an era of mutual competition, cooperation, and respect.

## The United States Suffers from Champion's Anxiety

After winning the Cold War, the United States didn't remain happy for long. It soon entered a deep state of champion's anxiety that trapped it in feelings of fear, inflated pride, doubt, conflict, and many more complicated moods, and the US has since found it very difficult to extricate itself.

## A Champion's Greatest Fear

After the Cold War, the US altered its goals and strategic interests toward building a national order led by itself and ensuring that its special position as champion could not be threatened or challenged. They saw the most serious challenge coming from the Eurasian mainland, believing the next potential champion nation would arise there.

In 1997 American strategist Brzezinski said that after the Cold War America was promoted to being the world's only superpower, which made America's need for a complete, comprehensive Eurasia strategy more pressing than ever, because most of the world's politically proud and active nations are located in Eurasia, most all the nations that have attempted to become world powers are located there. The most populous countries with ambitions to become regional hegemons, such as China and India, are also located in Eurasia. All but one of the publicly nuclear nations are located in Eurasia; and all but one of the nations that are nuclear-capable, yet not publicly so, are in Asia. This region is home to 75% of the world's population, produces 60% of the world's economic output, and houses 75% of the world's resources. The strength of the nations of Eurasia, added together, surpasses even that of America. The Eurasian landmass is the axis of the world. If a nation controls Eurasia, it controls two of the world's strongest economic regions, Western Europe and East Asia, and can exercise decisive influence. Take a look at a map and it is clear—if a nation controls the Eurasian mainland, they automatically control the Middle East and Africa. Given Eurasia's decisive significance on the political chessboard today, it will also have a decisive influence on America's leading position in the world and China's legacy.

To Brzezinski, America's position as the world's leading nation is its core national interest, and America uses its strategic leverage and strength to prevent the appearance of any global power with the strength to challenge it. And since the next potential champion nation will arise on the Eurasian mainland, the task of America is to prevent that from happening. Brzezinski believes America needs a continuing strategy for the Eurasian mainland, including a short-term and a mid-term strategy of 20 years, to prevent the eventual possibility of a hostile alliance rising that could challenge American dominance, much less a nation that actively seeks to threaten America. These possibilities must be reduced to nothing. This is America's "champion's anxiety"—a phobia of a potential champion nation arising in Eurasia.

## A Champion's Conceit

America's conceit comes from its confidence in its power, and from lack of knowledge about the unformed anti-American alliance of the future. Americans Stephen G. Brooks and William H. Wohlforth, in an article published in *Foreign Affairs* magazine, said the following: "As German political commentator Josef Joffe has put it, 'the history books say that Mr. Big always invites his own demise. Nos. 2, 3, 4 will gang up on him, form countervailing alliances and plot his downfall. That happened to Napoleon, as it happened to Louis xiv and the mighty Hapsburgs, to Hitler and to Stalin. Power begets superior counter-power; it's the oldest rule of world politics.' What such arguments fail to recognize are the features of America's post-Cold War position that make it likely to buck the historical trend. Bounded by oceans to the east and west and weak, friendly powers to the north and south, the United States is both less vulnerable than previous aspiring hegemons and less threatening to others. The main potential challengers to its unipolarity, meanwhile China, Russia, Japan, and Germany are in the opposite position. They cannot augment their military capabilities so as to balance the United States without simultaneously becoming an immediate threat to their neighbors. Politics, even international politics, is local. Although American power attracts a lot of attention globally, states are usually more concerned with their own neighborhoods than with the global equilibrium. Were any of the potential challengers to make a serious run at the United States, regional balancing efforts would almost certainly help contain them, as would the massive latent power capabilities of the United States, which could be mobilized as necessary to head off an emerging threat. Previous historical experiences of balancing, moreover, involved groups of status quo powers seeking to contain a rising revisionist one. The balancers had much to fear if the aspiring hegemon got its way. Today, however, U.S. dominance is the status quo. Several of the major powers in the system have been closely allied with the United States for decades and derive substantial benefits from their position. Not only would they have to forego those benefits if they tried to balance, but they would have to find some way of putting together a durable, coherent alliance while America was watching. This is a profoundly important point, because although there may be several precedents for a coalition of balancers preventing a hegemon from emerging, there is none for a group of subordinate powers joining to topple a hegemon once it has already emerged, which is what would have to happen today."[4]

American conceit believes that even if China's economy grows larger than America's, it will be impossible for China to unseat American power. Brooks and Wohlforth also said: "Most researchers looking at contending challengers America may face in the future turn their eyes to China, because China is the only nation with the potential to economically match America in the coming decades. Even if China's GDP catches up with America, technologically, militarily, and geographically, China still lags far behind America, and these gaps will persist. From the middle of the 1990s, Chinese strategists have become less and less confident about their ability to close the gap with America. They believe China doesn't have the capacity to do so in the short-term. The latest statistics from China show that, by 2020, China's economy will be ⅓–½ the size of America's. Half of China's labor force is employed in the agricultural sector and the technology sector only makes up a tiny portion of their economy. In the mid-1990s, American investment in new technology development was 20 times that of China's. Most of China's weapons lag decades behind America's. Furthermore, China has no way to change the fact of geography; China is surrounded by nations with the ability and the motives to check its power." Therefore, "for the foreseeable future, America will not face a global threat. No country, or group of countries, wish to make an enemy of America." During the Cold War, "America spent 5%–14% of its GDP on national defense, and maintained a vast nuclear deterrence arsenal. To demonstrate America's determination, 85,000 Americans died in two wars in Asia. At the same time, multiple American presidents maintained policies of nuclear brinkmanship that could have instantly brought forth a nuclear holocaust. In the coming decades, no country will be in a position to combine the resources, geographical advantages, and economic growth rate needed to unseat American power."

## Hegemony in Champion Nations

The worst expression of American hegemony is in its monopolization of its status as champion. In 1998 *A Military Strategy for a New Century* declared that America's goal was to lead the entire world and ensure that no other major power or group of powers could be allowed to challenge America's position. In February 1999 America's leaders declared again that American foreign policy in the 21st century would begin with the principle that the world can and must have only one leader, that the United States is the nation most capable of leading the world, and that its intentions were to bring all nations into a free world system. In *The National Security Strategy* report, published in September 2002, the United States government declared that no strong antagonistic military power will be allowed to rise, and that no foreign force will ever be again allowed to challenge American power as during the Cold War.

## The Game Destined to Be Civilized

What is the best path for America, the current champion among nations? America needs to abandon its Cold War mentality, escape the vicious cycle of hegemonic containment, and establish a new cooperative relationship with its potential successor, China. China and America will both find benefit, and it is a necessity for the creation of world peace.

## Understanding Civilized Powers

The United States is the most civilized hegemon in modern history, and China is the most civilized rising power in recent history. If we compare China and America, based on history and circumstance, China is a bit more civilized than America. So, the competition between the two over which becomes the champion among nations will surely be the most civilized of such competitions in the modern era. When two civilized great nations compete, the necessary result will be the creation of a new type of competition to be civilized, a completely new way for the world's great nations to compete—one that will take competition between civilizations to a truly more civilized plane, reduce the cost of competition between great nations, lower the cost of international progress, and raise the influence of competition between civilizations to a new level.

The difference between the civilized hegemon nation of America and past hegemonic nations is that America doesn't threaten the existence of rising powers, but it does try to limit and control their development. The significance of this is that its hegemony is a restrained hegemony, and its control is a restrained control. Comparatively speaking, it is a more civilized and cooperative hegemon.

In the history of Sino-American relations, the United States, this most civilized of hegemon nations, has certainly demonstrated its powerful, hegemonic side; however, it has also demonstrated its more civilized aspects. If we list America as an imperialist power and compare it to other imperialist powers, through Chinese eyes, American imperialism is a benign variety of imperialism—a reasonable imperialism, and the imperialism least resented by China's people.

## China's Rise Is America's Profit

Neither China nor America can beat the other in open conflict; this was decided during the Korean War. Neither China nor America can change the other: China made its mark on the world's revolutionary thought long ago, and America's attempts to Westernize and polarize China will not succeed. In today's globalized world, neither China nor America depends on the other, and neither can stand in for the other. For China and America, there is only live-and-let-live policy; peaceful, cooperative, mutually beneficial competition is necessary if both are to survive, shine, and win.

More than that, in the process of China's peaceful rise, another phenomenon has appeared: China's rise is America's profit. The United States has truly been the biggest beneficiary of China's rise. American commentator Thomas Friedman wrote in *The World Is*

*Flat: A Brief History of the Twenty-First Century* that while China's breakneck development would affect the employment of manufacturing workers in other workforces, for the world's consumers, China's cheap products would be an undisputed blessing. On October 4, 2004, *Fortune* magazine referenced a Morgan Stanley survey reporting that beginning in the 1990s, China's cheap products saved American consumers roughly $600 billion, and saved American components importers an inestimable amount. These savings allowed the Federal Reserve to maintain low interest rates for longer, helped American citizens buy houses, and gave entrepreneurs the capital to innovate. These phenomena instilled the idea that China's development benefits the world and China's rise is America's profit and were nothing short of miraculous in their influence on the American Economy.

## Hegemony Cannot Be the Core National Interest

All the champion nations in recent history have treated their status as hegemon as their core national interest, and acted to protect it, and the potential champion nations have treated the pursuit of hegemonic power as their core national interest. The result has been a vicious cycle of rises and containment. In China's patriotic atmosphere national interest comes first and is sacred; anything labeled as a national interest becomes unassailable—something that should be protected by a death oath. Anything labeled as a core national interest becomes even more of a bottom line, a line that if crossed could be very dangerous for the trespasser. The problem is, in international society, for a champion among nations, what is a core national interest? If a nation becomes the world's leading nation should it automatically regard hegemonic power as a national interest? It seems that the era in which champion nations place hegemonic power as a core national interest ought to be revolutionized. In the peaceful world ahead, a new kind of champion nation is required, one that doesn't regard hegemonic power as a core national interest.

Speaking in terms of the current champion nation of America, what does it mean to seek and protect core national interests? In reality, it consists of two parts: the first are the interests it gains from leading the world in scientific and economic strength, which are the necessary conditions and fruits of its status as a champion nation; the second are the interests it seizes using the hegemonic status granted to it as a champion nation. These are interests gained purely through hegemonic power and the rights and benefits it gains by exercising its role as hegemon. This kind of national benefit is gained through harming other nations, not benefit that is duly, rationally earned. Seeking the latter kind of national interest creates chaos in the world, and is the fundamental reason for the destruction of international peace. America's fear that potential champion nations will harm its core national interests is actually the fear that it will lose the corrupt benefits seized through exercising its power as a hegemon.

As China moves toward the world's leading nation it will struggle to become a new kind of champion nation, the significance of which is that China will never seek to become a global hegemon, and will never seek hegemonic benefits, and will never consider holding hegemonic power as a core national interest.

## China and America's Joint Responsibility to Lead the World

If America is the most civilized of the great powers that have struggled for and obtained hegemonic power in recent history, it is a new kind of hegemon, different from the others. China is the most civilized of the rising powers, and hopes to end the era of hegemonic nations. This means that the strategic competition between the potential champion nation of China and the incumbent champion nation of America will be the best opportunity for international society to make a historic, fundamental, and transformational step toward progress. It's a step that could reshape the world and create unprecedented accomplishment. The era of hegemon nations could potentially conclude with America. This is something that American strategists have foreseen and predicted. At the same time, the first non-hegemonic champion nation in history will appear, and that nation is China.

The appearance and existence of hegemonic nations is something that international society had to adjust to in the jungle age of international relations. With the appearance of non-hegemonic nations, humanity will be brought into a new, more civilized, lawful, democratic, and peaceful world. China has the potential to end the jungle age of international relations in which all is decided by size, might, and dominance. The creation of such a world is both China's mission and America's responsibility.

## III. A New Model for China and the US

How America and China will compete in the 21st century is a grave strategic choice faced by both nations. The mode of competition they choose is what will determine their methods of competition, the quality of the competition, and the rules of competition. China's declaration of its "peaceful development, peaceful rise" policy is actually a commitment to a peaceful mode of competition. It was a declaration of China's intent to bring its competition with America onto a peaceful, non-military path. Through this competition, both countries will promote the mutual development of one another and create prosperity for the world. The mode of competition chosen by China and America in the 21st century will decide the fate of both nations and the future of the world; this relationship is the weathervane for evolution toward a civilized strategic game between great nations. Analyzing the historical progress of how the champion nations of modern history have obtained their status and comparing the different modes of competition great nations have used is of critical importance for choosing and creating a new mode of competition for China and America.

## Steps and Remedies for the Struggles of a Champion Nation

The competition between champion nations and their potential successors is seen in how champion nations defend their title and how potential champion nations attempt to claim the title. These struggles for champion status primarily occur in three forms, which reflect three separate eras of history.

## Three Forms of Struggle for Champion Status

First, war is the ultimate form of competition. Nations fight for survival in large-scale battle. This fight for survival began with the modern world system and concluded with World War II. In the second form, nations don't fight for survival in major wars, but rather face off against one another in another Cold War. This form of competition continued for nearly half a century. The third form, as exemplified by China and America in the 21st century, not only exhibits characteristics and trends completely different from the previous two forms, it will bring about unprecedented innovations and changes to society, bring prosperity to both countries, and bring prosperity to the world.

## Three Steps in the Current Struggle for Champion Status

The 20th century was a century of war and antagonism for humanity. The 21st century will be a century of competition and cooperation. From the beginning of the 20th century to the middle of the 21st century, we can carve out three 50-year periods, each a different phase of competition.

The first phase, the competition among great powers in first 50 years of the 20th century, was an era of wild, jungle competition. The two world wars were duels in which the victors killed the losers. The precondition of "you are defeated, I gain victory" is a proclamation of the goal of "you die, I live."

The second phase corresponds with the second half of the 20th century. Although not as bloody and brutal as the first half, this was an era of competition conducted according to the principle of "you decline, I prosper." This was a zero-sum game. After nearly half a century of the Cold War, it was a boxing match, a competition in which the victor took shots at the loser in hopes to weaken and eventually knock them down. The preconditions of "you lose, I win" are "you fall, I stand," and "you decline, I prosper" and were omnipresent

In the third phase, China and America's new round of competition in the first half of the 21st century, the relationship between the competitors is not defined by "you live, I die," "you fall, I stand," or "you lose, I win." It will be more like a race: a "you chase, I run" and "you are second, I am first" model, in which both nations will continue to thrive and compete regardless of the outcome.

China and America's competition in the 21st century needs to move beyond duels and boxing matches to a track and field competition. China and America should create a new international civilization of competition, a new model for competition between great powers, and new rules for competition between nations. Just like humanity left the jungle and established civilization, international society also needs to leave the jungle behind and create a civilized world.

## War Is the Cruelest Competition

Clausewitz said, "War is the continuation of politics." Great wars are the continuation of great power struggles in politics and world wars are the continuation of struggles in world politics. Continuing politics through war is a brutal, bloody, and unnecessary solution. The progress of human civilization and world politics calls for new thought on the link between war and politics.

## Bismarck's Strategy for Duels Among Nations

After Germany's reunification after World War I, Bismarck warned Germany: "After a long split, the German people are finally united. We should cherish our hard-won fortune, and commit ourselves to peace and justice. Of those who resort to force to settle international disputes, after giving it some thought, simple dueling seems like an inappropriate way to solve these conflicts."

Bismarck introduced the concept of war as dueling, and refuted it as an effective method. Bismarck was a man who was brave enough to duel, both in his personal life, and in his blood and iron policy on German reunification. In international duels, he was brave enough to compete as a strong competitor and victor. Even this brilliant dueler, after sincere reflection on the method, decided that simple duels were inappropriate for solving international conflicts. But in the contention and replacement of champion nations, duels seem to be the only method. Duels always seem to become the guiding principle.

## The Historical Summary on Duels Among Nations

Robert Gilpin, contemporary renowned Western scholar of international relations, said there is not a single example to prove that to avoid war a dominant nation will give up its position to a nation rising in the international system.

Gilpin's theory fits with the reality of great power competition in recent history. Some experts point out that there were three nations that were able to become global hegemons in recent history; the 17th century Dutch Republic, 19th century Great Britain, and the 20th century United States; and that the global wars that produced these three hegemons each lasted about 30 years. After 1914–1945, the United States arose from the ruins of two world wars to take its place as the champion nation. In recent world history, every champion nation, without exception, has been a king of the jungle that beat down other claimants to the throne.

According to noted American political scientist George Modelski's Long Cycle Theory, put forth in the 1980s, turnover among world hegemons is accomplished by war between claimants to the title. From the emergence of the current international order, "hegemonic wars" have occurred according to a regular cycle, and the winners hold power over the international order for an average of a century. He believes that after 16th century Portugal, the 17th century Dutch Republic, the 18th and 19th century British Empire, and the 20th century United States, a new global leader is due to emerge in the 21st century, and that in the 2020s or 2030s, a new global war will engulf the world. His logic is that rising champion nations need to engage in a duel with the current champion, and that the handoff in status must be accomplished through war. This isn't just Cold War mentality, this is true warrior mentality. It's impossible to approve of a theory that predicts the explosion of a new world war, but analyzing theory using the last 500 years of duels between champion nations and contenders for the title seems to prove that it is inevitable. Looking at the turnover of champion nations in modern history, it seems it is a long process of wrestling in many aspects that eventually results in a duel, or war. Unfortunately, based on precedence, it seems this truly is historic law.

## *The Price America Paid to Become Champion*

When we speak of struggles among champion nations, America seems to be the model for a peaceful transition, because the United States supplanted Great Britain as the champion nation without a war. Actually, the price paid by America for its place was unprecedentedly large, but it was borne by other nations. The United States, in the process of taking Great Britain's place as hegemon, produced a peaceful transition that was the perfect product of an American strategy that incorporated trickiness and cleverness.

Although the transition from British to American hegemony wasn't decided by war, two major world wars had to occur before America became the final victor. If Germany, in its struggle for hegemony, hadn't deeply weakened Great Britain, it would have been impossible to avoid a war between Great Britain and the United States to accomplish the transition. Before the Second World War, the United States was constantly preparing for war against the British Empire, and Great Britain had its own plan for war against the United States. The so-called peaceful transition between Great Britain and America was actually a transition in which the United States paid the smallest price in history with relatively few military casualties, and the world paid the largest price in history with the unprecedented devastation of two world wars. War, especially global war, became the climax and necessary path for the transition of hegemony. The unusual form in which British hegemony was transferred to America was not an exception to the iron law of war between rising and falling champion nations.

## *The Cold War as a Boxing Match*

By looking at the Cold War as a boxing match, we can see the controlled yet merciless brutality of the Cold War in how one side had to utterly defeat the other. A winner had to be decided. The Cold War was progress from the duel model, in that the loser would still be allowed to exist because both contestants would survive the battle.

## *Cold War Mentality Is More Civilized than Duel Mentality*

After the Cold War, the world judged Cold War mentality as the devil that plagued competition between major powers. But looking at the shape of struggle to become the champion among nations in international society prior to the Cold War, it was an improvement over the bloody wars of the past, Cold War mentality was progress when compared to outright warrior mentality, and the Cold War was a much more civilized way of great powers tussling than in the past. The Cold War was more civilized than traditional war, even though that civility was forced, thanks to the evenly matched forces of the two sides, and the chilling effect of nuclear weapons on global war.

The historical significance of the Cold War was in the type of strategic competition it produced. It was a phase of competition between great nations. Its contribution to human civilization and the international relations process was the ability for great powers to compete without a global war. Theoretical questions left by the dissolution of the Soviet Union, the end of the Cold War, and the transition to a new era include the following: Why didn't the Cold War end because of a Soviet military defeat? And why didn't the arms race produce a third world war? We can judge the Cold War, but the Cold War was an era in which there were nuclear weapons, but no nuclear war; an era in which a massive arms race did not produce massive military conflict; and an era in which global conflicts did not produce global war. No matter if we compare the Cold War to the 50 years before it, the 20 years after it, or any 50-year period following the year 1500, it was the era with the fewest and smallest wars; it was the era in which superpowers paid the smallest possible price to decide the winners of their conflicts; it was the era in which the conflict was concluded without war. Given that, is it possible not to call the Cold War miraculous? We must further investigate the political wisdom behind the fact that no major wars came out of the Cold War.

## *The Calmness and Intellect of Cold War Mentality*

The Cold War was a strategic creation by the United States to overcome the Soviet Union, the invention of a civilized military imperialism to cope with Soviet hegemonic ambitions. In February 1946 George F. Kennan, Soviet relations expert and serving minister-counselor at the United States embassy in the USSR, wrote the exquisitely detailed, 8,000-word "Long Telegram," which was sent in five dispatches to the US on February 22. In the telegram, Kennan provided thorough analysis and advice about the theories, intents, policies, and methods of the Soviet Union and the means the United States should use to deal with them. Kennan believed the conflicts between the United States and the Soviet Union could be solved without recourse to a general military conflict, because "Soviet power, unlike that of Hitlerite Germany, is neither schematic nor adventustic. It does not work by fixed plans. It does not take unnecessary risks. Impervious to logic of reason, and it is highly sensitive to logic of force. For this reason it can easily withdraw—and usually does when strong resistance is encountered at any point. Thus, if the adversary has sufficient force and makes clear his readiness to use it, he rarely has to do so. If situations are properly handled there need be no prestige-engaging showdowns."[5] At the same time, the American government must strive to educate Americans about the true shape of Russia, which should strengthen the confidence, discipline, morale, and collective spirit of the American people. He advised that the US "must plan and point out more proactive and more constructive advice than we have in the past for other countries to create a picture of the kind of world we wish to see; and must courageously and confidently uphold our own methods and our views on society."

Kennan's "Long Telegram" put forth the view that the Soviet Union should be contained, a view that was approved of at executive levels. Kennan was immediately transferred back to the United States by the State Department, and made chief designer of State Department strategy. Secretary of the Navy James Forrestal ordered the telegram copied and made required reading for hundreds of high-ranking military officials. Later, Kennan expanded the "Long Telegram" into an article called "The Sources of Soviet Conduct," which was then published in the July 1947 edition of *Foreign Policy* magazine. It further developed the content of the telegram, and recommended a complete set of theories and policies with which to contain the Soviet Union. It should be apparent, given the historical conditions, that Cold War thinking was the product of calm, rational decision-making by the best minds of both sides. It was a comparatively reasonable approach, and the expression of both sides' strategic wisdom. The Cold War, and the containment of the Soviet Union, was the containment of a new world war.

## *The Cold Ware Era Has Come to an End*

The Cold War, as a historical period of competition between great powers, was civilized when compared to prior great power competition, but that does not give it any reasonable reason to exist beyond the four decades that it continued through. The Cold War was extremely antagonistic, and risky. It left the world surviving precariously under a sword of Damocles. It turned the planet into a giant bomb, and forced all of humanity to live under an uneasy peace enforced by the threat of destruction at any moment. Such a high price is something humanity cannot accept.

The Cold War fought by America and the Soviet Union for nearly half a century was actually a third world war in a unique form. The Cold War was not a duel between great nations; it was a boxing match between two global giants. In the previous two world wars, the nations seeking global hegemony treated the world as their battleground, which caused two worldwide wars in which nations fought bloody duels. In the Cold War, two superpowers treated the world as a boxing ring. The contest wasn't a lethal duel, but it was a contest to determine which would lose and be knocked down. In today's world, where peace, development, and cooperation are the trends and demands of the era, boxing-match-style competitions, despite not being lethal duels, have become as outdated and contemptible as the duels they replaced.

## *Track and Field Model: A New and Civilized Competition Model*

A track and field competition model between China and America is significant on two levels. The first is that the 21st century will hinge on the competition between America and China, which will be history's most civilized round of great power competition. It will not be a duel-style great war nor a boxing-match-style Cold War; it will be a track-and-field-style heat. The second is that the competition will be a century-long struggle, a track and field competition between the two nations. Not a hundred-meter or thousand-meter sprint, this will be a marathon that tests courage, will, and patience. The upcoming track and field event between China and America in the 21st century will be notable for two things: the civility and the length of the competition.

## *No Need to Avoid Mentioning the Challenge or Competitor*

There is no competitive event without challenge or competitors. The very nature of a competition is to face challengers; competition demands the existence of opponents. Competition between nations demands opponents as well. Objectively speaking, the struggle between champion nations and potential champion nations is precisely this type of relationship between a title-holding contender and a challenger seeking the title. Thus, there is no need to avoid mentioning the challenge or to fear the challenge.

The fundamental problem is not whether a challenge exists, but the nature and form of the challenge. Duel-type fights to the death are disastrous, and boxing-match-type challenges that demand a winner and loser come with a terrible price. But track-and-field-style challenges are a way for both sides to improve their athleticism. That is the natural result of normal competition—and a source of encouragement for all participants. Disallowing challenges is to disallow competition, and this is both impossible, and disadvantageous for providing the world the motive and strength to develop.

The challenger nations that have arisen in recent history have all been duelers and boxers, and rising hegemons have all had to challenge existing hegemons to take their own place as hegemons. After a period of time, their power and strength decline, and one or more challengers arise to take on the new hegemon. Spain challenged Portugal; France challenged the Dutch Republic; France and Germany each challenged Great Britain; the United States helped Great Britain meet the challenges of World War I, and then, after World War II, when the United States arose as the new hegemon nation, it faced a challenge from the Soviet Union. The resistance and wars caused by these challenges were disastrous for all nations involved and the entire world, and are diametrically opposed to the direction in which the world is moving today. While the world revokes challenges in the form of duels and boxing matches, it cannot revoke track and field challenges. International society is a kind of international stage on which each nation wants to perform its role—it is also an international arena, and every nation is an athlete. While nations as athletes and people as athletes have important differences, both share the common goal of wanting to perform and win. The arena of the past was an international dueling range, and it later evolved into an international boxing ring, but today, it has become an international racetrack. An Olympic event of national strength is ongoing. The challenge posed by the strategic competition between China and America is a sprint, a hurdle jump, and a marathon. It is an Olympic challenge to see who sprints faster, jumps higher, and runs farther. This is why the competition between China and America will provide enormous drive and vitality to the struggle for world progress, and will not be a disaster for the world.

## Eight Major Distinctions Between the Cold War and Sino-American Competition

Competition between China and America and competition between America and the Soviet Union are two qualitatively different competitions. Differences in eight important aspects tell us that the Sino-American competition will not be another Cold War.

**1. Different environments:** The Soviet-American competition was a competition between two societies, and two worlds, for one planet. The Soviet Union organized a unified society based on socialism, while the United States organized a so-called free society—a capitalist society. Humanity was split between two mutually exclusive societies, and the international world was split between two hostile and irreconcilable worlds—the free world and the totalitarian world. But the 21st century's competition between China and America is not a competition between two societies and two worlds, it is working together creating a peaceful, developed, open, and harmonious world. China does not want to build a separate world hostile to America; it wants to blend with the existing world and international order.

**2. Different competitive goals:** The Soviet-American competition was a competition over global hegemony. However, one of China's defining characteristics is that it does not desire hegemony. China wants to become the world's leading nation without becoming a despot. It wants to build a strong nation without becoming a king. China is not a Soviet-style promoter of a global revolution, and is not an American-style exporter of democracy. China is a peaceful, friendly, nation with unique characteristics and a purely defensive stance. Therefore, China does not need to use Cold War tactics as a tool in Sino-American relations.

**3. Different content:** America and the Soviet Union were both nations with a strong ideological identity, and their ideological attacks on one another were actually a renewed Crusades of sorts. However, China and America's competition in the 21st century is not an ideological battle. If China becomes a capitalist nation, America gains no major strategic interest. And if China remains a socialist nation, America's strategic interests aren't hurt. The competition between the Soviet Union and America was a competition to see whether American-style capitalism or Soviet-style socialism was a better system. The competition between China and America is simply an exchange of socialism with Chinese characteristics and American capitalism. Socialism with Chinese characteristics is a socialism that doesn't fight for hegemony and operates using a market economy; it is in line with the Western world, and shares common interests with the Western world. China and America's relationship is characterized as both civilized competition and intimate cooperation.

**4. Different allies:** The Soviet Union and America built huge strategic alliances that competed in concert as groups, and nations not in either group had to have their own ideology, stance, plan, and allies. The competition between China and America is largely conducted on an individual basis. Neither has a group of allies to speak of, and neither can accuse the other of ganging up.

**5. Different objectives:** The conflict between the Soviet Union and America was hostile, because the Soviet Union wanted to topple the American social order, and America wanted to change the Soviet social order. The Soviet Union wanted to turn the October Revolution into a worldwide revolution, and America wanted to turn the American democratic system into the world's democratic system. In the Soviet-American competition, both sides wanted to attack the other, and both wanted to export their own social model; the Soviets hoped to export Soviet socialism, and America hoped to export American democracy. Both sides wanted to change and shape the other, and the world, according to their model. Soviet socialism was an aggressive socialism that wanted to plant its red flag all over the world. American capitalism was just as aggressive and expansionist, attempting to turn the entire world into a democratic, free, capitalist world. The competition between China and America is different. China doesn't want to export revolution, it wants to maintain its special characteristics and integrate itself into a diverse world.

**6. Different risks:** The competition between the Soviet Union and America was a competition that at any moment could have exploded into global nuclear war. Several crises came close to sparking wars that could have obliterated humanity. The competition between America and China, militarily, is one without risk of major war, especially nuclear war.

**7. Different principles:** The competition between the Soviet Union and America was conducted upon the zero-sum principles of "you die, I live," "you fall, I rise," and "you are defeated, I am victorious." The competition between China and America is not one with the goals of pushing over and defeating the opponent; overall, it's one with goals of cooperation, mutual benefit, and mutual glory. The planet can't survive without the United States, and the planet can't survive without China; the future requires both a flourishing China and America.

**8. Different conclusions:** The competition between the Soviet Union and America made the world very nervous, and the price of such competition was too high. Sino-American competition, on the other hand, will be a process of creation, in which the two countries' competition in the political, economic, foreign relations, and military spheres will produce new innovations and the most civilized competition between powers in the history of mankind—especially since the establishment of the modern international system. It will push the competition between great nations into a more civilized phase, and make the world more civilized, more peaceful, more democratic, and more developed. The competition between China and America will be different from the campaign-style competitions before the two world wars, and different from the Cold War–style competition after World War II. This new phase of strategic competition between nations and in international society at large is a kind of strategic order, strategic rule, strategic culture, and strategic civilization. The United States cannot use the mentality it used to compete with the Soviet Union to compete with its new opponent, China.

## *American Prosperity Is Contingent on Chinese Prosperity*

A critical element that makes this new track and field model of competition the only possible future for Sino-American competition is the deepening economic ties between the two nations, which bind their prosperity together in a trade relationship. During Great Britain's ascendance, the UK and the United States shared deep economic ties. Great Britain relied on imported American grain and the United States was the largest market for Great Britain's fabric products; furthermore, Great Britain had huge amounts of capital invested in the United States. By the 1850s Great Britain owned more US government securities than all other European nations combined. In 1857 the seven American railways listed on the London Stock Exchange had a total value of 80 million British pounds. British prime minister Lord Liverpool said, "If we wish for England to prosper, we must allow America to prosper." Looking at the development of trade between China and the United States over the last 30 years, and the scale of Sino-American bilateral trade today, we can see a similar phenomenon today: if we wish America to prosper, we must allow China to prosper.

It was popular for a time among French Internet users to call for a boycott of Chinese goods. Other users responded to their comments with opposition: "To boycott China, we would first have to strip naked, and throw our cell phones, keyboards, computer monitors, TVs, MP3 players, watches, car parts, and motorcycles out the window. Is everyone ready to do that?" Today, every person in the world, on average, per year, buys one pair of Chinese-manufactured shoes, two meters of Chinese-produced fabric, and three pieces of Chinese-produced clothing. The lives of global consumers are inseparable from Chinese manufacturing. The bonds purchased by China with its export earnings keep the global financial system stable. If China's economy collapsed, it would spell disaster for the world, and even if China's growth simply slowed, there would be serious consequences for the global economy. Those in the West with vision have already seen that the real threat is not from China's development, but from interruptions in or the failure of China's development. From this perspective, when China develops, America benefits, and so does the world.

## *A New Competition Culture*

Taking the struggle between champion nations and potential champion nations from duels, to boxing matches, to track and field competitions, and then moving toward a runway model is a revolution in international politics—a historic innovation in the competition between major nations. The appearance of the European Union was a major innovation in this direction. In the 21st century, the competition between China and America will have deep significance for furthering this process.

In the 1,100 years before World War II, France and Germany fought more than 200 wars—on average, once every five years. Over the course of a millennium of hostility and war, the losers in this relationship lost horribly, and the winners won horribly. The painful lessons for both sides of this losing relationship provided the spark for their political enlightenment. The Second World War caused a significant change in the layout of Europe, and persuaded the long-extant thoughts of a European alliance and unified Europe to gain prominence. Even in 1942, as Churchill considered how to revive a postwar Europe, he raised the idea of a United States of Europe. In March 1943, the Pan-European Conference supported by European federalist Richard Coudenhove-Kalergi met for the fifth time in New York, where he advocated establishing a European Union after the war. In September 1946, Churchill delivered a speech at the University of Zurich titled "Europe's Tragedy," in which he called for "the establishment of an organization resembling the United States of Europe." From May 7 to 10, 1948, more than 800 representatives from every European country attended the Hague Congress, including such notable figures as Winston Churchill, Eduard Herriot, Paul van Zeeland, and Konrad Adenauer. The Hague Conference produced the "Notice to the People of Europe," which expressed a desire for a united Europe, a European Charter for Human Rights, and a court to enforce the charter. These federalist demands included the establishment of a federal government with supranational authority. After the Second World War, West Germany's first chancellor, Konrad Adenauer, and president of the Fifth French Republic, Charles de Gaulle, finally dissolved the centuries of enmity between the two nations. With France and Germany as the engines that drove Europe toward a new organization, a united market, a united currency, a common legislature, and even a common military force. With this, an incredibly powerful regional consortium was born.

The development and cooperation of postwar Europe was a historical miracle. Brzezinski said that the Europe Union was truly a pioneering effort—one that America had underestimated and criticized. Harvard Kennedy School professor Joseph Nye once hailed the creation of the European Union as a unique attempt in world history. In the past there were states that joined together to form a federation, like 18th century America. But Europe is unique because it did not form a federation, but rather established a more tightly organized union than other international organizations, and none of the member states lost their international status. This is a wonderful format, because it eliminates the competitive relationships that led to European nations fighting one another in the previous century, and avoids the destructive results of that fighting. Today, it's impossible to imagine how war between France and Germany could occur. The European Union will endure, and will benefit the European economy and politics, and it will continue to evolve. Some think it will become a federation and Europe will become a single country, like the United States. I am dubious of this possibility; I am optimistic about the European Union's development, but I don't think it will develop into a federation.

Unification of the European Union has progressed faster than even the most optimistic predictions. On November 11, 2009, the European Union adopted the Lisbon Treaty.

Shortly after, the European Union announced its new president and foreign minister, and a new European Union nation was born.

We can consider the first great step forward in this new era of international politics as Europe's historic transition from war to union to establishing a nation together. The European Union is the first major product of the positive competition between nations after the Second World War. Likewise, the next 50 years of competition between China and America will be the next major creation as these two nations forge an entirely new model of civilized conflict between major powers. The creation of this new model of Sino-American strategic creation will be an even more significant event than the appearance of the European Union. The European Union is a homogeneous coalition, a product of relations between countries with similar social and ideological backgrounds, as well as a common geographical area, which provides an important, limiting prerogative to cooperation. When China and the United States find a new way to cooperatively compete, it will be a fusion of two nations with dissimilar social systems and ideologies, a change of incredibly far-reaching significance for the world in the relationship between champion nations and potential successors, and an important contribution to the construction of a world based on democracy, cooperation, civility, and harmony.

## IV. A Non-Hegemonic World

The China Dream is China's dream for itself, as well as its dream for the world. China's national goals are linked to China's vision for the world. A major global power needs to consider what kind of a world it wants to build before it can understand what kind of a country it wants to become. China's aims cannot just be limited to itself; they need to be goals for the world.

Whether or not the human world of the 21st century will become one of peace, harmony, and cooperation depends on whether it can become a world without a hegemonic structure. Hegemony is the largest threat to global peace, harmony, and cooperation. China's major goal for the world in the 21st century is to create a non-hegemonic world. Ending the era of global hegemony is the historical mission of the century-long game between the US and China, and the necessary result of the century-long clash to come between China and America.

### Signs of Great Global Transformation

The world is always changing. The rise of great nations is the motivating force and the signpost of great global transformations. In modern history, as wave after wave of great nations have risen and clashed, three great historical transformations have taken place.

## *The Rise of Western Nations: The Transformation from Feudalism to Capitalism*

The first major transformation has been the transition from a feudal to capitalist world. The force that drove this change was the rise of a group of Western nations, including Spain, Portugal, the Netherlands, France, England, and the United States. This group of nations all made the transformation to capitalism during the rise of the capitalist world. The rise of capitalist nations in the West signaled the decline and death of feudalism. It fundamentally concluded the Middle Ages in Europe, ended the global age of feudalism, and allowed the feudal world to transition to a capitalist one.

The great nations that prompted the first major transition in modern history made their breakthroughs through becoming naval powers, expansionists, colonialists, and warriors. The rise of each was primal, cruel, savage, and marked by the original sins of military expansion and colonial conquest. In the bloody wars precipitated by their rise, the world made its first historical transformation.

## *The Answer to the Western Rise: The Founding of Socialism*

The second great historic transformation was the rise of the Soviet Union and a series of socialist nations, which took the world from an era of capitalist dominance to a model of "one world, two systems." The Soviet Union was the world's first socialist nation, and its rise was hostile and antagonistic toward the capitalist world. Its rise cleaved the world in a new era of two rival systems. Its rise ended the era of capitalism's dominance, and brought the world into an era in which capitalism and socialism stood apart yet dealt with each other on equal terms. It was a tense time for the world, but also a new age of civility. Traditional, primal capitalism was able to transform itself into a gentler, more civilized capitalism because two very different superpowers were struggling and competing. Socialist power forced capitalist power into civility. This second historical transformation produced the second round of historic improvement for the world in the modern area. The Soviet struggle with the West did not escape the vicious cycle of hegemonic struggle, however. The Soviet Union rose as it fought America's capitalist hegemony and died as it tried to take it.

## *The Rise of China: From Hegemony to a Hegemon-Free World*

The rise of China was different from the rise of Western nations and the Soviet Union, because it was an entirely new type of rise. There are three characteristics that make this new era distinctive.

**1. The Goals of China's Rise:** Becoming a global hegemon is not China's goal; China does not provoke existing hegemons nor threaten other powers and weaker nations. Instead, it

THE FIGHT FOR THE CENTURY

seeks to revive itself and benefit the world. "China opposes all forms of power politics and will never seek to engage in hegemony or empire expansion." This declaration from the 17th Party Congress is China's promise to the world and the defining goal of its rise.

**2. The Environment of China's Rise:** China arose from among the world's developing nations. China is not the only developing nation in the world with the conditions and strength to rise to the status of a great power; a number of developing nations have risen to the level of global influence that China holds. China's rise has taken place with the support of the global tide of development and has deep, structural mass support on the global stage.

**3. The Means of China's Rise:** China's rise has been conducted through peaceful development. China's rise has not been a colonial rise accompanied by warships and cannons, nor has it been accompanied by campaigns of conquest and military might, nor has it been a Cold War–style rise demanding the fall and demise of other nations. China's rise is a historically unprecedented peaceful rise, a rise in which we don't attack others, and we don't allow others to attack us. It has been a rise based on peaceful development, mutually beneficial cooperation, and mutual prosperity. Therefore China's rise is a profoundly more moral type of rise.

## A Hegemon-Free and Nuclear-Free World

Not long after Barack Obama took over as US president, he asked that we build a nuclear-free world and create a world without nuclear weapons. Building a nuclear-free world is a systematic process that will require efforts on many fronts, but the key to building a nuclear-free world will be building a hegemon-free world.

## The Greatest Danger to World Peace Is not the Nuclear Threat but a Hegemonic Threat

Prior to production of nuclear weapons, the greatest danger to world peace was hegemony. The root causes of the two world wars were to fight for world hegemony, rather than control via new and profoundly powerful weapons. After World War II, a 50-year Cold War broke out. The root cause of the Cold War was to seek global hegemony, and both the United States and the Soviet Union wanted to achieve ultimate power. Nuclear weapons became a tool for the US and the Soviet Union to gain strategic and military leverage in their quest for global hegemony.

After the Cold War, as the world became unipolar and the United States became the only superpower, the proliferation of nuclear weapons became a serious problem as rising nations strove to research and develop their own nuclear weapons. The entire world saw that the United States, without the Soviet Union to check its power, had began to lose its restraint and exercise its hegemonic power. Relying purely on military superiority, it launched the Gulf War, Kosovo War, Afghanistan War, and Iraq War to cement its hegemonic interests. The list of countries that have been attacked is growing. Some countries, feeling the threat of American hegemony, and without any strategic reassurance to prevent an attack by the United States, began to see the possession of nuclear weapons as a guarantee of safety, and have gone to tremendous lengths to get them. American hegemony is the root cause of the current attempts at nuclear weapons proliferation. American war has not stopped since the Cold War concluded, and the reason is not nuclear weapons, but America's imposed hegemony. The first strategic task necessary to guarantee world peace is not denuclearization, it is the end of hegemony. Only if America halts its hegemonic campaigns can the world denuclearize.

## A Hegemon-Free World Cannot be Created by a Hegemon

In a world with a hegemon, countries most likely to feel threatened by hegemonic power are non-nuclear nations. These nations face tremendous pressure that threatens their function and survival, and in situations without strategic guarantees that they will not face attack and invasion by the hegemon, or even the most basic guarantees of their safety, they will do anything necessary to obtain what has become the nuclear guarantee of safety.

Building a hegemon-free world is the only strategic guarantee for a nuclear-free world. In a world where threats from hegemonic power exist, both hegemon nations and non-hegemon nations will demand nuclear weapons. In a hegemon-free world, nuclear weapons will become a thing of the past—in places where it's not necessary to lock your doors at night, any kind of weapon is unnecessary. Thus, without a hegemon-free world, we will never see a nuclear-free world. Hegemony is the catalyst for the spread of nuclear weapons. Moving toward a world without weapons means moving toward a world without hegemons. The "denuclearization" of certain countries is closely tied to the progress of the de-hegemonization of others.

## Strategic Reassurance Cannot Be Provided for Global Hegemony

In 2009 America's Deputy Secretary of State James Steinberg proposed a new slogan of strategic reassurance. He said, "Just as we and our allies must show, we are ready to welcome the arrival of China as a flourishing, successful major power, but China must provide the world with strategic reassurance that its development and growing global role will not come at the expense of the safety and happiness of other nations."

China's development and rise will not come at the expense of the safety and happiness of other nations, but they will also not be traded to protect America's hegemony. Hegemony is a product and expression of the law of the jungle. A peaceful, harmonious, democratic world, where the weak are not preyed upon by the strong, does not need a king of the jungle. The civilized major powers of the 21st century have a responsibility to abandon hegemonic thought, leave behind hegemonic struggles, and conclude the cycle of hegemony they have sustained. China's strategic reassurance to the world is that it will not seek or engage in hegemony and contribute to the building of a hegemon-free world.

## Strategic Reassurance: China Won't Become a World Hegemon Successor

On August 10, 2009, Japanese prime minister Hatoyama stated in his feature article in the September issue of the political commentary magazine *Voice* that Japan exists between the United States, which struggles to maintain its hegemonic position, and China, which seeks to become a hegemon. How to maintain true independence, and how to protect our own national interests, are the problems facing Japan and Asia's other small and mid-size nations. Actually, Prime Minister Hatoyama was only half-right. The United States is certainly struggling to maintain its hegemonic position, but the goal of China's rise is not to become a hegemonic nation, but instead to become a strong non-hegemonic nation.

China's rise is not the rise of a hegemon; it marks the end of global hegemony. The goal of the competition between China and the United States is not to unseat and replace a hegemon, it is to put to rest an old world of hegemons and create a new world with cooperative superpowers. The world is at a turning point in history; wealth and power are moving from the West to the East. This turning point marks the transition from a hegemonic world to a non-hegemonic one. China's rise is driving the rise of a new, multipolar world.

The strategic game between the United States and China will change the face of the globe, and deeply impact the fates of both nations. During this strategic game, the United States will transition from being a hegemon to a pole in global dynamics—and China will become the first non-hegemon champion nation in human history. America will not seek to maintain global hegemony, and China will not seek to obtain it. This should be the strategic reassurance that China and America exchange.

## Rescuing America: Exclusive Power Is not America's Lifeblood

America is truly in need of rescue. When American Secretary of State Hillary Clinton expressed that China and America were in the same boat, on some level, she was expressing that need. Rescuing America from the financial crisis and providing support and help during that time was an acute treatment to a symptom. If China wants to cure America, we need to help it overcome its hegemon syndrome, a disease that threatens the world and wreaks havoc on America's national fortunes.

All the things troubling America have a common root, because they are the common troubles of a hegemon; all the crises America faces are the crises of their self-imposed status of hegemony; the decline of America is a decline from this status. In today's world, relying on hegemony to revitalize and strengthen a nation is going against the tide of history. Any nation that tries to maintain global hegemony will decline and fall. Only by transitioning toward becoming a pole in a balanced global structure can a nation fundamentally and permanently escape the loss of initiative.

Unipolarity is a cancer of strong nations; it kills great nations. The logic of history tells us that it slays, misleads, and brings down nations. For the United States, hegemony is a road to decline and collapse—a threat to the world, and a trap for America. America needs to pull itself out of that trap and save itself. It needs to escape from the trap of hegemony. The fundamental problem American strategy needs to address is not challenges or threats from others who wish to claim a leading position, it is saving itself from the trap of power and control.

America's future path, and its escape, is a complete transformation of its ideas about reviving and strengthening itself through hegemony—to turn away from hegemonic thought, strategy, and goals, and completely transform itself from a hegemon nation into a cooperative, supportive nation and a normal member of the global community. This will be the deepest revolution in American history.

## Waving Goodbye to Hegemony: The Mission and Contribution of China's Rise

The fundamental conflict between China and America is that America's strategic goals are to maintain a unipolar world and maintain its hegemonic position in that world. But in the tide of the transition to a multipolar world, China is leading the way. The core question of the conflict between China and America is whether the future world order will be unipolar or multipolar; whether the world of the future is a multipolar, democratic world, or a hegemonic, unipolar world; whether we continue to live in a world with a unipolar power, or whether we put an end to the hegemonic world and create a world of cooperative competition.

The stake in the great game between major powers in recent history has been the replacement of global leaders. At the end of each round, an old hegemon steps down, and a new hegemon begins its reign. This became the fate of all great nations, and the cycle of competition between powers.

The game that will be played between China and America in the 21st century is of a new kind—unprecedented in history. What makes this round unprecedented is that the stakes of the game are not who will be a global hegemon, but whether the age of global hegemony will come to a close or not. The game between China and America is both a historical mission and the end of an era, and the mission is to end the historical struggle over singular global leadership.

China and America should provide the world with a strategic guarantee, and swear a strategic promise that they will create a world without hegemons. America should cease being a global hegemon, and China should not seek to take its place as that role. Just like the nuclear-free world Obama wants to build, China should strive to build a hegemon-free world.

# CHAPTER 3

# THE CHINESE CENTURY:

# AN AGE OF GLOBAL PROSPERITY

The appearance of every champion nation begins a new era. Launching the China Age is China's historical responsibility; it will be a milestone of China's revitalization and successful rise, and a necessary step for the progress of history. The China Age, at its most basic, will be an age of prosperity. In Sun Yat-sen's evaluation of the West's conception of Yellow Peril, he said that in the future, China's era would not be one of Yellow Peril, but of Yellow Favor. The China Age will not be one in which China threatens the world, it will be one in which China enriches the world.

## I. China's Leadership in the Global Age

The first sign that the Age of China has arrived will be when China establishes its leadership in the world economy and plays a leading role in the international community. At a Global Think Tank Summit held in Beijing on July 3, 2009, a reporter from the *Times Weekly* intensely questioned former European Commission president Romano Prodi. The journalist asked, "Is the world's power structure currently undergoing dramatic changes, and if so, where is China's place in this process?" Prodi answered, "The Olympics showed a 'Smiling China' to the world, and made an important impression on international society. Not long ago, when China's leaders made an appearance at the G20, their political influence was unprecedented. Without China, the G20 would be a failure, and this shows that China is taking steps toward a role of leadership in the world."

Prodi's statement that China is taking steps toward a leadership role in the world reflects an already acknowledged fact in international society. For a long period of time, China was excluded from the ranks of world leaders. Today China is entering their ranks as a necessary member in this new, global era of world history.

## China Has No Original Sin

To date, all the great nations that have arisen in history have a list of black marks—a criminal record of sorts. They have all been guilty of invasion, colonialism, and theft; their hands have all been steeped in blood. China's rise has been a civilized rise, a clean rise. China did not discover a New World, it did not seize territory to establish colonies, it did not sell opium, and it did not invade other nations. China is the only major nation in the world today without any original sin. China's hands are clean, its history is free of guilt, and it holds moral high ground. This is an important moral qualification as China takes on a leadership role.

The history of the rise of the West's great nations is a history of committing original sin. The original sin of the West was in shaping a backward Africa to create a developed Europe. The development of the Atlantic slave trade and its consequences are sufficient proof of the original sin of the West. Early in the age of great geographical discoveries, Africa was considered to be a primitive accumulation of capital for Europe to exploit, and grounds for the commercial hunting of black people. In 1492 Columbus announced the discovery of the American mainland, and laid the foundation for the black slave trade. According to statistics, at the beginning of the 17th century, Africa exported an average of over 10,000 slaves per year. The Atlantic slave trade persisted in Africa for four centuries, and was at its most rampant during the 17th and 18th centuries. Beyond the Portuguese and Spanish slave traders, there were British, Dutch, and French slavers. In 1714 after the War of Spanish Succession, the Treaty of Utrecht granted England the exclusive right to sell slaves to Spain's Western colonies for 30 years. The speed of development of plantations in the Americas demanded more slave labor, so more slave ships were needed. Using England as an example, in 1709, only one slave ship operated out of Liverpool; in 1730, there were 15; by 1771, there were 105; by 1792, there were 132. Marx said that Liverpool was built on the slave trade. From 1709 to 1787 the tonnage of Britain's foreign trade fleet increased 14 times over, and slave ships accounted for the majority of this increase. Other European nations profited hugely from the African slave trade. Ports like France's Nantes and Bordeaux, Amsterdam in the Netherlands, New York, Boston, and Philadelphia in the United States all relied on the slave trade to some extent. In the 18th century, the Triangular Trade had reached its peak. The Triangular Trade was composed of three shipping routes: the first from the ports of Europe to the west coast of Africa, where cheap manufactured goods (liquor, fabrics, jewelry, arms) were traded for slaves, or slaves were simply kidnapped, and then driven onto ships and sent to the Americas, where they were exchanged for minerals and agricultural products, which were then shipped back to Europe for sale. The Triangular Trade allowed a slave trip to earn 100–300% profit on a single journey. A black slave could be purchase in Africa for $50 USD and then sold for $400 USD in the Americas. African historians split modern history's African slave trade into three stages: the first stage was from the 15th century to the middle 17th century, when the Atlantic slave trade arose, and was primarily between the eastern and western Atlantic coasts. The second stage was the middle 17th century to the latter half of the 18th century, when the African slave trade was at its most intense. The third phase was from the latter half of the 18th century to the latter half of the 19th century, when the slave trade (especially the Atlantic slave trade) declined. The book *The African Slave Trade from the Fifteenth to the Nineteenth Century* reports that from the 16th to 19th centuries, Africa exported 15–30 million slaves, and if the number of slaves who died in transit is added, the total reaches up to 210 million. African-American equal rights activist W. E. B. Du Bois thought that from the 16th to 19th centuries, at least 10 million African slaves were exported to the Americas, and if the number who died in transit is counted, at least 60 million. American history professor Philip D. Curtis compiled documents and produced a new estimate. He believed that from the middle of the 15th century to the 19th century, Africa exported 11 million slaves (not including those who died during capture or transit). The slave trade was a disaster for African society, causing a complete collapse. Many thinkers the world around believe Western nations should establish a repatriation fund for Africa.

Spain committed the original sin of religious persecution. For example, in 1526 Spain's King Charles V ordered that every fleet must carry missionaries, or it could not leave his ports. In 1532 Charles V asked the pope for 200 missionaries to send to Latin America. The records of famous missionary Las Casas report that wherever Spanish conquistadores claimed new territory, they immediately forced the native population to convert to Christianity through brutal executions and physical punishments, and demanded submission to the king of Spain. Anyone who would not submit was killed immediately. As an extreme example, the original Native American population of the Antilles was 3 million. That was reduced to 14,000 by 1514, and ultimately to only 200.

Marx said that to occupy Malacca, the Dutch were asked to pay the Portuguese governor a bribe. In 1641, to save a bribe of 21,875 pounds, they went to the governor's home and murdered him. Anyplace they went became desolate and depopulated. Java's Banten and Bankit had 80,000 residents in 1750, and only 8,000 by 1811! And this is peaceful commerce!

Japan, a nation some have called the "bandit among bandits," committed the original sin of unbridled slaughter. Japan's brutality is well known even in the West. In November 1894 Japan occupied Dalian and Port Arthur, burned and looted the city, and massacred the inhabitants. Nearly 20,000 Chinese people lost their lives; only 36 were kept alive to bury the bodies. European and American newspapers reported on the Japanese violence. The *New York World* reported that Japan was a monster dressed in the skin of civilization with bones of barbarism. In the 15 years of Japan's occupation of China, there were 35 million Chinese casualties, including over 20 million civilian deaths, $100 billion USD in direct property damages, and $500 billion USD in economic losses. During the Pacific War, 1.11 million Filipinos died in battle or were massacred, and just between 1944 and 1945 more than 2 million Vietnamese starved. Roughly 2 million labor captives taken by the Japanese died in Indonesia. In Malaysia the Japanese army massacred over 100,000 people. In Thailand and Burma in the forced labor project of the Thai-Burma Railway (also known as the Death Railway), 12,000 prisoners of war and 250,000 labor captives died.

The United States is a nation ridden with original sin. On September 16, 1620 102 English Puritans boarded the *Mayflower*, and after a 66-day journey, they reached North America. By the next year, only 50 were left. Sixteen twenty-one was a year of bumper harvests, so they held a feast to thank the Lord for his bounty. In 1863 President Lincoln announced a new national holiday, Thanksgiving, on the fourth Thursday of ever November and commemorated with a four-day national holiday. Thanksgiving is the most unique holiday in America, and to Americans, on some levels, it is even more important than Christmas. But to speak of thanks, it cannot be forgotten that the white colonists who stepped onto the American mainland owed their deepest gratitude to the Native Americans. American gratitude soon turned to vengeance. At a meeting of their legislature in 1703 the colonists decided to offer a reward of 40 pounds for every red scalp taken or every red man captured. In 1720 that was increased to 100 pounds. In 1744 the scalp of a 12-year-old Indian boy brought 100 pounds, the scalp of an Indian war prisoner brought 105 pounds, and the scalp of a woman or infant brought 50 pounds. On the North American mainland, Native Americans suffered the tragedy of white oppression for four centuries. In the 16th century these peoples numbered at least 3 million, but by 1860, they numbered 340,000, by 1890, they numbered 270,000, and by 1910, there were only 220,000 left. At the beginning of the 20th century, although Native Americans had been granted US citizenship, they had not been granted the associated rights; although they paid taxes and were conscripted into the military, they were confined to reservations mired in poverty.

## China Has the Most Excellent Cultural Gene

The cultural strengths and insight of a people are the cultural conditions with which a nation leads the world. The United States has only one kind of culture—capitalist culture. China is a museum of human culture, civilization, and tradition. The Chinese people possess the world's longest-running civilization and the world's only surviving classical civilization; the Chinese people possess a socialist culture guided by Marxism, a revolutionary culture that, despite global socialism being sidetracked or trapped in ruts, has not been overthrown; the Chinese people also possess the largest, most successful example of a culture opening up; it has been successfully reforming itself, and absorbing the lessons of capitalist culture, forming a distinctive open culture along the way. China's culture today is a tolerant, diverse entity, and China today possesses excellent cultural genes and cultural attainments worthy of a world leader.

## China Has the Resume and Experience to Lead the World

There is a viewpoint that states that China should become a strong country, but not a leader. This is worth deliberation. Taking China's rise and development, and the great revitalization of the Chinese people, and placing them within the limits of being a strong nation but not a leader may be comforting to Americans, but placing limits like that on China's rise and revitalization is a kind of self-containment. China's great goals in the 21st century absolutely cannot be restricted to simply becoming a strong country.

In our globalized age humanity finds itself, more and more, crowded onto the same boat. Who gets to be the boat's helmsman affects the future and fate of the entire world. As America continues as the helmsman, they seem less and less capable of steering the ship, and the passengers are becoming less and less confident. President Obama's November 2009 visit to China touched off a round of intense debate in the world media about China's world leadership role. The *Wall Street Journal* wrote that an anxious international community looks to China to lead the world.

Leading China into a world leadership role prematurely may be an American trap. But America cannot be allowed to remain helmsman of the world's ship; it has caused crises all over the world, and riddled the ship with holes. If China wants to save itself, and the world, it needs to prepare itself to be the helmsman. Of course, the situation on this global ship is complex. Global problems are multilayered and difficult, and as a multipolar world slowly forms, no one nation will truly be able to act as global helmsman. But this cannot become a reason for China not to become a global leader.

Being a leading nation is not equivalent to being a hegemon nation. Great Britain and the United States were both the world's leading nations, and they were also both global hegemons, but that doesn't mean that the leading nation of the post-American era also needs to be a global hegemon. The significance of China becoming a global leader is that it will sever the dual destiny of leading nations and also forcing their will on nations. China will demonstrate that a leading nation need not be a hegemon nation and it will open a new historical era in which there are global leaders, but no global hegemons.

Democratic nations are not leaderless; they are nations where the leaders are produced democratically. A democratic, multipolar world is also not leaderless world; it's a world without tyrant nations. A democratic world requires leading nations that do not seek control, and a multipolar world, even more so, requires leading nations that can preserve harmony among its poles. Both democratic nations and a democratic world need leaders, but these leaders need to be produced democratically, and need to be democratic leaders, not aristocratic or tyrannical leaders.

When can China become a global leader? When can China take over the post? There will be a process, and when it's time for China to take over as helmsman, it will steer the boat with everyone's input. If China gives up the goal of becoming a leading nation because the task of helmsman seems too heavy, and rides in a boat forever steered by America, it will only be because of a lack of confidence and initiative.

China will never seek to lead, and never take the lead. This is brilliant strategy. However, China needs to critically apply the strategy of never taking the lead. Because all previous leaders have also been hegemons, being a leader meant being a hegemon, and China can never be that kind of leader. Some leaders of the past have been alliance chiefs, in which certain nations form an alliance and engage in hostilities with another alliance of nations. China cannot take on that kind of leadership, either. China cannot take on the antagonistic leadership role, but that does not mean China will never use its role and position as a leading nation. China has a role as a global leader in driving economic development, preserving world peace, promoting mutual development, solving global problems, strengthening international cooperation, and encouraging global progress. If China creates a more stable, fair, and peaceful world order abroad, and helps its citizens lead secure, happy lives at home, what could go wrong? As 21st century China becomes a strong nation, it can't refuse a leadership role.

China has a thousand years of experience as the world's leading nation and excellent traditions as a global leader. These are invaluable assets. Today, China has brought about the revitalization of the Chinese people, and is in the process of making itself the world's leading nation and retaking the title of champion nation for a second time. China's history of rising, falling, and then rising again, of going from the world's leading nation to a nation backward and abused, and then back to world's leading nation will make China the most experienced global leader in history. When China takes over as world leader, it will be the best leader the world has had so far.

## Broad-Mindedness Is the Key to Global Leadership

George Washington, the first president of the United States, made two impressive demonstrations of his broad-mindedness. First, at a time when monarchies were universal, and despite the encouragement and support of military officials to take over as king, he resisted the temptation of monarchy, and instead allowed the United States to form as the world's first modern republic. Second, after serving two consecutive terms as president, despite unanimous support for him serving a third consecutive term, he refused, actualizing the American concept to limit presidential terms. The generosity Washington showed as a leader should be the same generosity shown by a leading nation. The generosity he showed in his domestic politics should be the generosity America shows in international politics.

Regrettably, the United States, as a leader in the international sphere, has been incredibly selfish. A report by the RAND Corporation called "From Containment to Global Leadership: Post-War America and the World" said, "As the victor of the Cold War, America has several strategic choices. It can abandon the responsibilities of global leadership and turn its attention inward. It can slowly hand off global leadership, and use the reductions in its global role to encourage the reappearance of a balanced power arrangement in the world. It can also choose to entrench its role as global leader and prevent the rise of any global rival."[1] Of America's choices, "Taking up the responsibilities of global leadership and preventing the rise of another global rival or a multipolar world is the best long-term objective. The benefits of an American-led world outweigh other strategies: first, American values like openness, democracy, a free market, and rule of law will be more accepted. Second, it will be easier to prevent nuclear proliferation, threats from regional powers, low-intensity conflicts, and other major problems. Third, we can prevent the rise of another global rival, thereby avoiding another global Cold War or hot war and the resulting calamities, including nuclear proliferation. An American-led world is more conducive to global stability than a bipolar or multipolar world."

Where global leadership is concerned, America needs to learn from George Washington. Nations, like people, ought not to lust for power. Such restraint would show America's civility and insight, and bring the world happiness and prosperity. The good news is that many of America's citizens are not proponents of American hegemony; they are proponents of a democratic world. In his 1999 article "The Lonely Superpower" published in *Foreign Affairs* Samuel T. Huntington said that officials "boast of American power and American virtue, hailing the United States as a benevolent hegemon"and the "first non-imperialist superpower."[2] In 1997, a public opinion poll reported that "13 percent [of Americans] preferred a preeminent role for the United States in world affairs, while 74 percent said they wanted the United States to share power with other countries. Other polls have produced similar results. Public disinterest in international affairs is pervasive, abetted by the drastically shrinking media coverage of foreign events. However much foreign policy elites may ignore or deplore it, the United States lacks the domestic political base to create a unipolar world."

## *A Leading Nation Needn't Be a Hegemonic Nation*

In modern history, all the leading nations in the international community have been nations that are hegemons at the same time they are leaders. But when the China of the future leads the world, it will change the nature of leadership; it will be the first leading nation in a post-American world that is not a hegemonic leader.

Ever since Europe's explorers linked the world's geographical regions and regional societies scattered over them into a global community, there has been a new kind of demand, a demand for a world order—a need for the world to be led and managed. This world order requires a long, formative process. Today, with an international community that has existed for over 500 years, a fully formed international order has still not taken shape. There is still a long road before the international order can develop to the completeness of the current nation-state.

The evolution of global leadership can be split into three broad phases. The first phase was a leaderless phase, in which there was an international community but no leader. This period was marked by banditry and piracy by those with the strength or capability. A few nations used force to kill, exploit, loot, and destroy other civilizations. Early Spain, Portugal, and the Netherlands are classic examples; in the primal jungle of a freshly formed international society, they engaged in Hobbesian predation. This was the original state of the international community. It lasted from 1500 to 1648, before the conclusion of the Thirty Years' War, roughly a 150-year period. The second phase was the hegemonic phase, in which the strongest nations were masters and tyrants. From 1648, after the conclusion of the Thirty Years' War, international society emerged from its primal stage and entered a phase in which the international hegemons were produced by war; the international order was founded and supported by hegemons. The classic examples of hegemons in the hegemonic phase are Great Britain and the United States, and models for hegemonic-era international orders are Pax Britannica and Pax Americana. This phase has lasted three and a half centuries from 1648 to the present. The third phase is the democratic phase. When China takes over as world leader, it will mark the beginning of this phase and the democratization of international relations and international society.

American global hegemony is falling behind the times. Its leadership has been incompetent and is the subject of a growing amount of criticism. The Malaysian prime minister, in an interview on Chinese television, said, "America had a very good chance to show its civilized side, but unfortunately its leaders choose to show its power through invasion. Including pre-emptive invasion, even when no other country has attacked it. America thinks it has the right to invade and conquer other countries. That makes some small countries afraid. This is not the role that America should take. America should be a good global citizen. It should respect the supervision of international relations by organizations like the United Nations and the opinions of other countries. I think America can be a good country, I think it can handle the responsibilities of being a global leader. But unless equality is established between America and other countries, America will abuse those weaker than itself. A good leader should not be invasive, it should act according to morality. Engaging in wars of conquest against other nations, and killing people; this is not a good leader. A nation should work on itself and provide good lives for its people, it shouldn't attack and invade other countries and steal what belongs to others. It shouldn't conquer another nation, say, rich in petroleum to provide a good life for its own people, it should accomplish that through hard work and developing its industry. You can work hard to provide a good life for your people, but you can't sacrifice other nations as the price for that. Conquering another nation, taking their resources away and using them for yourself, that's holding on to old ideas of empire, and it's wrong." China, as the new world leader, will not take the American road of hegemony. Instead, it will preserve global peace and harmony.

## China Must Learn from America

America's GDP surpassed Great Britain's in 1895 to become the world's largest. But it was only after 1945, half a century after America's GDP outpaced Great Britain's, that the United States replaced Great Britain as world leader. China's GDP is still smaller than America's; it may take China 50 years to overtake America's GDP and replace it as world leader. There is still no need for America to be nervous. China needs to fight, so when it takes over the heavy responsibilities of global leadership, it will be ready. China should not be in a rush to be a leader; it should allow America to keep the position until a time that is best for all sides.

America's slow rise to leadership wasn't a choice: it was forced. Long ago, America had ambitions to dominate the world. Even before the United States existed as a nation, the pilgrims who crossed the sea from Europe wanted to build a "city on a hill" in North America, and had dreams of igniting a global lighthouse that could guide humanity. They believed they were God's chosen people, and that leading the world was, to use a later phrase, their "manifest destiny." The limits of America's strength kept it fixed in isolationism before the late 19th century. World War I severely weakened the major powers of Europe and was an important turning point for American power. During the war, America's GDP surpassed the combined GDP of Europe, which fed the American desire to lead the world. President Woodrow Wilson's Fourteen Points advocated establishing the League of Nations, unveiled America's policy agenda for world leadership, and presented a blueprint for an American-led world. It was an important theoretical foundation and implementation for a world designed and led by America. But this upstart power had just appeared on the world stage, and its significant economic strength could not be transformed into the strategic ability to lead the world. American prestige alone was not enough to convince the global public. While it had to compete with old empires like Great Britain and France, Wilson's American Dream for the world suffered on the global stage and domestically. In the end, America couldn't become the world leader, and Wilson died in despair, worn out from his tours of the globe to lobby for the American Dream. Because America couldn't fulfill its dream of leading the world, its only choice was to turn back to isolationism.

Before China can take over as world leader in the 21st century, it will need half a century to work through three stages. The first will be catching up to America and actively taking a leading role where it can in the world; the second will be racing neck-and-neck with America, and leading the world as an equal partner with America; and the third stage will be guiding the world through exercising leadership and management in the world, and thereby becoming the world's leading nation. China is already actively participating in leadership where it can, and moving toward becoming America's equal. This stage will last for another 20 to 30 years.

China's road to global leadership will be one of taking root and eventually dominating by joining and then leading the international order. If a people can't take root and stand independently in a forest of people and nations, it has no right to enter the world. And entering the world and aligning with the world system are not just goals for China; they are what *must* be done to become a nation that can lead the world.

## II. China's New Development Model

The competition between nations, especially the competition between champion nations and potential champion nations, at its core is a competition of models, models of establishing and developing nations. A nation's competitiveness is, at its core, the competitiveness of its models, and the history of a nation's choice of models and the advantages and disadvantages of those models are what decides a nation's position, future, and fate. And the competition of models between great nations is, at root, a competition of levels of civility and happiness indicators. It is a competition watched by the entire world, as people observe which model is more vital and more innovative, and which model is more attractive and more cohesive.

### Three Development Models

In the 20th century, three competing models appeared that produced a lasting impact on history and the future of mankind: the Western model, the Northern model, and the Eastern model. The United States represents the Western model, the Soviet Union represents the Northern model, and China, with its socialism with Chinese characteristics created in the 30 years since Opening Up and Reform, represents the Eastern model. The competition between the Soviet model and the American model permeated the 20th century. The competition between the Chinese model and the American model will permeate the 21st century. The latter competition will have a much deeper and longer-lasting impact on history.

After the Cold War, belief in an "End of History" was common in the West. This notion stated that the Western democratic political model was the last, and best, political model that mankind would develop, that the Western world had a duty to use Western democracy to shape and mold the world, and that the West's democracy and liberty were the soft power that would win over the rest of the world. The West very quickly saw that history had only ended the Soviet model, and that the end of the Soviet model and socialism were not one and the same. The competition that followed World War II was a competition between national models, and the Soviet Union's defeat was the failure of a particular national model.

After the end of the Soviet model, the Chinese model began, a model that showed global adaptability, persuasion, influence, and competitiveness, a model that signaled the opening of new horizons for the progress of human society and world development, but that at the same time showed its immaturity. On the global stage of the 21st century, the competition between models of establishing and developing a country will primarily be a competition between the Western and Eastern models, the American and Chinese models. After the American model defeated the Soviet model, the former reached its peak. The arrogant American model is showing signs of decline in its competition with the Chinese model in the 21st century; the global financial crisis severely damaged America's position and influence. In today's world, the American model still occupies the high ground of the global leader. Even though the Chinese model has produced astonishing accomplishments, it is still in its infancy, and it still has a lot of work to do before it becomes synonymous with innovation. If China wants to win the global competition, it needs to make its own model more advanced and superior to the American one.

## *Lessons from the Soviet Model*

The Soviet model was one of modern history's most notable achievements, because it accomplished three historic tasks. The first was providing the bulk of the force that defeated global fascism in the Second World War. It suffered more than any other nation in World War II, with at least 6 million military casualties, 27 million dead, more than 1,700 cities and 70,000 villages looted, and 679 billion rubles in property damage. The Soviet Union alone suffered 41% of all the damage incurred in World War II. After the war, it was publicly acknowledged as the world's foremost military nation. America's President Franklin D. Roosevelt said, "It was the Red Army and the Soviet people who set Hitler's mighty forces on the road to utter failure, and thereby won the deepest, everlasting admiration of the American people." The second was the enormous feat of building the Soviet economy and GDP into the world's second-largest national economy.

The third was forcing capitalism onto a path of civility. Early, primal capitalism was bloody, savage capitalism; monopolistic capitalism was brutal capitalism; and fascism was an even more extreme form of capitalism. But the Soviet Union's socialism was a rival, and their struggle forced capitalism into the more civil modern form we see today, and in doing so made the world a more civilized place. The Soviet model may have vanished, but it won a brilliant victory for Marxism and socialism, because the savage early capitalism Marx wanted to overturn was gone, and the world wars driven by predatory, melon-carving capitalism that Lenin and Stalin wanted to eliminate ceased to exist long ago.

If the harsh exploitation and oppression of primal capitalism prompted the formation of a revolutionary proletariat socialism, then revolutionary socialism forced capitalism into a more civilized form. Later, thanks to stagnation, rigidity, and even corruption in the Soviet model, the pressure from competition with modern capitalism forced the Soviet model to dissolve. The collapse of the doomed Soviet model and advantages of the American model forced China to produce the socialism of Reform and Opening Up, a Chinese model fundamentally different from the Soviet model, and one that can compete with the American model. The competition of different models is a cycle of victory and elimination that drives the tide of world progress and historical development. If any globally influential model, no matter how many miracles it has produced, ever becomes too arrogant, it will become rigid, mutated, and corrupt, doomed to be swept into the dustbin of history. If the Chinese model wants to retain its vitality and competitiveness, it needs to be durable and innovative—more innovative than the American model it is competing with.

## Tolerance to Diversity: The Secret of the Singapore Model

Former Singapore prime minister Lee Kuan Yew said, "There is no Great Wall separating capitalism and socialism. They can be used to supplement and perfect each other." Singapore's People's Action Party cofounder S. Rajaratnam said, "What people call the Singapore way is actually socialist government and capitalist economics. We use capitalist means to create wealth, and use socialist means to distribute it." The rise of the tiny nation of Singapore within a few decades has been miraculous. But what is the secret of the Singapore miracle? Lee Kuan Yew and S. Rajaratnam tell us the secret is its diverse synthesis. This is what makes the Singapore model distinctive. Its success is in using capitalism and socialism to supplement one another and create a more perfect result.

What is Marxism? Marxism is a critical, revolutionary, and creative synthesis of doctrine. Marxism takes everything valuable created by primitive society, slave society, feudal society, and capitalist society, and combines them into a synthesis of human civilization.

What is socialism? Socialism is a critical, revolutionary, and creative synthesis of doctrine. In 1918, Lenin pointed out in *The Immediate Tasks of the Soviet Regime* that if socialism did not use the technological and cultural achievements of capitalism, it would be impossible to build a socialist society. He stressed that socialist nations had to be happy to absorb good things from abroad: the Soviet regime + Prussian rail organization + American technology and corporate trusts + American educational organizations + etc. = synthesis = socialism.

Socialism with Chinese characteristics will naturally be different from Singaporean synthesis. China's Reform and Opening Up is also a process of synthesis accomplished by studying the wider world. Synthesis is an important strategy in Marxism, and underlies the strength of socialism with Chinese characteristics. Socialism with Chinese characteristics is a combination of the best from China and the best from abroad, especially the best products of global capitalism.

## Leading the World by Innovation: The Mission of the China Model

Without exception, the world's champion nations and leading nations create a new model. They build unique nations and bring life to their nations through innovation. They don't replicate, imitate, or copy other countries. America had characteristics different from Great Britain, and China has characteristics different from America. If China wants to become a leading nation, it needs to create a new model for the world. This means China cannot copy others, as China's model will not be replicable by others. Champion nations and leading nations, as models and examples for the world, can only be studied, never copied, which is why the essence of Chinese characteristics is innovation and the mission of the Chinese model is to innovate. The Chinese model shows its creativity and innovation in three aspects:

1. From socialism's perspective, the task of the Chinese model is to solve the problems left unsolved by the Soviet model, and in this aspect, the Chinese model has had huge successes.

2. From the perspective of the development of civilization, the Chinese model needs to solve the problems left unsolved by the American model, like the serious problems exposed by the global financial crisis of 2008, or hegemonic tendencies in international relations. In this aspect, China and America's cooperation to lead the world and solve related issues has been increasing, and has produced obvious results. The road ahead for such cooperation is broad.

3. China also has to solve the bottlenecks affecting scientific development, like the income gap, corruption, etc. The model used by a leading nation is necessarily a model that produces healthy scientific development, and is a model that effectively solves global conflicts, disputes, problems, and challenges. The vitality, competitiveness, and influence of the Chinese model is dependent on whether it can effectively address China's problems and its ability and potential to address the world's problems. That ability and potential, at root, is creativity and innovation.

## III. Leading the World with Chinese Values

There is a saying that first-tier nations export culture and values, second-tier nations export technology and rules, and third-tier nations export products and labor. The China Age will be more than just a time when China's production capacity leads the world; it will be a time when the Chinese spirit and Chinese values become the cultural foundation of a new era.

### *Westernization Gives Way to Easternization*

Speaking of attempts to Westernize and divide China causes indifference. Some people say that just as the landlords and bourgeois feared the "communization" of society after the Communist Party came to power, what's stopping us from turning "Westernization" into "Easternization," or turning the "Americanization" of globalization into "Sinification"? Aren't those the goals China will be fighting for several generations from now? Won't that be an indicator of China's success several decades from now? Won't that be the landmark of China's cultural success as a leading nation?

Chinese culture is already the most vital culture in the world. Not only is it the world's only extant classical culture, but it has the power to conquer its conquerors. The Chinese nation has certainly been defeated militarily in the past, but it has no record of cultural defeat. The Chinese people can be conquered militarily, but not long after, the conquerors are assimilated into Chinese culture and conquered by their victims. Conquering China is like plunging your sword into the ocean. You'll meet very little resistance, but soon after, the iron will rust, and the sword will decompose and be absorbed. It will be absorbed utterly. In a few generations, only philosophers will know who was the conqueror and who was the conquered.

Chinese culture's incredible cohesiveness makes it the world's most difficult culture to assimilate. America is an immigrant nation, and it's been called a "melting pot" of different cultures. But the biggest headache for this cultural melting pot is Chinese culture, because American culture finds it very difficult to assimilate, to the point that it was one of the causes of the Chinese exclusion movement at the close of the 19th century. After the American Civil War, the country made a major push for rail construction, and brought in large numbers of Chinese immigrants as labor. In 1882, pressure grew in places like California to ban the Chinese, which led to the passing of the Chinese Exclusion Act. It banned the immigration of people of Chinese ethnic origin for 10 years, and later was extended permanently. In 1889, it was upheld as constitutional by the US Supreme Court, because the Chinese were of a different race, unable to assimilate and different in every aspect. They lived independently and maintained the habits of their original country. If this Oriental invasion was not limited, it would soon become a threat to US civilization.

Chinese culture is a profound heritage that stretches back 5,000 years. How could it be assimilated by American culture, which took shape in just a few hundred years? Obviously, in the modern era, Chinese culture faced the challenge of Westernization as well, and the erosion of European rain and Western wind. Even today, the Western world is making attempts to Westernize and divide China. The Western wind and Westernization refer to the Western world's attempts to attack and influence China. The West and the Western world have geographical significance, and also political significance. We can split Western civilization or Western history into three stages. The first is the Mediterranean Stage, the second is the Western European Stage, and the third is the North Atlantic Stage. The Mediterranean Stage and the Western European Stage span the classical era to the modern era, in which the Western world meant the Western part of Europe. After the 15th century, Europeans began moving across the ocean in great numbers. From a geographical standpoint, the world of the West was a world of oceans. Europe is a peninsula, and many smaller peninsulas jut out from it. The old saying "China opens its front door and sees mountains" applies to Europe, with a slight alteration: "Europe opens its front door and sees the ocean." Geographically, today the Western world means Europe and North America, and politically, it means capitalist society.

For centuries, Western civilization has been changed by the world, and the world has undergone Westernization. China has also changed under the attack and influence of Western culture, because in both material offerings and culture, the West has held the advantage. Even today China has to be vigilant against and suppress the Western world's attempts to Westernize and divide it, which reflects that Chinese culture is still in a position of weakness. In the Chinese Age, China's economic strength and material wealth will surpass that of America, but it will also create a culture that exerts greater influence and is more attractive globally than America's, a culture that cannot be peacefully shaped by America, but that instead can peacefully shape America's culture. When China has the power to do that, Easternizing the Western world and forcing America to embrace the peaceful changes caused by Chinese culture, we will truly be in the spiritual and cultural Chinese Age.

In the Chinese Age, when China has the world's most material wealth and cultural offerings, it will not attempt to Easternize or peacefully shape the Western world, especially America, and in this respect, China is more civil than the West. But the more natural and more civilized something is, the more widely it will spread across the world. The Easternization and Sinification of the future will spread without being forced, and when that happens, America will find it hard to avoid being peacefully shaped into a form more civilized than it is today.

## *The Country Without a Cultural Flag Cannot Lead the World*

Leading nations are the world's cultural flag bearers. Nations that guide the world guide it first with culture. Nations with influential value systems, nations that can plant their cultural flag on the world's cultural high ground, are the only nations that can lead the world. America is a nation that excels at occupying the international moral high ground. The earliest representative of American idealism and liberty was Thomas Jefferson, who was later followed by Woodrow Wilson, Franklin D. Roosevelt, and Bill Clinton. They turned their ideals into strategic means and principles, and considered their ideals to be strategic goals. Jefferson linked American liberty to American territorial expansion; Wilson linked world peace with establishing American-style democracy abroad; Roosevelt linked the four major powers of the postwar world with his four freedoms; and Clinton linked the international order with democracy and human rights. These became the cultural flags of American thought.

Any country that leads the world needs a value system that can provide cohesive force for itself and influence and inspire the world. Some countries, despite not being the world's most materially wealthy, have the world's most innovative cultural creations; by raising their cultural flags, they influence and guide world culture. The Soviet Union, when it raised the world's first flag of socialist victory, became one such nation. On the evening of the day after their victory in the October Revolution, the Second All-Russian Congress of Soviets of Workers' and Soldiers' Deputies unanimously passed the milestone *Decree on Peace*. This document was written by Lenin himself; it described the fundamental principles of the first socialist nation's foreign policy, expressed policies against imperialist wars and invasion, and expressed a strong desire for peace, equality among nations, national self-determination, and the abolition of secret diplomacy. In Lenin's *Letter to American Workers*, he described Soviet Russia's foreign policy: Soviet Russia would strip off the wars of imperialism and raise the flags of peace and socialism for the world.

The Soviet Russian government's peaceful foreign policy shocked the world, and shocked America's President Wilson. Wilson stepped onto the world stage under new historical traditions, and tried to put a new face on American diplomacy. The Fourteen Points was his attempt to create a new diplomacy and a world constitution after the war. Open diplomacy, national self-determination, and an international league were the pillars of Wilson's new diplomacy. It was both targeted at the old imperialist diplomacy and an attempt to contain Leninism.

Lenin and Wilson, as the two great politicians of the Soviet Union and America, each represented an innovative worldview and set of values unique to their countries, and both struggled to plant their own cultural flag on the global high ground. This would be the flag of the world's leading nation.

But a nation's awareness and a politician's understanding proceed at different rates. When a people lack sufficient preparation and necessary awareness to lead the world, and when a nation's cultural flag to lead the world can't be raised, lofty ideals become tragedies. The tragedy of Wilsonian ideals is the classic example. Wilson was a noble idealist who raised America's cultural flag for the world and hoped to plant America's cultural banner on the world's cultural high ground, but that proved impossible. American historian Warren I. Cohen, in *The Cambridge History of American Foreign Relations*, wrote: "As hegemony died out in Europe, Wilsonian ideals defined a foreign relations framework for America, and combined American military strength, economic resources, and cultural innovations to go beyond the traditional pattern of sovereign nations caring only about their own self-interests and at the expense of the world's interests, a world in which war and preparation for war were normal acts, and in which diplomatic balance was the goal."[3] Wilson issued a challenge to these practices and ideas. He wanted nations to serve not just their own interests, but the interests of the world. He said America should use its capacity to "serve the whole of humanity," and that other countries should do the same. The final result was a theory in which nationalism and internationalism were fused, and in which national sovereignty was only significant in the larger web of international relations. The realists who followed him for the next decade called Wilson's internationalism a form of naïve idealism. But the internationalism that informed Wilson's thinking was not idealism, it was an internationalism informed by a deep understanding of the common interests of every nation and the common desires of every person on earth that transcended national borders, among the basic forces that drive culture. On some level, Wilsonianism placed culture at the center of international relations. America's rise on the global stage at the beginning of the 20th century was important not simply because it became the primary military and economic power; it also introduced cultural factors into world affairs, and because America's globalization was already one of the most important affairs of the 20th century. But the opposition he faced to his peace treaties in Congress was tragic. To gain the support of the American people, he began a national tour of approximately 8,000 miles over 21 days in November 1919. Before he could see the fruits of his tour, he collapsed in Colorado, turning this trip into an unattainable dream. Congress and the American people weren't ready for Wilson's new international order, and other nations were even less ready. America never joined the League of Nations, which meant that the United States had decided to stop at the level of other nations. Wilson's failure did not mean the death of Wilsonianism; in Europe and many countries around the world, more and more Wilsonian thinkers appeared, and in the shaping of the post-war world, their influence and unifying strength were powerful as Wilson's own. Wilson was a pioneer in using American culture to guide the world, and the fate of pioneers is always tragic. America's cultural banner was finally planted on the global high ground after World War II, and America became the world's leading nation.

## Raising the Chinese Flag to Inspire the World

During World War I, US President Wilson was the first to raise the banner of anti-colonialism, self-determination, and collective security, through which he gained universal recognition in the international community for the rising United States. Today's America has raised the banners of freedom, democracy, and human rights to use its core values to influence the world. China, rising today in a globalizing world, has raised the banners of peace, development, cooperation, and building a harmonious world.

Building a hegemon-free democratic world is an important component of China's core values, and an element of tremendous appeal that allows China to guide and inspire the world. As the Three Transformations sweep the world—the multi-polarization of power, the democratization of international relations, and the diversification of development—"building a democratic world" is becoming a common aspiration. If we say that building a democratic nation is something all people desire, then building a democratic world is something all nations desire, something all sides in the international community are calling for. And an important characteristic of a democratic world is its lack of hegemony. And if we are to de-hegemonize the world, we will need to achieve the Three Equalities: equality of social systems, equality of development models, and equality of social faiths.

Building a democratic world is the key to driving progress in the world forward, and is our most urgent task. If power is not supervised and restricted, it will become corrupt power. International power without balance or restriction is hegemonic power. The key problem to be solved in the construction of a democratic world is the problem of global hegemons. The hegemon problem is the root problem affecting world peace and world harmony. A democratic world is a peaceful and harmonious world. Only with a democratic world in place can nations cooperate on a truly equal level.

The most critical step in building a democratic world is not to transform every nation in the world into an American-style democracy; it is to ensure that there is no hegemon in the international community, and that no one seeks hegemony. There is nothing more damaging to world democracy than the existence of a global hegemon, and hegemony is the biggest threat to world peace. When America brings up the democratic nation theory of peace, China will answer with the democratic world theory of peace and anti-hegemon theory of peace. Hegemony is the root cause of war, and a democratic world is a guarantee of peace.

What kind of world is the ideal democratic world? It includes three key elements. First, every nation on earth is transformed into a democratic nation, and of course this means every nation will be democratic in its own uniquely characteristic way, as diversely democratic nations, not only Western democracies, and especially not only American democracies. The standards of democracy are not only America's to decide, and America is not the only arbiter of democracy. Second, every sovereign nation in the world enjoys equal sovereignty, and can effectively supervise and restrain nations that seek hegemony. Third, no one nation can monopolize the position of leading nation, or set term limits on world leadership. If a world leader declines, it should step down. This is an important aspect of a global, international democratic system.

Some people say, "Protecting human rights is America's political nuclear weapon. Resisting hegemony is China's political nuclear weapon." People also say, "Building democratic nations is the weapon with which America attacks China, and building a democratic world is the weapon with which China attacks America." Actually, protecting human rights and building democratic nations are also important elements written on China's cultural banner. But on America's cultural banner, there is no anti-hegemonic, democratic world. This puts China's cultural flag on higher ground than America's, and makes China's cultural flag more suited in guiding the world.

The cultural flags that lead the world are those held high by nations for the world to follow, and inscribed with ideas that resonate beyond national borders. They are a leading nation's strongest soft power, and the trademarks of a leading nation's national brand. China's international banner demonstrates its international sentiment and mind, and expresses the common interests and aspirations of the world. China's flag stands in China, but flies for all the world to see, and is one that both China and the world can unite behind.

## Creating a Chinese Spirit Suitable for the 21st Century

Nations that lead the world must be global spirit leaders. America's ability to lead the world is inseparable from the American spirit. The American spirit is what led America to rise, and has influenced the world. If China wants to become a leading nation, it needs its own Chinese spirit. China is a nation of great spirit, a traditional spirit formed over thousands of years, a revolutionary spirit formed over decades of war, and a spirit of openness formed over the last 30 years of Reform and Opening Up. British historian Arnold Toynbee once called the global spirit incubated by China over the ages an important legacy left to the future world. There is no need to be circumspect: the 30 years after the Cultural Revolution, in some places, among some people, has been an age of materialism and benefit. Some people, in placing their priorities upon economy-building, have allowed themselves to be led by material profit. Some people have allowed their economic brains to demolish their spiritual homes. Some Chinese people have become monetarily wealthy, a new bourgeoisie, but remain mired in spiritual and cultural poverty, far below the basic necessities required to remain healthy.

Westerners think that a market economy without a church becomes a terrible market, run on the devil's economics. At the center of every market economy is a church, there to limit the madness of greed. Despite their presence, crises always seem to happen. At the center of China's market economy, you won't find a church, but we need to have spirit. A socialist market economy is the unification of the market and spirit. China's planned-economy era was a time of spirit without the market, but today, China has the market without spirit. We need to build a Chinese spirit suited to the times. To foster this spirit, China again needs to undergo an age of spirit, a flourishing era of culture. Until China becomes the world's foremost great nation of spirit, it will never become a world leader.

The Chinese spirit is a system, and at its core is faith in ideals. *The Memoirs of Zhang*

*Xueliang* includes this passage: "In the years when the Northern Expeditionary Army was crushing its enemies and tearing the Zhili Clique and the Fengtian Clique to tatters, Fengtian commander Zhang Zuolin asked his son Zhang Xueliang to look into why. Zhang Zuolin said, 'Son, I don't understand, we have guns, we have mortars, we even have a German artillery squad, we should be able to bomb them…so why doesn't it work when we bomb them?' His son replied, 'Dad, we have guns, mortars, and a German artillery squad, they don't have that… But have you ever thought, they have the Three Principles of the People, and we don't!' Zhang Zuolin wasn't convinced, 'What's so special about their three principles? I have as many principles as you want!' But a few days later, Zhang Zuolin came back and said, 'Son, you were right! We really don't have the Three Principles of the People! I'm still hungry for the wheat stubble of the northeast. Let's leave.'"[4] The Three Principles of the People are ideals and faith, and if we have those, we have power, we have strength, and we have direction, and those can overcome any warlord. That's true in the military and in all other aspects, including China's rise to global leadership.

A nation that leads the world is a nation that produces spirit and exports culture. China is a major producer of material goods, but it still isn't a major producer of spirit and culture. China needs to become a world factory of culture and bring Chinese culture out to the world. China imports more than ten thousand books from abroad, and they occupy 10%–15% of the domestic book market, but China only exports just over a thousand books each year, which make up 0.3% of the world book market. No amount of material trade can make up for that kind of cultural trade gap. Today the world uses vast amounts of Chinese material products, but when the world uses the same proportion of Chinese cultural products, when the bulk of the world's cultural products are made in China, the age of Chinese spirit and Chinese culture will have truly arrived.

## Chinese Culture Leads the World in the 21st Century

In November 2007, the First China Strategic Culture Forum was held in Beijing's Great Hall of the People. Leading academic Ji Xianlin wrote a congratulatory letter to the forum, in which he said, "In *21st century: The Age of Eastern Culture*, I wrote, 'Looking at the world today, it seems Chinese culture will occupy a leading position in the world within 20 years. At the end of the Ming Dynasty, Western culture emerged from the Catholic tradition, and in the several centuries since, Western capitalism has brought the world enormous material wealth, but it has also given the world cancer, AIDS, a lack of freshwater resources, global pollution, ecological imbalance, and many more catastrophes. So what's to be done? Today, we are 30 years from the end of Western ascendancy. We have to take the baton of the West, and based on what they've built, use the comprehensive analysis of Eastern thinking to solve the problems it has left to us.' I also said, 'I think the segmentation of Western thinking has exhausted its usefulness, and that the Eastern tendency to seek overall summaries will substitute it. Segmentation-based Western culture will decline, and an Eastern culture of comprehensive analysis will replace it. "Replace" does not mean "eliminate"; it means, upon the foundation laid by the West over the last few centuries, using the comprehensive eye of Eastern culture to connect and summarize it, and using Eastern culture as a curator to select and absorb the best of Western culture to push global culture to a new level of development. We will see this replacement in the 21st century. The 21st century will be a time of Eastern culture. We are watching this go from a subjective wish to an objective fact.' These words are my hopes and congratulations as you begin the First China Strategic Culture Forum."

Ji Xianlin's cultural dream, cultural ideal, and cultural prophecy is this: the 21st century will be an age of Eastern culture, in which Chinese culture takes a leading role in the world, and the arrival of this era is transforming from a subjective wish to an objective fact. Just like in a relay race, China, based on the foundation laid by the West, needs to take the baton.

# CHAPTER 4

# BUILDING A BENEVOLENT CHINA

On November 28, 1924, Sun Yat-sen published *Speech for the Kobe Chamber of Commerce and Other Groups*, when attending the welcome meeting in Japan held by five groups, including the Kobe Chamber of Commerce. He stated that Eastern culture is benevolent government, Western culture is hegemon government; benevolent government advocates virtue and morality, while hegemon government advocates utility and power; virtue and morality can exert influence on people by justice and axiom, but utility and power oppress people by firearms.

The nature of benevolent government is virtue and morality, which adheres to equality, fairness, integrity, and a generous attitude in accordance with the principle of doing as you would be done by others. It uses virtue and moral strength to influence people, rather than to oppress people; virtue must be equipped instead of fear; truth must be applied to make people obey, rather than force to rule the people. In the 21st century a benevolent China must build power without engaging in hegemony or oppressing people, but rather with high morality and amiable and respectable characteristics.

## I. The Charm of Chinese Character

Nations have a certain personality. That personality shows in the character of a country. China has a certain personality, which shows in China's character.

### *Peace and Order*

Several philosophers, including British philosopher Bertrand Russell, have argued that the Chinese desire to rule others is notably weaker than that of the white race. If there exists a people that takes pride in a refusal to go to war, the Chinese are that people. The natural Chinese disposition is tolerant and gregarious, and courteous in the hope that courtesy is shown in return. Russell believed that the Chinese character was not conducive to war, and indeed aspired toward peace. He was surprised at the deep spirit of tolerance and forbearance he found in the Chinese character. The Chinese Empire, at its peak, could have looked at the world in disdain, because there was no other nation strong enough to challenge it, and if China had had the desire to expand, no other nation could have resisted. Howerver, the Chinese Empire made the choice to not much impose its central authority on the ethnicities or territory of other nations.

As we can see, China is a nation that does not invade smaller or weaker nations, and does not threaten neighboring countries. Beyond simply refraining from treating weaker nations as enemies and threatening to turn to war at every turn, China has a history of solving conflicts with humility, settling disputes by offering moral and actual aid to enemies, and even marrying enemies to make them relatives. Qing Emperor Kangxi once married his own daughter to rebellious Mongol leader Galdan. It was only after repeated rebellions that the choice was made to eliminate him.

The Chinese people are a loving, benevolent people who live by the principle of not harming unless harmed; a people who love peace and despise war, a kind and gentle people. As Sun Yat-sen put it: the Chinese people desire peace and order. Except in self-defense, the Chinese people rarely go to war.

### *Matteo Ricci's Observations*

The Chinese are different from Europeans in that China is a large, powerful country, but it has no desire for conquest. That was the conclusion of Matteo Ricci, the Italian missionary who spent 30 years in China four centuries ago.

Of the most notable Europeans who made the long journey to China in historical times, two always stand out: one is Marco Polo, who came during the Yuan Dynasty, and the other is Ricci. Matteo Ricci arrived in August 1582 in Macau, and from there traveled to Zhaoqing, Shaoguan, Nanchang, Nanjing, and finally Beijing. In May 1610 he died and was buried in Beijing. To Ricci, China was strangely different from Europe. China was a country with vast territory, a countless population, and incredible riches. Such a strong, centralized kingdom, with plentiful provisions, could have easily faced down the armies and navies of its surrounding nations, but neither the king nor his subjects ever thought to launch an invasion. They were satisfied with what they had, and had no desire for conquest. In this respect, they were stunningly different from Europeans. Europeans were often dissatisfied with their governments, and coveted the things subjects of other countries enjoyed. The nations of Europe were utterly exhausted after struggling among themselves over who would rule the world, and they couldn't even accomplish what the Chinese had done—maintaining the heritage of their ancestors for thousands of years. Ricci, as a European, truly reveled in the peaceful nature of the Chinese people, who from the emperor to the commoner rejected wars of invasion and conquest. Ricci revealed his own integrity by speaking frankly about Europe.

Matteo Ricci experienced China's personality as a visitor from Italy, halfway across the world. From China's border, Malaysia's Prime Minister Mahathid Mohamed has his own experience of China's personality as a neighbor. "Malaysia and China have traded for more than 1,000 years, and there are many Chinese people in Malaysia, but we have never been conquered by China. But, from 8,000 miles away in Europe, England came to conquer us. China and Europe's attitudes are different. China comes for trade, but the Europeans don't come for trade, they come for war. In the end, they're conquering their own trading partners. So we're not worried about China, but we are worried about Europe."

China was a major power for thousands of years, but the small countries bordering it, like Annam, Burma, Goryeo, and Siam, all maintained their independence. Then, as Europe came east, Annam was swallowed by France, Burma was swallowed by Great Britain, and Goryeo was swallowed by Japan. China's aid for weak nations and the West's preying upon them were a stark contrast.

China's powerful but non-conquering personality, according to Sun Yat-sen, began forming in the Han Dynasty. Most political theorists during the Han Dynasty were virulently against imperialism. Best known among the period's anti-expansionist works is *A Proposal for the Abandonment of Zhuya (Hainan)*, which argued that the empire should not fight over territory with the southern barbarians. That is why, during the Han Dynasty, China did not support wars with outsiders. China was already a very non-aggressive power during the Han Dynasty. By the Song Dynasty, China was even less aggressive. It was invaded by foreign powers and eventually destroyed by the Mongolians. The country was finally revived during the Ming Dynasty; and in the Ming Dynasty, China was even less aggressive.

There are some Europeans who understand today that if China had been a conquering nation, Europe's history would have to be rewritten. Yale University professor Paul Bracken said people forget that 500 years ago, China was the world's only superpower. At a time when many Europeans were living in mud huts, China had the world's biggest economy and the most powerful military. Before Europe began its conquest of the Americas, China had the world's largest, best navy. If not for certain accidents of history, Europeans could very well be speaking Chinese today.

## China's Resources Are Strained

People often describe China as a "vast country, rich in resources," but thanks to China's equally vast population, China's resources are strained. Constraints on resources lead to more intense competition and sharper conflicts. The Western strategy is to export conflict and convert internal disputes into external disputes through territorial expansion in order to prevent crises at home. A unique characteristic of China is that, no matter how strained its resources become, it would rather fight to the death internally than start wars of aggression abroad or invade foreign territory. China has no colonies.

Climate and geographical reasons (large mountainous and desert regions) mean China's ratio of arable land to total territory is far below the international average. People have inhabited China since ancient times, but by the end of the 20th century, China's proportion of arable land was 10%, while Europe's proportion of arable land is over 25%. China's average arable land per agricultural worker is only one-third hectare, against 99 hectares in the United States. In the past 1,000 years, China's population has expanded from 55 million to 1.3 billion, a 22-fold increase. Compared with Europe and the Americas, China has always put much more pressure on its land. Over the past millennium, if we compare the Chinese diet to the medieval or modern Western diet, Chinese people eat far less meat, adults do not drink milk, and dairy products are almost nonexistent. China's dependence on grain is tied to its scarcity of land, because obtaining protein and calories from grain, rather than animals, makes for lower demands on the soil. But despite these conditions, China has never expanded abroad. No matter how strained resources become, China has never invaded other countries to steal their resources. China has never engaged in a resource war with other nations. China would rather starve than steal.

## A Self-Defense Policy Without Invasion

China is a civilized nation built on peace; a-live-and-let-live philosophy; no pre-emptive attacks; in self-defense, to be reasonable, protect the interests of both sides, and exercise proper restraint; and repaying grudges with kindness, rather than seeking revenge. These principles exemplify another unique characteristic of China's personality: not being the one to attack first.

Noted Japanese religious and cultural figure and social activist Daisaku Ikeda has argued that China is a nation that desires a robust stability to guarantee its own safety and security. Actually, if China is not threatened, it never preemptively dispatches its troops. In modern history, the Opium Wars, the Sino-Japanese War, the Korean War, and all conflicts involving China are actually wars of self-defense. There is no example of a preemptive strike at any time in the modern era.

Japanese cultural critic Shuichi Kato said, in a CCTV interview, "Japan takes a very aggressive stance in its foreign relations. When it feels danger, it prefers to attack first. We prepare our military for explosive, extreme, spasmodic campaigns that deliver sudden blows in the shortest time possible. China is more stable, and it's hard to find places where China has attacked first."

China's military civility has shocked the world. After victory in the Second Sino-Japanese War, China gave up demands for war reparations and released Japanese war criminals after reeducation, and welcomed the war orphans left by Japan. During the Korean War, China maintained a humanitarian policy toward prisoners of war. An American POW said, "China is the most civilized country in the world." Their mothers wrote letters to the Chinese army praising their treatment of war prisoners as "the same kind of treatment a mother would give them." In the Sino-Indian War, Chinese forces on the brink of total victory instead immediately stopped their advance and withdrew behind the pre-conflict Actual Line of Control to express their desire for a peaceful resolution. They also released all war prisoners, and returned all weapons and military supplies seized back to India. Returning the enemy's weapons was unprecedented in the history of war.

## Civilized and Tolerant Without Conflict

Chinese civilization has a wide embrace, and within the embrace of Chinese civilization, you won't find cultural conflict and hostility, you'll find different cultures linking hands, embracing, tolerating, fusing into, and saving one another. Former Israeli prime minister Ehud Olmert once said, "We have a deep affection for the Chinese people, and undying gratitude for the warmth and friendship shown to the Jews in Shanghai and Harbin during the early 20th century and the Second World War."

Historically, some Jewish people made their way to China and set up communities in the Kaifeng region. All over the world, Jewish communities have remained cohesive, due to the serious discrimination and incredible oppression they face from outsiders everywhere. But in China they found a unique exception. Only in China did Jewish communities not meet with oppression and discrimination. Instead, a natural fusion of the two cultures was formed, and by the 19th Century, when Westerners came to China, the Jewish communities they found had absorbed so many elements of Chinese culture that they were nearly impossible to distinguish, leaving the Europeans shocked and in disbelief. The personality of Western culture produces a conflict of civilizations; the personality of Chinese culture produces a fusion of civilizations.

From ancient times to the founding of the Qing Dynasty, China maintained close operations with its neighbors, and had no discrimination whatsoever against foreign merchants or missionaries. The Nestorian Stele in Xi'an is proof that as early as the 7th century, foreign missionaries were at work spreading their religion in China. Buddhism was introduced by a Han Dynasty emperor, and China's people enthusiastically adopted this new religion. It flourished in later times, and eventually became one of China's three major faiths. Both missionaries and merchants were permitted to freely travel the empire. Even into the Ming Dynasty, there wasn't a trace of discrimination against foreigners in China. More than 100 years ago, Sun Yat-sen appealed to America's people, saying that China was not a closed, conservative, exclusionary society. So where did the xenophobia that later emerged come from? It was carried in on invading Western gunboats and formed as a response from China's people. More accurately speaking, it wasn't xenophobia; it was resistance.

## Sun Yat-sen's Generalizations

China's personality is a kingly personality, not a hegemon's personality; China was founded on kingliness, not hegemony. Kingliness is China's national principle, and China's national morality. Sun Yat-sen explained how kingliness upholds and guides Chinese ethics in *The Three Principles of the People* in 1924: China's ancient values, which its people have never forgotten, are fidelity first, benevolence second, honor third, and concord last. Foreigners who have done business for long periods in China will often say the word of a Chinese businessman is far more reliable than a contract with a foreign businessman. To speak of honor, even at the height of its power, China never obliterated another nation. Take Goryeo, which in name was a Chinese vassal state, but was actually an independent country. After thousands of years in the shadow of Chinese power, Goryeo remained. Japan, after only 20 years as a strong nation, destroyed Goryeo. China's millennia-long love of peace is innate. Individually, it finds expression in humility, and in politics, it finds expression in the refusal to swallow other countries, which is very different from the foreigners. So when we appeal to these ancient Chinese values of fidelity, benevolence, honor, and concord, we are as ever appealing to foreigners. When we speak of the morality of peace, we are also appealing to foreigners. These outstanding values are the spirit of our people, and in the future, we will preserve these values, raise them, and spread them.

## A Kingly Culture

In books on contemporary history, the stories of opposing cultures and great nations, or of the competition between Eastern and Western culture, often involve comparisons and conflicts between a kingly culture and a hegemonic one.

In his speech to the Kobe commercial associations on November 28, 1924, in Japan, Sun Yat-sen raised this question: would a kingly culture or a hegemonic culture be more just and humane? Which would produce better results for a people and a country? In the speech, he answers the question: the rule of might, Europe's culture of aggression and power, would give way to the benevolent, moral rule of the Orient. Hegemony would give way to kingliness, and presage a bright future for world civilization. He concluded this speech with a warning for Japan: Japan today has become acquainted with Western civilization's rule of might, but retains the characteristics of Oriental civilization's rule of right. Now the question remains whether Japan will be the hawk of Western civilization's rule of might, or the tower of strength of the Orient. This is the choice that lies before the people of Japan.

In *Choose Life*, British historian Arnold Toynbee predicted that the world's political unification would be the only way for humanity to avoid destroying itself, and he estimated that global unification would appear in peacetime. And for this goal, no people on earth is better prepared than the Chinese people, who have spent 2,000 years developing a unique way of thinking.

## II. The Chinese Phenomenon

Hegemonic nations exhibit symptoms of hegemony: force, invasion, occupation, colonialism, etc. These are the most basic expressions of hegemony's nature. But the behavior of kingly nations shows in the Chinese phenomenon, the special nobility, civility, and benevolence that characterize China. These are the expressions of China's nature.

## *Only One Chinese-Speaking Nation*

Of the UN's six working languages, five are the official languages of more than one country. Chinese is the only working language spoken only in one country: China. According to statistics, there are 45 nations in the world that use English as an official language. The United Kingdom, United States, Canada, Australia, and New Zealand are all nations where English is the native language. There are 200 million people in the world who speak French, but only 60 million of them are French. There are more than 20 countries where French is an official language. There are 110 million German speakers in the world, and three nations where German is the only official language spoken: Germany, Austria, and Luxembourg. There are 350 million Spanish speakers in the world, and more than 20 countries use Spanish as an official language. Russian was the official language of the Soviet Union, and the Soviet Union split into 15 countries, of which Russian is an official language in four: Russia, Belarus, Kazakhstan, and Kyrgyzstan. Today, there is just one country in the world where Chinese is the native language, and where Chinese is used as an official language: China.

In the world today, after all of recorded history, there is only one nation that uses Chinese as an official language. This is proof that this nation has never invaded other countries, and never tried to expand its territory. The existence of dozens of English-speaking nations in the world today comes from the fact that they were conquered and colonized by the British Empire. They were occupied, and then owned, by the British.

## China Has Not Expanded Overseas

The rise of Western nations is inextricably tied to the rise of overseas invasion, expansionism, colonies, and the African slave trade. The history of Europeans directly selling slaves taken from Africa began when Henry the Navigator of Portugal brought a dozen slaves to Europe obtained in Africa by one of his exploration teams. After that, his expeditions combined exploration, colonialism, and slavery. Discovery and occupation became one and the same. Wherever his expeditions set foot was claimed as Spanish territory. Especially in 1481, after Joao II took the Spanish throne and announced the Portuguese Empire. China has never, neither by design nor practice, established an overseas China.

Why has China never established an overseas China? It's not because China lacked ships or the capacity to do so, it's because China never had the desire to expand. In the West, discovery was paired with occupation for the naval powers. For China, discovery was paired not with occupation, but with friendly relations.

Western countries also create rumors and confusion and attack China about China's problems in Tibet and Xinjiang, but a young Chinese man's rebuttal of those accusations was posted online and spread widely. A 21-year old Chinese student studying in Canada created a video called *Tibet Was, Is, and Always Will Be a Part of China*, and in it he said: if Westerners pack up and leave from the Americas, the Pacific, Africa, and Asia, and return to Europe, China will leave Tibet. Otherwise, don't raise problems like this with China. If the West actually did this, half of the nations of the Western world would vanish.

## The Chinese Strive to Return

When Chinese people left their country, they were always sad to go, and planned to return. But when the British left their country, it was with plans to occupy prime new territory and establish a home there—new countries where they were in charge. They spread their seed, and planned to take root. In the Han Dynasty, the Three Kingdoms period, the Sui Dynasty, and all the way to the beginning of the 13th century, China traded along the Silk Road and the Maritime Silk Route. China knew about many of the places along those trade routes long before the Europeans, but to China they were only discoveries, never places to be occupied.

Migration from China exhibits the same pattern. China never had dreams of establishing new countries abroad, but backed by the threat of ships bristling with cannons, Europeans founded one overseas colony after another. During Europe's rise more than 60 million Europeans moved overseas and established colonies. English colonists moved overseas, set up new colonies, and founded several New Englands. China always stayed in its own territory and used its own strength to solve its own problems. China's government never organized major colonial initiatives, and although for many reasons there were 60 million Chinese people living overseas, China never once founded an overseas colony directly governed by the home country, and never tried to build overseas Chinas.

Today, although the many English-speaking countries ceased to be one country long ago, their blood relations have kept them close, and they are quick to form alliances, especially where they see a common strategic interest. On March 5, 1946, in his famous "Iron Curtain Speech," Churchill suggested a special relationship between the United Kingdom and Great Britain to unify the English-speaking world: "Neither the sure prevention of war, nor the continuous rise of world organization will be gained without what I have called the fraternal association of the English-speaking peoples."

## China Doesn't Plan to Conquer the Globe

All the great nations that have arisen in modern history formed and carried out strategies to divide and rule the world, even at the cost of pushing humanity toward destruction. China, since ancient times, has been a civilized, courteous, just, sincere, and self-protective state. This is why the Chinese notion of "all under heaven" has never extended beyond China's borders. China's history of brilliant politicians and heroes discussing the state of the world, drafting strategies in their command tents, and outmaneuvering political rivals only happened on China's own soil. From the Qin Dynasty to the People's Republic, the idea of conquering and unifying the world has never appeared in Chinese thought. China never produced an outline to conquer the world like the Tanaka Memorial, which said, "In order to take over the world, you need to take over China. In order to take over China, you need to take over Manchuria and Mongolia."

China has never produced a strategy outline like Germany's *German Imperial Designs for War* (originally called *The Emperor's War Plans*), which proposed that Germany conquer France, ally with Japan, and fight America to the death. These strategic war goals were made even more specific on December 18, 1940, in Hitler's Directive No. 21, a war order for an operation code-named "Operation Barbarossa," in which Hitler ordered that the Soviet Union be crippled in a single devastating stroke before the conclusion of the war with Great Britain. After the Soviet Union and Great Britain were eliminated, Germany and Japan would clear the Anglo-Saxon forces from North America. They planned to launch a massive naval invasion of the east coast of North America from Scotland, Iceland, the Azores, and Brazil, and of the west coast from Hawaii and the Aleutian Islands. German high command did not just have detailed plans to invade the Soviet Union; they had plans to attack Great Britain and the United States, and eventually, to conquer and dominate the world.

China never produced a war plan like the *Will of Peter the Great*, in which Peter the

Great declared that the light of God forever shone on the Russian people and that they would forever be blessed with divine aid, so it was their responsibility to conquer Europe. In an age when Europe was the center of the world, to conquer and unite Europe was to conquer and unite the world. China has also never had any strategic designs to convert the Pacific Ocean into its own lake.

## China's Naval Strength

During the Ming Dynasty, China was the economic center of the world, producing 45% of the world's output. Iron production was 2.5 times that of the Northern Song, and in the early years of Emperor Yongle's reign, reached 9,700 tons a year. At the time, Russia was Europe's biggest iron producer, and it produced only 2,400 tons a year. The Ming Dynasty's military strength, especially its naval strength, was immense. Noted technology historian Li Yuese thinks the Ming Dynasty's navy may have been larger than any other Asian navy in history, end even larger than the European navies of the period. Even allied, the nations of Europe could never have defeated the Ming Dynasty's navy. Paul Kennedy said: one-third of global steel output was Ming Empire weapons production. The Ming Dynasty was strong, but did not engage in long-distance campaigns. This was because the Ming Dynasty did not want to expand.

Ming Dynasty navigator Zheng He set out on July 11, 1405, with a massive fleet on the first of seven voyages into the Western Ocean. By 1433, over nearly 30 years, Zheng He's fleets had visited the Pacific Ocean, the Indian Ocean, the Red Sea, and even the eastern coast of Africa, and left traces of their visits in more than 30 countries and regions. On each of Zheng He's seven trips to the Western Ocean, he brought an average of 27,000 people and more than 260 ships, of which 60 were large or mid-size treasure ships, each with a displacement of roughly 1,500 tons.

On Columbus's many trips to the Americas during his lifetime, the least number of ships he took was three, and the most was 17. Each of his ships had a displacement of 100–200 tons. The lowest number of people accompanying him on his journeys was 90, and the most was 1,200–1,500. On his two voyages to India, the displacement of Vasco da Gama's ships was 50–120 tons.

In 30 years of sea voyages, China's ships reached over 30 countries. Not one was subjected to military conquest, not a single colony was founded, and not a single nation's wealth was stolen. Instead, these voyages brought ambassadors who promoted economic and cultural exchange. They were voyages of friendship and peace. The places conquered and colonized by the West on their extended journeys east were the same places Zheng He had visited only decades before. Why were China's long-distance expeditions not long-distance campaigns? Because even though China had the strength to expand and colonize, it didn't have the desire.

In 1433, during the seventh of Zheng He's journeys, he died of illness. Resistance to the maritime expeditions from several high ministers caused the new Ming emperor to issue an edict: journeys to the Western Ocean by the various treasure fleets are stopped. China's naval industry was abandoned, Zheng He's treasure ships were left to rot in the harbors of Taicang, and worst of all, imperial soldiers burned Zheng He's shipyards, which he had operated for years, and all his blueprints.

The 15th century was a turning point in humanity's shift from land to the ocean, and China was the world's preeminent maritime power, but in the end it withdrew from the sea. Hegel once said that the Chinese turned away and left the ocean at their backs. And just as China turned away from the oceans, Europeans forged ahead into them, beginning the era of great maritime discoveries, colonial occupation, and robbery of overseas wealth. Paul Kennedy pointed out that China was the most developed and most advanced civilization of its era. He believes that the reason China ended its sea voyages was the conservativeness of Confucian officials. The important officials cared about protecting and restoring the past, not about a future based on overseas expansion or trade, which was responsible for the empire's widespread distaste for commerce and private capital. If this is Western commentary on China's abandonment of maritime expeditions, is it not just proof from another perspective of China's attitudes at the time against expansion, robbery, and colonialism?

## China's Nuclear Strategy

There are eight (including North Korea) publicly nuclear nations in the world today. Several have more nuclear weapons than China, and several have fewer, but the only nuclear power to ever announce a no-first-strike policy is China.

The United States was the world's first nuclear power, and the first nation to use nuclear weapons. It is the nation with the most nuclear weapons and the most advanced nuclear technology, and it is the nation with the strongest conventional military, but it has not announced a no-first-strike nuclear policy. China was the first and is the only nation with a no-first-strike nuclear policy. The United States and China have shown vastly different attitudes toward their nuclear weapons.

China is not just the first nation to disavow a nuclear first strike. China also has publicly announced that it will not use nuclear weapons against non-nuclear nations or regions, shouldering a responsibility that no other nuclear power has dared to. China has never helped another nation develop nuclear weapons, and China's government has a policy that puts it resolutely against the use, encouragement, or proliferation of nuclear weapons.

China's nuclear weapons are purely for self-defense. China will never use its weapons for murder; it possesses them only for self-defense. The entire world was happy to hear President Obama's calls for a nuclear-free world. The road to a nuclear-free world will be long and hard, but will first require a world in which nuclear powers disavow nuclear first strikes. But can America, which leads the calls for a nuclear-free world, follow China's example and swear to the world that it will never use nuclear weapons first?

## China Has "Will Nots" for the United States

With China's rise has come the rise of theories about the "Chinese threat." While other countries can be forgiven for such fears, American fears of a "Chinese threat" are laughable. China's personality guarantees that the United States will face no threat from China. China has "Will Nots" for the United States, which should be enough to provide Eight Reassurances for Americans about China. Can China reassure the US?

**1.** China is not pre-1945 Japan—China will not cause another Pearl Harbor for America.

**2.** China is not interwar Germany—China will not challenge the world militarily or fire the first shot or drop the first bomb in a war against America.

**3.** China is not pre-1991 Russia—China does not need to engage in Cold War, and will not engage in Cold War against America.

**4.** China's military technology may lag behind the United States, but China will not mistakenly bomb any United States embassy. The United States has no need to safeguard its embassies anywhere in the world against misaimed attacks by Chinese bombers.

**5.** China's military reconnaissance planes will not reach the west coast of the United States, and there will never be a collision with a US military aircraft, and American pilots launched into the sea.

**6.** If any part of the United States declares independence or wants to secede, China will not intervene, or establish a regional relationship with that portion of the United States, nor will China provide it military aid.

**7.** China will not use a strategy of Easternization or division against the United States, or adopt a strategy of trying to cause peaceful change in the United States.

**8.** China will not organize or attempt to shape any form of alliance against the United States.

## III. The Chinese Art of War

The character of a nation or people can be witnessed directly in their military culture. China is a major military power, and the Chinese art of war is a jewel of China's military culture. China's political culture crystallizes in its military expression. The Chinese art of war offers an important perspective on the personality of China.

### A Peaceful Art of War

China's arming to stop the swinging of axes is a peaceful art of war. The goal and aim of arming is to stop axes, which is to say that the ultimate aim of military struggle is peace rather than victory. To put it another way, China's military culture isn't one that fights to win, that seeks victory; it's a military culture that fights to stop war and win peace.

Five thousand years ago, when China's ancestors carved the *wu*, or martial character, on tortoise shells, they did so in the spirit of stopping axes, to ask for the peace. The ancient tradition of stopping axes decided that China's martial spirit would be for the purpose of stopping axes, which meant that actually, China's martial spirit was a spirit of peace.

The slogan of China's art of war is "since ancient times wise soldiers resist war," and the ideal of China's military experts is "since ancient times wise soldiers fight for peace." Investigating military matters and developing the world's most advanced army was not to defeat the enemy, but to win peace. The core value of China's art of war is not victory first; it is peace first.

America's ability to defeat its enemies is without doubt the world's foremost, but its ability to win peace is lacking. Since the end of the Cold War, the United States has defeated every enemy militarily, and failed at every attempt to win peace. Every battlefield it has won with ease has become a mire of difficulty after the victory. America's military technology and art of war haven't solved the difficulties facing US military forces, so perhaps Americans would do well to study the Chinese art of war?

### Responsive Strike and Defensive Strategy

China's responsive strike and defensive strategy mean that China doesn't attack. China doesn't make preemptive strikes, doesn't provoke war with others, and doesn't fire the first shot. The slogans on the lips of China's soldiers of the past were be prepared and always be ready. The key was always preparation. China's army and China's soldiers didn't try to gain the strategic initiative by making preemptive attacks; they gained victory by being prepared to meet enemy attacks, and gained security through preparedness.

Not firing the first shot, fighting with reason, and striking in response are the basic strategic principles. And these are the fundamental factors that decided the non-aggressive, non-invasive, and non-provocative nature of China's military culture. They settled China's military culture, at the strategic level, as a non-offensive, but rather defensive, protective one that specializes in counterstriking, not striking first.

Although China's art of war is recognized the world over as a history of brilliant military strategies, they are primarily not strategies of offense; they are primarily strategies of defense and protection; they stress counterattack, not striking first. The most distinctive feature of China's military culture is active defense, but this doesn't deny the value of China's art of war as a tool of attack. It indicates that the value of attacks in China's art of war is primarily defensive, rather than as a tool of occupation; that they are tools to hold the line, rather than expand. Emperor Wu of Han's brilliant campaigns deep into the desert to attack the Xiongnu were defensive attacks—attacks to prevent further attacks. These, too, were an active defense at work.

The defensive nature of China's military culture is widely acknowledged. Noted American Sinologist John K. Fairbank wrote, "China's strategists, throughout history, have stressed defensive war, which is starkly different from the aggressive commercial expansionism found in the military actions of European empires." Thomas Cleary said, "China's use of military might has been limited to defensive purposes, and been influenced by Buddhist and Confucian thought. War is a method of last resort, something that can only be undertaken with a very good reason; this usually applies to defensive wars, but doesn't rule out punitive wars, to prevent oppression through strength." Matteo Ricci, a Western missionary who lived in China for 30 years during Emperor Wanli's reign in the Ming Dynasty, said, "The Ming army is the largest, best-equipped army I have ever seen, but this Chinese army is only used to defend the country. It has no designs to invade other nations."

A Russian historian estimates that between 1700 and 1870, Russians engaged in 38 wars, and of those only two were defensive; the other 36 were offensive wars. But in the thousands of years of China's history, it's hard to find even one example of China attacking a country or people without being attacked first.

## Tactical Art of War

The tactical art of war, of winning without fighting, is the art of winning military struggles through tactics rather than battles. China's ancient military strategists stressed the use of tricks before battle, deciding conspiracy before moving to war, and using conspiracy as your primary weapon and force as a secondary one. They stressed the use of tactics, conspiracy, and strategy—of frightening opponents with military might, or achieving peace through marriage, or using forts to contain opponents, or of using rank and titles to appease opponents, or using trade to enrich opponents, or of using religion to pacify opponents; all forms of achieving victory with little or no war. Ancient China had a history of using tricks. The legendary 36 Strategies are a profound heritage. China's art of war is to promote tactics and use strategy and aims to achieve victory without using soldiers and lower the cost of war. American scholar Arthur Waldron gave this summary of China's art of war: "The history of China's military strategy is one of using the least possible troop strength (Strength), and using tactics and strategy (Craft) to gain the largest possible objective benefit (Advantage)."

The essence of the tactical art of war is to refuse savagery and reduce the number of deaths. The Chinese art of war prefers to take its cities intact, rather than destroy the city's strategic defenses, sack it, and butcher its citizens. It is a civilized art of war, a benevolent art of war. Attaining victory through strategy is the most civilized, most beneficial form of victory, reduces the costs of military struggle, and cuts down on the price of obtaining victory and winning peace. China's art of war shows the civility of its military culture.

## Differences Between Europe's On War and China's Art of War

Germany was home to General Carl von Clausewitz, whose On War is seen as a German masterpiece. The passion with which Germans read On War is no less than the passion with which the Chinese read Sun Tzu's Art of War. Among Germany's politicians and military experts, who hasn't read On War?

On War has been called Europe's Art of War. But the character of European and Chinese military strategy is as different as their representative works. Europe's great wars shaped its military strategy, and Europe's military strategy was the catalyst for its great wars and even world wars. After two world wars, many of Europe's strategists and military experts shared a common regret—they didn't read Art of War sooner.

Kaiser Wilhelm II began the First World War, and after the war, he read China's Art of War. His reaction upon reading it was grief: "If I had read Art of War 20 years earlier, I could have prevented the tragedy of Germany's demise." B. H. Liddel Hart, the great Western military strategist known as the "20th century Clausewitz," wrote in the forward of a new translation of Sun Tzu's Art of War in 1963, "In the era prior to the First World War, European military thought was strongly influenced by Clausewitz's On War. But if that influence had been counterbalanced by Sun Tzu's influence, humanity could have avoided much of the destruction caused by the two world wars." Art of War sold incredibly well in postwar Europe, and later became a global favorite. The appeal of Art of War is actually a reflection of the appeal of China's military culture.

China is a major contributor to military thinking around the world, but it has never been a major contributor of wars to the world. China's art of war is a peaceful, defensive, strategic, benevolent, moral, civilized art of war, one that uses softness to overpower steel, and quiet to overcome force. Sun Tzu's Art of War is a classic expression of China's military culture, a concentrated reflection of China's military personality, and a breakthrough work in the military expression of China's political characteristics.

## IV. The Chinese Empire Is Powerful but Arbitrary

The Chinese Empire was history's longest-lasting empire; an immortal empire made real. But the principle the Chinese Empire lived by was that emperors do not abuse their neighbors. The Chinese Empire was large but not harsh and strong but not tyrannical. This mighty empire and its mighty emperor displayed distinctive kingly characteristics.

### Constructing the Great Wall

The symptoms of empire are strength, attack, invasion, and expansion. The Chinese Empire was one of history's strongest empires, but it was different from almost every other empire in the world. It remained a very introverted empire through the course of its history. It was a conservative empire, a defensive empire, a self-protective empire, a moral empire, a peaceful empire, and an approachable empire.

China's imperial history begins with Qin Shihuang, who was China's first emperor and the creator of the Chinese empire. He also created the Great Wall, making him the designer and leader who ordered the construction of the largest defensive structure on earth. After he unified China, the new empire was a powerful military force, and he ordered a defensive campaign north against the Xiongnu. After banishing the Xiongnu and taking back the territory they occupied, he ordered the construction of the Great Wall to stop the barbarians from invading Chinese territory. But the Great Wall wasn't constructed along the Qin borders; it was built inside Qin borders. That kind of self-defensive restraint, despite the power and advantages held by the empire, was only possible in China.

The Qin construction of the Great Wall shows the conservative nature of the Chinese Empire. Each time the Great Wall was repaired, it wasn't during a period of decline in China, it was during a period of strength and prosperity. The Qin and Ming construction of the Great Wall were major engineering projects that occurred while Chinese strength was at its height. The Great Wall was a signal from the Chinese Empire, and a symbol of the Chinese Empire. What it stood for was conservative non-aggression and peaceful coexistence.

### Han and Tang Fear of Tribute

While one is investigating the global systems at work in history, the comparison of two systems is very telling: Asia's tribute system and Europe's colonial system. In East Asia's tribute system, China was the superior state, and many of its neighboring states were vassal states, and they maintained a relationship of tribute and rewards. This was a special regional system through which they maintained friendly relations and provided mutual aid. The appeal and influence of ancient China's political, economic, and cultural advantages were such that smaller neighboring states naturally fell into orbit around China, and many of the small countries nominally attached to China's ruling dynasty sent regular tribute. The commercial ties and cultural exchange that were the core content and defining features of this tribute system were very different from the actual duties imposed on China's political subordinates, and even more different from the colonial relationship the West shared with its partners. China was never a colonialist power, and there is no area of the world today that was once a colony of China.

In the Han and Tang eras, while China's relations with its neighbors was called a tribute system by the West, it was actually more of a reciprocal exchange, like the exchange between relatives, not a relationship of domination, obedience, and control, or of a leader and subordinates. The universal spread of China's civilization and the variety of nations that sent emissaries to China were simply a reflection of the attractiveness of the central nation, and the admiration that neighboring countries had for China's civilization. The small nations bordering China gained more than material benefits from their tributary relationship with China. Their rulers were granted royal titles by the mighty central empire, which enhanced their legitimacy, giving them political benefits as well.

What did foreigners think of East Asia's tribute system? In *De Christiana expeditione apud Sinas suscepta ab Societate Jesu*, Matteo Ricci said, "There are 3 nations in the East, more than 53 nations in the West, more than 55 nations in the south, and 3 nations in the north, and all grant tribute to the Chinese Empire. But in truth, when these tributary nations exchange gifts in China, they take away far more valuable gifts than those they contribute, so the Chinese authorities seem not to care at all about the tribute they receive."[1]

Ricci had discovered the secret of the tribute system China shared with its bordering countries, and actually, it was a late discovery. The tribute from neighboring countries was always a source of trouble for China. China's policy of generosity with its neighboring vassal states became over time a responsibility to maintain a decent relationship. Even in the Han and Tang eras, etiquette demanded that gifts returned to the visiting emissaries of foreign powers be several times, sometimes up to ten times, more than the value of their tribute, and over time this emptied the national treasure. By the Tang Dynasty, the burden of returning gifts to foreign emissaries was so heavy that the court had no choice but to issue a rule limiting tribute missions to one a year at most.

## Rural Uprisings in China

There is another interesting phenomenon in modern history: China experienced a great number of civil wars, while Western empires experienced a great number of external wars. China had more, and larger, rural uprisings than anywhere else in the world, and far more internal warfare than external.

The Chinese Empire didn't invade other countries while it was strong, and during periods of resource scarcity or internal conflict, it never used provoking incidents or war abroad, expanding its territory, or stealing resources to solve its problems, ease conflicts, or address crises. An important reason for the frequency and scale of China's rural uprisings is how the scarcity of land and intense competition for resources catalyzed social conflicts. Historically, Western countries solved these problems by sending their excess population to open new colonies, seizing territory by provoking war, exporting conflict, and diverting their population's attention abroad to ease internal relations and guarantee social stability. This form of distraction is actually easing internal conflicts by stoking international conflicts, using struggle with foreign peoples to ease domestic class struggles, and using foreign wars to ease internal competition. The Chinese Empire never used these methods of exporting problems abroad, instead preferring to internalize all problems and solve them domestically. The result was intense class struggle, the collapse of existing political orders, and new dynasties—a steep price to pay. This was the Chinese Empire, an empire that even at times of crisis and collapse turned its conflict inward, preferring to trouble itself rather than look outward, export conflicts, and provoke wars.

## The Relationship Between the Chinese Emperor and the Empire

The character of the Chinese Empire was intimately linked to the character of the emperors who founded and led it. The great emperors of China's history, from Qin Shihuang to Emperor Wu of Han to the Ming emperors, were not invaders and conquerors; they were preventative, defensive emperors. When Qin Shihuang conquered the six states competing with him, he was solving the problem of uniting the empire, and once it was done, he built the Great Wall.

All the great emperors of China's history, whether they founded or inherited a dynasty, only exercised their power within China's borders. The only exceptions were when the people of the Chinese heartland were faced with obliteration by an outside group like the Mongolians. China's emperors were very different than European emperors like Napoleon or Louis XIX, who wanted to use the sword to redraw the map of Europe. As Europe entered the Age of Discovery and began to expand, China was doing exactly the opposite. The founder of the Ming Dynasty was adamant about maintaining China's borders as they were, and not expanding abroad. He left specific instructions for his heirs, listing 15 countries that were not to be conquered, including Korea, Japan, and Annam.

In 1421, at one point, the number of foreign emissaries and merchants visiting Nanjing reached 1,200 at the same time. They were met with hospitality by the emperor and his ministers, and then seen off by the court ministers. These kings, queens, and high officials were delighted to have been able to visit the capital of China. The Chinese Empire treated smaller, weaker countries well. China's emperors treated the kings of smaller nations like little brothers. Strong and not abusive to the weak, large but leaving room for the small; governing ethically, treating all benevolently—these are the values that define China's personality.

# V. Differences Between China and America

In a world full of competitive, hostile, and antagonistic relationships, can a strong country and a mighty people pursue a higher realm of ideals?

## *The Two Realms, as Described in Sun Tzu's* Art of War

In his *Art of War*, Sun Tzu writes that to fight and conquer in all your battles is not supreme excellence; supreme excellence consists in breaking the enemy's resistance without fighting. The book discusses two realms of excellence: breaking the enemy's resistance without fighting is the highest, most ideal result of conflict, the realm of supreme excellence. To fight and conquer in all your battles is a lower realm, a lesser ability, and not supreme excellence. While China and America both seek to be without rival, they seek supremacy in two different realms. There is a basic difference in the type of supremacy they want.

America seeks to be without rival in its ability to defeat its rivals. It seeks strength. China seeks to be without rival in not creating rivalries, which is another realm. America's personality is adapted to being a hegemon; China's is adapted to tolerance. America seeks to maintain its place as a world hegemon without rival. China seeks a world in which none wish to rival it.

## *A Benevolent Nation Without Rival*

China becomes without rival by not creating rivals. China has not defined any nation in the world as its enemy. And in that sense, China is a nation without enemies, which makes it free of any guilt—in this world, no country calls China its enemy. China's goal of becoming without rival is significant in three specific respects.

**1.** China will not seek to become world hegemon or treat the world as an enemy. Countries that seek hegemony will always need to find other countries to be subjects to their power, and these must be countries that are guilty of a sin, to have become enemies of the world. China does not seek world hegemony, so China's relations with other countries will not be one of a hegemon and subject, which means China will not make enemies of other countries.

**2.** China will not seek to establish another country as its enemy. America has a long tradition of establishing others as its enemy, and this is an important factor in America's strategic thinking. Americans feel lost without an enemy, they feel their nation loses cohesion and drive, so they are constantly seeking and locking on to enemies. This is one of America's strategic needs. But China seeks a universal peace. China tries to create an environment in which there are no enemies. China considers a world in which the four seas contain no opponents its ideal world, and one in which friends cover the five continents as its landmark of success. And in today's world, China doesn't list a single nation as its enemy.

3. China doesn't glorify violence and victory. China's military culture is one that believes in meeting bare axes with jade and silk. An example is ancient China's peace and kinship policy, through which by marrying into the imperial family, enemies were made relatives. China resolves its differences peacefully, doesn't glorify military achievement or meeting axes with axes, and doesn't believe that war or military force will solve problems. Meeting bare axes with jade and silk is true peace. Meeting axes with axes is a temporary victory that plants the seeds for eternal hate; it is mere victory, not peace. And when the price of victory and the aftermath cost more than what victory has gained, victory becomes hollow. Winning this kind of victory is only creating a more powerful, longer-lasting foe for oneself. The highest achievements of China's military culture is not to fight and conquer in all its battles; it is to break the enemy's resistance without fighting. This kind of victory doesn't create a new enemy for the victor.

Put simply, China seeks to be without rival in having no enemies. If China seeks to become without rival in the realm of not having enemies and gaining the submission of all nations without weapons, then America seeks to be without rival in strength. It seeks might by raising its fists, to create a strength that can overcome any rival. The supremacy America seeks means returning violence with violence. The result is that the more enemies it defeats, the more enemies it will have to defeat. After the Cold War, the United States possessed overwhelming strength, but at the same time, it became the most insecure nation in the world, because even though it was without rivals militarily, it lacked moral strength.

## *The Biggest Danger Is to Become the World's Enemy*

America is an unrivalled hegemon and making enemies is the most insecure act possible. After the Cold War, the United States produced one list of enemies after another. The rogue nations, the Axis of Evil, the list of countries against which the use of nuclear weapons would be considered, the more than 40 non-democratic nations, etc. It essentially listed half of the world as its rivals and enemies. After 9/11, the United States listed Iran, Iraq, and North Korea as the modern Axis of Evil. After that, it added Cuba, Libya, and Syria to the list. In the *Nuclear Posture Report* put out regularly by the US Department of Defense, China, Russia, Iraq, North Korea, Iran, Libya, and Syria were listed as potential targets of nuclear first strikes. In the *2009 National Intelligence Strategy*, China and Russia were listed as America's main challengers, along with a list of other secondary ones.

"Today America is where Britain was around the turn of the/ century," wrote MIT economist Lester Thurow in 1985. "Rome lasted a thousand years, the British Empire about 200; why are we slipping after about 50 years?"[2] If a country declares dozens of other countries are its enemies, is it possible for that country not to decline?

In his 2007 book *Second Chance: Three Presidents and the Crisis of American Superpower* Zbigniew Brzezinski summarized the lessons learned from the terms of America's three presidents over the past 15 years: George H. W. Bush, Bill Clinton, and George W. Bush.[3] He claimed that after the Cold War, America's presidents were actually the kings of the world, and that America in 1991 was in a much more secure position than America in 1945. America had no enemies or rivals in the world, and had a rare opportunity to pursue peace. But 15 years after becoming the world's only superpower, America found itself in a politically hostile world, and stood as a democracy that was frighteningly alone in the world. Anti-American sentiment in the Muslim world grew by the day, the Middle East was in chaos, Iranian power was growing in the Persian Gulf, Russia was indignant, China was promoting economic cooperation in the Far East, Japan was more and more isolated in Asia, tides of populism and anti-Americanism were sweeping Latin America, the non-proliferation regime was on the verge of collapse, and America's moral image and credibility were severely damaged—the three presidents had pushed the United States into a dangerous corner. The younger Bush's counterterrorism strategy was to cry wolf every chance he got, intentionally creating a climate of fear in the country and inflating the scattered terrorist actors across the globe into an enemy that would win him the mission and approval ratings of a wartime president, and turning the United States into a closed, paranoid, and lonely nation. In the 15 years following the Cold War, the presidents of the sole superpower leading the world did a terrible job. George W. Bush was a disastrous president. George H. W. Bush envisioned the role of the United States as the world's police, Clinton imagine the United States as the trumpeter for social welfare, and George W. Bush made the United States chief of the world's security force. Brzezinski graded the three presidents: a B for the first Bush, a C for Clinton, and an emphatic F for the younger Bush. He said, at the moment when America led the world, at the height of American power, they turned America into a terrified, paranoid country, and left the world's strongest nation without a shred of security. From this we can see that a country that makes enemies everywhere in the world, no matter how large or powerful, is a country that will never be safe.

# VI. Tracing the Roots of the Chinese People

What were the conditions and factors that formed the unique Chinese character? What elements made the Chinese people into a peaceful, gentle, non-invasive, non-expansionist, benevolent, friendly people? This isn't a simple question to answer.

## *Agricultural, Nomadic, and Maritime Civilizations*

Human civilizations are created through the ways humans survive and develop, and more than anything, human civilizations are ways of surviving and developing. However many ways there are for humans to survive and develop is how many types of civilizations you'll find. The personality of a people is how that people survives and develops, and these factors are linked in primal, direct, and important ways. Looking at history tells us that there are agricultural civilizations, nomadic civilizations, and maritime civilizations, each based on one of three different ways people survive. These three civilizations lead to the three different characters of agricultural peoples, herding peoples, and maritime peoples, and the differences are very big.

Herding peoples need wars of conquest, and are very good at them. They are natural warriors. These are the peoples who exist on horseback and depend on the speed of their horses and arrows and migration to survive. They are naturally aggressive peoples. They move with their camps, and everyone who can raise a blade or spear is a warrior. They are herders, hunters, and conquerors all in one, and in winter or times of cold or drought, invading or raiding agricultural regions for resources is necessary to survive, which is why herding peoples are naturally nomadic and aggressive.

Maritime peoples are actually herding peoples in a marine setting. The places where maritime peoples live are usually barren peninsulas not suited for farming, so they have to rely on the ocean and shipping to provide a living. They gain wealth and resources through expanding overseas, opening up new trade markets, and establishing colonies, and by taking over monopolies on trade and finding the resources to develop their societies. So for them, trade and conquest are closely linked. Their fleets include both merchant ships and warships; expansion and war are how they gain wealth. War itself is a form of wealth creation and becomes a way to survive and develop—eventually becoming these peoples' means of survival.

Agricultural societies are self-sufficient, self-reliant civilizations. Agriculture is a more civilized means of survival than herding or maritime trade; it exposes its practitioners to less danger and risk, and makes their civilizations more stable and inward-looking. Social unrest and upheaval is disastrous for agricultural civilizations. Stability, safety, and security are the requirements for an agricultural civilization. So, agricultural civilizations are non-aggressive, non-warlike civilizations. China, since ancient times, has been an agricultural civilization, and it shows an agricultural civilization's desire for stability and safety, and an agricultural civilization's love of peace and non-expansionist strategic stance.

## *Continental Tradition Versus Marine Tradition*

Geographical factors are the objective conditions on which the people who live in a place depend to survive and develop. And geographical factors play a large part in forming how peoples and countries position themselves strategically. Typically speaking, a region's geography shapes that region's culture and traditions.

The Chinese people exhibit typical continental traditions. Chinese civilization originated in East Asia's Mesopotamia, the region between the Yellow River and Yangtze River. This vast, fertile, rich river valley gave Chinese civilization the room to develop, and protecting this fertile piece of land became the core interest of the Chinese people. Preventing raids from the herding tribes to the north was the long-term national defense project of the Chinese people. After 1840, threats of attack from the ocean became the primary threat to China's people, and in the fight between China's land power and Western sea power, keeping China's power over its land was China's primary objective, not beating Western sea power. China's struggle was never for more than to keep power over its land. China's culture is one that evolved to protect and defend its continental base, not one that evolved sea power to attack and plunder. That is what defined China's regional, continental, inward-looking culture.

One of Western culture's distinctive features is that it formed in a triple-sea region, on a landmass between and interwoven with the Mediterranean Sea, the Adriatic Sea, and the Aegean Sea. The Mediterranean Sea is the cradle of Western civilization, which expanded through Portugal, Spain, and the Netherlands and along the western coast of the European mainland.

## *The West Was Competing, While China Was Maintaining*

Western nations took shape much later than China, and Western civilization arose in a very fractured, fragmented world. The struggles, clashes, and competition between Western nations deepened by the day. The Thirty Years' War eventually involved the whole continent. If we say that Western culture evolved in an environment of hostility and competition between nations, and has always had strong outward-looking tendencies, then Chinese culture evolved through the rise and fall of empire and the transitions between dynasties, and has strong inward-looking tendencies.

From a larger view of history, we can see that China's history of internal conflict is far richer than its history of foreign conflict and war. China's internal conflict can be seen first in the power struggles between and within different political classes, and second in the wars between China's governing class and the laboring class. China's rural uprisings were by far the world's largest in scale and number. China was unified long ago, and its political crises, power struggles, and struggles to attain balance and integration always involved the rise and fall of dynasties and the succession of power, and what characterized these struggles was always their introversion. According to *The Modern World System* author and American scholar Immanuel Wallerstein, Chinese civilization took the road of internal expansion and developed internally; no Chinese dynasty ever considered external expansion to be a basic national policy.

The primary challenges faced by the Western world came from intense competition abroad, and the questions Western nations had to solve were how survive and develop by winning wars, expanding, and beating competitors. So, the distinctive feature of Western thinking was that it was outward-looking. As the fifteenth president of the United States, James Buchanan said, "The law by which our nation survives is expansion, and even if we wish to disobey it, it is impossible." The effect of China and the West's differing outlooks on security and national direction on the character of these nations and peoples is a factor that cannot be overlooked.

## The "Irreproachable Law of Survival"

The character of a people is a concentrated expression of their culture and core values. China's Confucian-dominated mainstream ideology is a value system founded on ethics and morals. An important feature of China's culture and core values is a very strong concept of right and wrong and good and evil. Morality is seen as a source of strength, and a high priority is placed on such concepts as morality wins support from many, losing morality means losing support, and immoral conduct dooms the doer. In war, values such as dispatching troops with reason, using just force, and conducting just wars take precedence.

Very different from China's pursuit of moralism is Western culture's utilitarianism. In international relations, the West engages in realist diplomacy, pursues power and interest goals, uses force and strength as negotiating tools, and seeks balance in trade-offs between things beneficial and damaging to its interests. The rise of the West was a Darwinian process governed by natural law, in which the weak were consumed by the strong, and it produced a culture that glorified power and military force, and loved war and conflict. Bismarck said, "The strong subduing the weak is simply the irreproachable law of survival."

The Western world has long advocated interests above all else, while China since ancient times has advocated morality above all else, and this forms one of the most fundamental differences in values between it and Western culture. And this is one of the formative characteristics of Chinese culture. The Chinese character gives pride of place to morality, and morality plays a critical role in Chinese strategic thinking, and its importance in Chinese culture informs moral judgment and considerations, and thus it becomes an important factor in how Chinese strategy is decided. The United States made several strategic errors concerning China during the Korean War, and although they were caused by many factors, one of the main reasons was that they underestimated the weight given to morality in Chinese military strategy.

## VII. The Unchanging, Kingly Nature of China

Kingliness is China's national character. When China becomes the most powerful nation in the world, this character must not change. But how can we ensure that China remains a kingly country? How can we keep China's national character from mutating?

### *"We Wouldn't Invade in a Hundred or Even Ten Thousand Years"*

On January 30, 1962, at a speech to the Enlarged Central Work Committee, Mao Zedong said, "In 1961 I had a discussion with Montgomery, at which we talked about these ideas again. He said: 'In another fifty years you will be terrific.' What he meant was that after fifty years we might become powerful and 'invade' other countries, but not within fifty years. He had expounded his opinions to me when he came to China in 1960. I said: 'We are Marxist-Leninists, our state is a socialist state, not a capitalist state, therefore we wouldn't invade in a hundred years, or even ten thousand years.'"[4]

On May 29, 1984, Deng Xiaoping pointed out during an important speech that, while China is a Third World country, once it develops and becomes rich, it will remain a Third World country. China will never seek hegemony, and will never abuse another country. On April 4, 1986, during another speech, he said, "If China, with its one billion people, abandoned the policy of peace and opposition to hegemony or if, as the economy developed, it sought hegemony, that would also be a disaster for the world, a retrogression of history. But if China, with its one billion people, keeps to socialism and adheres to the policy of peace, it will be following the right course and will be able to make greater contributions to humanity."[5]

During a century of suffering disastrous abuse at the hands of others, China stuck to the principle of never abusing others. Sun Yat-sen reminded us again before he left us: when China is revived, it cannot follow the West's example of hegemony and go on vengeful campaigns of conquest. It should maintain Oriental kingliness, and uphold fairness and justice for the world. Mao Zedong also announced to the world: China will not seek hegemony. That it will never abuse others is China's solemn promise to the future world, and will forever be the foundation of China's national policy.

### *Fighting Injustice*

In *The Three Principles of the People*, Sun Yat-sen wrote, "It is our duty to revive the spirit of Chinese nationalism and to use the strength of our four hundred millions to uphold justice and humanity."[6] Sun Yat-sen believed that once China took a leading place in the world, China had to do more than just restore democracy to its proper place; it had to take on a major responsibility in the world. If China couldn't shoulder this responsibility,

China's wealth and power would only harm the world, not help it. So what is the responsibility China owes the world? Establishing policies to help the weak and the poor has been the duty of China. China's duty is to support small, weak peoples, and resist the power of strong tyrants. Only if everyone in the country took that ambition to heart, he believed, could the Chinese people ever develop. If the Chinese people couldn't take that to heart, then there was no hope for them. To Sun Yat-sen, after China became strong, it had more than just a duty to not use its strength to prey upon the weak: it had a duty to support the weak, uphold fairness, shoulder responsibilities, and fight injustice.

## Counterbalance Between the US and China

On October 27, 2009, at the twenty-fifth anniversary banquet of the US-ASEAN Business Council in Washington, D.C., Lee Kuan Yew gave a speech entitled "On the Rebalancing of the Global Order," which was a classic example of the international community's balanced China theory. Lee Kuan Yew thinks that when China becomes the leading global power, the other nations of Asia will have no way to resist it. If the United States gives up an active role in Asia-Pacific affairs and fails to counterbalance China's military power, it will lose its position as global leader.

But how should China be counterbalanced? There are only three possible ways. One is a strategy of counterbalancing with containment at its core, and this in essence is just a containment policy. Counterbalancing China will mean containing China, and of course China must resist a policy like that. The second kind of counterbalancing would be one with adapting at its core, which features timely reordering of the system as the balance of strength changes, and we should actively encourage a policy like this. The third kind of counterbalancing would be a strategy to check China, which would mean to ensure that a nation rapidly gaining strength and moving toward becoming the world's most powerful country is not left without an effective means of supervising, limiting, and guiding its growth, to prevent a serious loss of balance. China should welcome this kind of counterbalancing with open arms.

The internal reason hegemonies form is that strong nations pursue hegemonic policies. The external reason hegemonies form is a lack of external restraining factors. After the Cold War, the reason American hegemony was so rampant—the reason America waved its guns on the world stage—was that it was overwhelmingly powerful, without anything to counterbalance or limit its strength.

Building a kingly China, maintaining China's characteristics, and stopping China from dirtying its hands with American-style hegemonic vices as it becomes the world's leading nation and the world's strongest country will require not only ethnical governance and self-restraint, but also force of law and external checks and counterbalances. Millennia of China's kingly traditions aren't enough to guarantee that China will be kingly when it ascends to the heights of power, or that its character won't mutate into something horrible. An America without effective international supervision or counterbalance has given the world rampant hegemony, caused untold disaster, and sent America into decline. A world out of balance is a world difficult to keep stable or at peace. As China rises, it doesn't want to rise as an unconstrained superpower that shakes off the limits of the international community. China wants to build a peaceful world, and that means China first needs to be at harmony and in balance with the world. On May 7, 1978 Deng Xiaoping said in a speech entitled "Four Modernizations, Do Not Seek Hegemony" that "China will never seek hegemony. People today can understand this thought now, because China today is still a very poor country indisputably in the Third World. The problem is that as we develop in the future, will we engage in hegemony? If at that time China raises its tail, begins to seek world hegemony, and starts making threatening gestures, then it has given up its citizenship in the 'Third World', and is no longer a socialist nation at all."[7] Deng Xiaoping's warning is worth consideration.

The world of the future requires a rebalanced China. The China of the future requires a balanced world. China welcomes an active American strategy of counterbalancing China, and China welcomes the world to actively do the same. In the end, ensuring that a kingly China never changes will require building a strong nation that never abuses others, that fights injustice in the world, and that helps others in danger, a strong nation that can both counterbalance hegemons and be effectively checked and controlled by the world.

# CHAPTER 5

# A GREAT STRATEGY REQUIRES

# GREAT THINKING

Strategy decides the direction and the future of a nation and a people. Strategy is the life-blood of a nation and a people. The rise and fall of every great nation can be traced back to the rise and fall of that great nation's strategy. With the right strategy, small nations can rise; with the wrong strategy, great nations decline. Weak nations, at root, are weak in strategy. While strong nations have strong strategies, the moment they lose their strategic advantage, they become weak. Revived nations are those with revived strategies. The rise of every great nation is the rise of a great strategy. With strategy in place, everything else follows.

## I. A Great Country's Strategy

Countries without a strategy can never be great nations, and nations without the right strategy can never become strong nations. What makes great nations great is great strategy, and the strength of strong nations comes from the strength of their strategy. For a great nation to rise, it first needs a rise of strategy; the competition of great nations is at heart a competition of strategies. Strategy is a nation's lifeblood, and its core competitive strength.

## *Ignorant Strategy Is a Fatal Mistake!*

China, since ancient times, has had a rich history of strategic thought, and it is an invaluable storehouse of strategic thought for the world. In this respect, it has contributed greatly to the world. But, in modern world history, China's strategies have lagged behind. Fall behind, and you'll be whipped. China's backwardness shows in its level of technological and economic development, but on a deeper level, China's strategy and strategic thinking are backward. The tragedy of modern China is a kind of strategic backwardness and passiveness. These flaws are the root cause of the disasters that have befallen this country and its people.

China's rise began with updating and innovating its strategic thinking. Sun Yat-sen's and Mao Zedong's revolutionary strategies and Deng Xiaoping's Reform and Opening Up were both innovations in strategy by the Chinese people. To adapt to the needs of China's rise and rejuvenation, 21st century China will have to create a strategic China. A strategic China is one that can make a historic leap in strategy to become a strategic powerhouse. China's strategy will involve three things: first, a long-term strategy that sees past the present; second, a global strategy that sees past parts of the world; and third, the ability to turn strategic thinking into strategic principle, a strategic compass, strategic behaviors, and the ability to convert strategy into action.

Twenty-first century China is making progress toward becoming a more strategic China: China's strategy is already long-term, as China is working its way through a century-long development strategy that began at the founding of the country; this is China's century strategy. In terms of comprehensiveness, China has already gone from entering the world to leading the world and designing its future; this is China's world strategy. In terms of execution, China's strategic thinking has become policy, and China's ability to turn strategy into action has begun to inform science, which in turn informs strategy, and forms a healthy cycle of strategic thought and execution, This flow does not leave China trapped in empty thinking. The long time scale, global vision, and execution of China's strategy are an important landmark for a strategic China. But today, China still has some distance to go before it can become the strategic China it wants to be.

Countries are like people in that sometimes it's impossible for them to avoid mistakes. However, nations can't afford to make strategic mistakes, because when nations make strategic mistakes, some can be fatal. In recent history, in the competition between nations, the nations that have fallen behind and declined are nations whose strategies had problems and had made fatal mistakes. Germany, which began another world war, Japan in the Second World War, and the Soviet Union, which lost the Cold War, were all nations that made fatal strategic mistakes. Among Western nations, the United States has an excellent strategic record. Over two centuries, despite making its share of mistakes and barely surviving a series of major crises (including the 2008 financial crisis), it has rarely made the kind of strategic mistakes that lead to significant setbacks. The United States has maintained a level of stability, inventiveness, and vitality, and it still has a lot of life. The competition between great nations is first a competition not to make mistakes, or perhaps to make the least mistakes possible.

## Why Did Japan Lead China to Make Mistakes?

A Chinese expert told this story: In September 2009 a Japanese right-wing politician toured Beijing, Xi'an, Chongqing, and Shanghai, then went back to Japan. At a meeting of high-level Japanese right-wing politicians, he said, "From looking at the modernization of China and Japan, Japan has basically lost, because Japan studies to gain the technological edge, and that's given us 100 years of prosperity. But now China is starting to study. It's only a matter of time before Chinese technology catches up to Japan; it's not a matter of 'if' anymore. And once they get close to us, China's natural advantage, its geographical advantages, mean it will be the king of Asia. So long as China doesn't make any major mistakes, even if it never stops making minor ones, China's rise is inevitable." Someone asked him, "What should we do then?" He replied, "We have to trick China into making major mistakes. Japan can do it. All we have to do now is tempt them into making a major mistake to slow down China's rise." He was then asked, "Then what if China doesn't make a major mistake?" The old politician said, "Get used to becoming dependent on China." This shows Japan's deep sensitivity, which comes from their deep anxiety, which means that they've already started to think of the possibility. Of course, China's development goal isn't just to be king of Asia, China wants to become king of the world. This means China can even less afford to make mistakes.

In the competition between great nations, misleading the opponent into making vital mistakes is a common tactic. It's the most difficult and the least costly kind of containment. The first thing a country needs for national security is strategic security. Guaranteeing a nation's strategic security is guaranteeing that it won't make lethal strategic mistakes, which means ensuring that a nation has the most advanced, most correct strategy. Leading China into making mistakes to reduce China's competitiveness and secure Japan's own place in the world and its own competitive advantages may be something Japan hopes to do, but isn't that also exactly what America wants?

## The Rise of China Requires Advanced Strategy

In 1987 American history professor Paul Kennedy of Yale University researched the favorable and adverse conditions surrounding China's rise. He pointed out that China was the poorest of the countries wishing to be a great power and occupied the worst strategic position. These, he said, were two adverse conditions that would limit China's rise, but he also pointed out two favorable conditions: one was that China's leaders had "an ambitious, coherent, and visionary strategy, one that could beat Moscow, Washington, and Tokyo, not to mention Western Europe"; the other was that "China would continue to develop economically, and could be a vastly different country within several decades."

These words from Paul Kennedy, an American strategist, show three deep strategic insights on his part: first was his recognition that China had a strategy, one that was ambitious, coherent, and visionary; second was his belief that this strategy could beat Moscow, Washington, Tokyo, and Western Europe; third was his understanding that this strategy would bring China massive strategic benefits: it would ensure China's economy continued growth, and produce massive change within the country in the next few decades. His analysis of China's strategy was very accurate. China's rise began with the transformation and innovation of China's strategy. China's rise was, before all else, the rise of its strategy. It China wanted to be a great power, it needed to produce the strategy of a great power, a grand strategy. Without the rise of a grand strategy, China would never rise. China's strategy is what guided its rise.

## II. The Four Phases of China's Plan

China, as a great world power, will have a huge impact on the world no matter whether it rises or falls. The Communist Party of China's grand strategy to save and revive the nation features two distinctive breakthroughs: first is the strategy's global reach—it is intimately linked with the world beyond China; second is its phased implementation—it is a process of development that proceeds in four phases, four strategic forms.

### Surviving Through Strategy

Before the People's Republic of China was founded, the basic problem facing China's grand strategy was how the Chinese people would stand on their own two feet in the world. China's strategy during this period was a strategy to save and preserve China and ensure that the Chinese people could survive. This strategy was executed through revolutionary strategy. The founding of the country up to the Reform and Opening Up 30 years ago was actually all one phase, a phase in which China had to find ways to survive and remain independent despite being alone and locked out of world politics. During this phase, Mao Zedong thought was the theoretical shape of China's grand strategy.

### How to Lead the World

After the Cultural Revolution, China's strategy underwent a fundamental turn in the direction of Reform and Opening Up. The Reform and Opening Up policy was actually

China's strategy of entering the world. China's strategy transitioned from being one of China standing apart from the world to one of China actively participating in it. China's goal moved from survival to development, from being a nation that functioned outside world systems to one that functioned within them. It was a new phase in China's grand strategy, represented theoretically by Deng Xiaoping's Three Represents ideology.

## Rising Strategy

After entering the new century, China's rise toward its great power status sped up. In this new phase of China's grand strategy, it will quickly catch up to developed Western countries until it becomes the most developed country, and then it will sprint toward the goal of leading the world. The transition from entering the world and developing to rising to a leading position in the world raises new strategic demands for China. In this phase of China's grand strategy, scientific development is the basic theoretical shape of China's strategy.

## Leadership Strategy

In several decades, China's development will surpass America's. This is something even Americans are discussing. China and the United States will lead, manage, and govern the world together, and this is something also raised first by Americans. Economically, China is already showing the ability and potential to lead the world, and China's responsibilities and duties as world leader seem to be growing by the day. China's strategy has gone from being one of independent survival, to one of participation and development, to one of rising to lead the world, and finally, it will be one of leading and guiding the world. This is the strategic path down which a great people and a great nation will proceed. A strategy that can lead and guide the world is the highest possible stage and highest possible realm of Chinese strategy, and is the greatest contribution that a grand Chinese strategy can make to China and the world.

From this, we can see the progression of China's strategy from establishment, to development, to transitions, and to upgrades, each of which represents an adaption to the needs and tasks of the country and its people during different phases of history. The tasks faced by the nation are what catalyze the nation's grand strategy, and the creation of the nation's strategy is what guides the nation's tasks to completion and guarantees that the nation's strategic goals are met.

## III. The Three Phases of Chinese Strategy

China's strategy is decided by its goals. The kind of goals China pursues decide the kind of strategy it should pursue. China, as a rising nation, a rejuvenated nation, and a leading nation, is a nation whose grand strategy can't just be limited to designing China; it has to design Asia and the world. China's grand strategy is a combination of its China strategy, its Asia strategy, and its global strategy. These three organic parts form a strategic system. China's strategy is to deal with itself first, then Asia, then the world. The grand strategy of 21st century China has to answer three questions: what kind of a China should we build, what kind of an Asia should we build, and what kind of a world should we build?

## What Kind of China Should Be Built?

What kind of China should be built? This is the first question Chinese strategy needs to address. Mao Zedong led the construction of a socialist China; Deng Xiaoping led the construction of a China built on socialism with Chinese characteristics. Both were strategic designs and systems for a different kind of China. The first layer of China's grand strategy is deciding what kind of China we should build, and how to build it.

As China races toward its rise and revival, some people have proposed theories of a "China threat." In a world where some countries have misgivings about several of China's future development scenarios, if China is to be a major world power, it has work to do presenting, explaining, and promoting itself. But China's rise and revival cannot be limited to a strictly economic rise, and China's role as a great power cannot be limited to a major economic role. Those who think China's rise is not an ideological and military rise, or who think China's rise is just an economic rise, and that China is only rising to become an economic power or a GDP power are making a strategic mistake. Positioning China's rise in those terms, or assuming the Chinese people's revival is only an economic revival, is seriously mistaking the motives of this nation and its people.

A China that rises and develops without an ideology is a China without a soul, a brawny China without the IQ to match. A rich nation without a strong military is an insecure power. A nation without technological innovation is a country that can't produce a scientific rise, and in an era where the knowledge economy is the most productive force, it is a country that can't be strong economically. If China limits its rise to purely economic goals, it will produce a hobbled global power, a kind of global power that doesn't last. To create a nation like that would be equivalent to cutting short China's rise and the revival of the Chinese people.

## What Kind of Asia Should Be Built?

While the China of today is developing in a globalized environment, it also exists in a regional environment. To lead the world, China first needs to lead Asia. More than half the world's population lives in Asia, 6 of the world's 10 largest countries are in Asia, and 30% of global exports originate in Asia. If China wants to manage the world, it first needs to manage Asia. Kissinger believes that the global system is undergoing a fundamental change; the center of the world is moving from the Atlantic to the Pacific. Most of the world's key nations are in Asia, or will be Asian nations in the future. We must manage their rise, and they will resist our management. One could say that Asia is the region with the most vitality and potential in the 21st century. The kind of Asia we build will be critical in deciding what kind of world we build. After the Second World War, Europeans' strategic plans and designs for the continent were a success. The success of the European Union today is strong proof of that.

The era of the Warring States in Europe has come to a close. The conflict of the past has become an alliance, one that shows great strength and potential on the world stage. But Asia's Warring States era has just begun, and today China, Japan, and India are acting out the Wars of the Three Kingdoms over the entire continent. In Asia, it's not just one or two countries that want to control the continent's destiny. India's politicians declared long ago that the 21st century will belong to India. In answer to the question of what kind of Europe to build and how to build it, Europeans have already produced a grand European strategy, and putting that strategy into practice, they have produced remarkable achievements.

What kind of Asia to build, and how to build it, are questions that Asians have begun to consider. The leaders of Australia, Japan, and other countries have proposed an Asian community. Asia needs to look to the European Union for experience, but there is no possibility of copying the European model. The building of Asia will take Asian wisdom and innovation. And in the creation of Asian goals, an Asian model, Asian methods, and Asian strategies, China will serve a unique role.

## What Kind of World Should Be Built?

What kind of a China does the world need, and what kind of a world does China need? These questions are closely linked. Building a successful China will be beneficial in the building of a better world. And what kind of a world is built in the future will be critical for China. What kind of a world China needs and how China will use its leading role to create that world are questions that China's grand strategy for the 21st century must answer.

The essence of China's grand strategy is a champion nation strategy and a leading nation strategy. China's grand strategy, when China becomes the world's leading power, will be China's plan for leading the world, the plan through which China leads the globe in the creation of a new world. So at its highest levels, China's grand strategy is its overall, long-term design for the world. If China is to guide and lead the world, it needs to have a plan and a design for it.

## The World Is Too Important to Give to the United States

Historical experience shows that how the international order is arranged is a question that decides war, peace, and the happiness of humankind. After the Napoleonic Wars, from 1815 to 1914 Europe saw nearly 100 years of peace. The 19th century was a golden age of stability for Western civilization. This was made possible by the 1815 Congress of Vienna, held after the wars, where the European order was redrawn along more intelligent and more civilized lines. The conference allowed Europe to maintain a roughly equal balance of power that produced nearly a century of peace. But from 1914-1945 the wars of Europe drew in the entire world. And one of the primary reasons was that the international order after World War I was designed very poorly. It was far less enduring than the one produced after the Congress of Vienna in 1815. On June 28, 1919, at the signing ceremony of the Treaty of Versailles in Paris, which ended the First World War, Marshal Ferdinand Foch, commander of the French forces, said of the treaty, "This is not peace. It is an armistice for 20 years." His words were prophetic. The Paris Peace Conference bought Europe 20 years of peace with four years of war.

The strategic wisdom and strategic contributions of great nations lie in the organizations, orders, and frameworks they establish to promote peace and development. They need to do more than win wars, they need to win peace as well. History proves that it's much easier to create war than peace. The conclusion of the Cold War was a fantastic opportunity to create a better world order, but instead the United States embarked down the path of unilateralism and hegemony. America's mistake harmed itself and the world.

Joseph Nye, American political scientist and Harvard University John F. Kennedy School of Government professor, has argued that the principle of a world power is that it cannot just seek its own interests; it needs to seek methods that benefit its own interests as well as the interests of others. The ideal world power should have a wide view of its national interests, should have a combination of appealing soft power and hard power, and if it cares about other nations, should strengthen its soft power. The ideal world power looks at the international system in a broader context, and rather than only serving its national interests, also serves other national interests. In this, China is more suited to lead the world and rebuild the world order than America.

French politician Georges Clemençeau said, "War is too important to be left to the generals." Charles de Gaulle said, "Politics is too important to be left to the politicians." A Chinese expert said, "The world is too important to be left to America. China must become the world's designer. China needs to 'design the world.' China must lead the world toward a better future." As a designer, China needs to produce a better blueprint for the world than America's. As a world leader, China needs to produce a better policy agenda than America's. China has said it wants to build a harmonious world, and this is what China's design for the world offers.

## IV. China's Strategy: Learn from America

Among the rises of all the great nations, the experience of the United States is the most significant. America's rise was the fastest, smoothest, least costly, most effective, smartest, wisest, most artful, and most dramatic. America rose against numerous competitors who were very strong. In succession, American strategy outcompeted and subdued Germany, Japan, and the Soviet Union.

The importance of America's rise is primarily concentrated in three aspects: first is how America broke out of containment and rose despite it; second is how America contained other nations and protected its position as hegemon; and third is how America prevented secession and kept its territory united. America's methods in these three areas provide a wealth of experience for China to study. But China's research into American containment methods and how it preserves its hegemony is primarily looking at how America has contained others to learn how to cope with American containment. In the world today, the only country capable of containing China's rise is the United States. If China's rise is to succeed, China needs to study America and overcome it. In the subject of how a great country should rise, we could ask for no better teacher than the United States.

### America Is a Strategically Powerful Country

When people compare Japan and America, many say that Japan is better at small-scale scheming than America. In terms of grand strategy, America is far beyond Japan. America has the heart of a small nation, and the strategy of a great nation. The rise of great nations is great in terms of national strategies. The successful rise of a great nation is the success of its strategy. In the 200 years of American history it has made more than a few mistakes, but it has made very few mistakes that caused a great setback in America's strategic goals. The history of America's rise proves it is one of the great strategic nations, and that it will leave its mark on the world's history of grand strategy.

George Washington first advocated isolationism, and out of it, America's independent protectionist strategy was born. Isolationism, at the time of America's founding, was its first grand strategy, the first historical phase of its grand strategy, and its first ideology. Isolationism has deep historical roots in America. It took form as an American tradition in the days of George Washington. He believed that the New World (the Western Hemisphere) was superior to the Old World. He wanted to cut ties with a corrupt, declining Europe, and wanted even less to be involved in their disputes. The basic tenets of isolationism were that the United States would not involve itself in Europe's affairs, and would pursue an independent foreign policy free of European constraints. Isolationism was, in essence, a reflection of American independence, an insistence on an independent American foreign policy, but it was also an expression of the fact that the newly founded United States didn't have the strength to hold its own in a conflict with Europe.

America's isolationist thinking was given its deepest expression in George Washington's farewell speech on September 17, 1796. French political theorist Alexis de Tocqueville provided a brilliant description in his book *De la Démocratie en Amérique*: "There are two men who gave the policy of the Americans a direction that is still followed today; the first is Washington, and Jefferson is the second. Washington said, in this admirable letter addressed to his fellow citizens that forms the political testament of this great man: 'The great rule of conduct for us in regard to foreign nations is, in extending our commercial relations, to have with them as little political connection as possible. So far as we have already formed engagements, let them be fulfilled with perfect good faith. Here let us stop. Europe has a set of primary interests, which to us have none, or a very remote relation. Hence she must be engaged in frequent controversies, the causes of which are essentially foreign to our concerns. Hence therefore it must be unwise in us to implicate ourselves, by artificial ties, in the ordinary vicissitudes of her politics, or the ordinary combinations and collisions of her friendships, or enmities. Our detached and distant situation invites and enables us to pursue a different course. If we remain one People, under an efficient government, the period is not far off, when we may defy material injury from external annoyance; when we may take such an attitude as will cause the neutrality we may at any time resolve upon to be scrupulously respected; when belligerent nations, under the impossibility of making acquisitions upon us, will not lightly hazard the giving us provocation; when we may choose peace or war, as our interest guided by justice shall Counsel. Why forego the advantages of so peculiar a situation? Why quit our own to stand upon foreign ground? Why, by interweaving our destiny with that of any part of Europe, entangle our peace and prosperity in the toils of European Ambition, Rivalship, Interest, Humor or Caprice? 'Tis our true policy to steer clear of permanent Alliances with any portion of the foreign world. So far, I mean, as we are not at liberty to do it; for let me not be understood as capable of patronizing infidelity to existing engagements (I hold the maxim no less applicable to public than to private affairs, that honesty is the best policy). I repeat it, therefore, let those engagements be observed in their genuine sense. But, in my opinion, it is unnecessary and would be unwise to extend them. Taking care to always keep ourselves, by suitable engagements, on a respectable defensive posture, we may safely trust to temporary alliances for extraordinary circumstances.' Previously Washington had expressed this excellent and sound idea: 'The Nation, which indulges towards another an habitual hatred, or an habitual fondness, is in some degree a slave. It is a slave to its animosity or to its affection.' The political action of Washington always aimed to follow his maxims. He succeeded in keeping his country at peace, when all the rest of the universe was at war, and he established as a point of doctrine that the well-understood interest of Americans was to never take part in the internal quarrels of Europe. Jefferson went still farther, and he introduced to the policy of the Union this other maxim: "That the Americans should never ask for privileges from foreign nations, so that they are never obligated them to grant such privileges. The foreign policy of the United States is eminently one of wait-and-see; it consists much more of refraining from action than of doing."[1]

Washington's political farewell speech was the manifesto of American foreign policy. It's been called a distillation of the principles of American isolationist policy, and was no less influential than Alfred Thayer Mahan's *The Influence of Sea Power on History*. Washington's last will and testament was a crystallization of the wisdom of America's founding fathers. It was a creation of American strategic wisdom of the time, and directed American strategy for a century afterward. Washington's farewell speech was America's grand strategy and compass, and the thinking and theory behind its grand strategy. It was a document that can stand next to any of the world's great political works. In the history of American strategic thought, Washington's farewell speech and Mahan's masterpiece were the guiding lights of American strategy until the expansionist era.

## The Monroe Doctrine: America's Regional Hegemonic Strategy

If the isolationism in Washington's farewell speech was the first historical phase and ideology of the grand strategy of the United States, then the Monroe Doctrine was the second phase and the second ideology. Isolationism at its root was the former British colony and now independent nation declaring its foreign policy's independence from European systems and disputes. It wanted to avoid getting involved in European struggles to avoid being a pawn on Europe's chessboard. The new American nation wanted its own foreign policy. The Monroe Doctrine built on America's independent foreign policy to move from the domestic sphere of isolationism to the role of a regional hegemon. The Monroe Doctrine was United States hegemony in the Americas; it was a US strategy of regional hegemony; it was the US strategy of snatching the Americas from Europe. It was an important stage in path of the United States toward global hegemony, and an intermediary one.

Washington's isolationist policy kept the United States out of foreign alliances and out of European conflicts, but in the early 19th century the United States started viewing Latin America as its backyard. In 1823 the US government announced the Monroe Doctrine, as the core belief that the Americas belong to the people of the Americas, but which in practice meant that the Americas belonged to the United States. The Monroe Doctrine was another great leap in United States foreign policy—the leap from isolationism to regional hegemony.

On December 2, 1823, American president James Monroe, in the State of the Union address to Congress, explained a new foreign relations policy that was later called the Monroe Doctrine. It covered three essential principles: resistance to any European attempt to establish colonies in the Americas; the non-interference principle; and the American system. In "resistance to any European attempt to establish colonies in the Americas," Monroe said, the "American continents, by the free and independent condition which they have assumed and maintain, are henceforth not to be considered as subjects for future colonization by any

European powers." Although there was an element of anticolonialism in this declaration, its true significance was in securing the right of the United States to expand its territory by limiting and preventing new European expansion in the Americas and resisting the establishment or colonization of any new territory on the American continents by Europe. In an environment where the United States lacked the strength to enforce its will, this was a diplomatic principle to ensure the United States had room to expand.

Non-interference contained two layers of meaning. The first was to keep Europe from interfering in affairs on the American continents. In the State of the Union, Monroe said, "Governments who have declared their independence and maintained it, and whose independence we have, on great consideration and on just principles, acknowledged, we could not view any interposition for the purpose of oppressing them, or controlling in any other manner their destiny, by any European power in any other light than as the manifestation of an unfriendly disposition toward the United States." The second was that the United States would not intervene in European affairs. He continued, "With the existing colonies or dependencies of any European power we have not interfered and shall not interfere." The "non-interference" principle actually contained both "interference" and "non-interference." It meant that the United States would resist interference in the affairs of the Americas by any other nations, but it maintained the right to interfere in the affairs of the continent. Interfering in American affairs was deemed to be the exclusive right of the United States. So the Monroe Doctrine became a policy tool that the United States used to oppose interference on the American continents by any nation but itself.

As for the American system, Monroe's State of the Union address says, "The political system of the allied powers (the Holy Alliance) is essentially different in this respect from that of America . . . we should consider any attempt on their part to extend their system to any portion of this hemisphere as dangerous to our peace and safety." He continues, "It is impossible that the allied powers should extend their political system to any portion of either continent without endangering our peace and happiness; . . . It is equally impossible, therefore, that we should behold such interposition in any form with indifference." Monroe's State of the Union praised the republican system of the Americas, and called the American system a different system set apart from European monarchy. This was the "American system" principle. The "American system" signified that "the Americas belong to the people of the Americas," but the actual meaning was that "the Americas belong to the people of the United States," and was meant to prevent and reduce the influence of Europe in the Western Hemisphere, stop further contact between the Americas and Europe, and clear the way for United States expansion in the Western Hemisphere.

This address was representative of the United States government's policies toward Latin America, but the United States hadn't discussed this with Latin American nations; it had simply declared itself their guardian. The Monroe Doctrine was an international reaction to the Holy Alliance's very real designs for armed interference in Latin America, part of an intense grab by the capitalist classes of Great Britain and the United States for Latin America, and a declaration of intent in the sharp international conflicts between the United States and Russia. It was an attempt to protect the present interests and future expansion of the US capitalist class.

The Monroe Doctrine was a basic principle of United States foreign policy. It was a declaration of resistance by the republican capitalist classes against the European feudal monarchy, and in its objective support for the independence of Latin American nations, and it how it cut short the ambitions of powerful European nations like Britain, France, and Russia to assert their political and economic influence and establish new colonies in the Americas, it was a step in the direction of progress. But the idea that the Americas belong to the people of the Americas was only a cover; the United States was actually establishing the Americas as its own sphere of influence and pushing out strong European powers, especially Britain. It was actually a declaration of United States power over the Americas, and a declaration of American intent to seize regional hegemony from Europe. And later in America's history, the Monroe Doctrine, once a step for progress, became a tool for the United States to invade and expand in the Americas, becoming eventually the justification that the Americas belong to the people of the United States. Under the banner of the Monroe Doctrine, the United States went on a wild expansion binge. In the 1830s and 1840s the United States seized Texas from Mexico; from 1842–1844 it forced Great Britain out of Oregon; from 1846–1848 US president James K. Polk invaded Mexico and annexed more than half of its territory. From 1819 to 1853, through land seizures, annexation, and cheap land purchases, the US expanded its territory by more than 1.3 million square miles, 80% of its territory in 1819, and including the territory of six large states: California, Nevada, Utah, Colorado, Arizona, and New Mexico. By the latter half of the 19th century, the north-to-south stretch of the original 13 states along the Atlantic coast was matched and exceeded all the way across the continent to the Pacific.

The Monroe Doctrine was a declaration that the United States would take over as master of the Americas. It subtly bound the interests of the United States and the American continents together in a brilliant, unique fusion: it resisted European monarchy through capitalist republicanism, and European colonialism through self-determination and national independence. And through these two kinds of resistance, it pulled in the Americas, pushed out Europe, and left the Americas for the United States to swallow and control alone.

The landmark work of the third stage and ideology of America's grand strategy was Alfred Thayer Mahan's concept of sea power. The sea power concept expanded America's strategy from dominating the American continents to a Pacific empire maritime strategy. America's capitalism entered its imperialist phase just as its territory reached the Pacific coast. The United States stretched across the North American mainland, accomplishing the goal of connecting the two coasts, but with all the territory in America's West now under cultivation and the domestic market clearly segmented, class conflicts began to sharpen, so America's monopoly capitalists turned their eyes overseas. But by this time, the rest of the world's territory had been carved and split up among the old colonialist powers. Only the three sick men of China, Persia, and Turkey were left in a half-independent state, and contention over them was fierce. The United States demanded that the world be repartitioned. Around this time, America produced a raft of expansionists like Mahan, Theodore Roosevelt, and Henry Cabot Lodge. There weren't many of them, but they held prominent positions and were very active. Theodore Roosevelt served as assistant secretary of the navy, then later as vice president and president. Lodge served as a senator for many years, and as chairman of the Senate Committee on Foreign Affairs. They advocated a so-called "Pacific empire theory" that was the distillation of the Wall Street consortium's intense desire to expand abroad, and they all had a significant influence on the formulation and execution of America's foreign policy. They were adherents of Mahan's sea power theory and the Pacific empire theory, and they were the creators of big policy. They tried to expand the navy, seize territory, and rule the sea. Their big policy was to take Cuba, establish a base in the Caribbean, dig the Panama Canal, take Hawaii and the Philippines, and establish an empire in the Pacific. At the close of the 19th century, this policy led America to undertake a series of invasions. The Spanish-American War and the Open Door Policy were this rising power's challenges to the old colonial empires of Europe, and the result of its designs to expand its international influence.

## The Design of Franklin D. Roosevelt's Globalism

Before the conclusion of the Second World War, the ideals and designs of Franklin D. Roosevelt's globalism became the third stage and ideology of America's grand strategy. After World War I, Wilson experienced setbacks in his plans for the world. But Wilson's efforts were only America's first attempt. World War II provided another chance for America to establish hegemony over the world. After 1943, Roosevelt explicitly stated, "The power which we [America] have already obtained—moral, political, economic, and military power," gave the United States "the responsibility to lead the international community and the opportunity which will shortly follow." Before the end of World War II, the American leadership represented by Roosevelt and Cordell Hull put forward a series of ideas on how to rebuild the postwar world order. These were later collectively termed "globalism" by historian Arthur Schlesinger Jr.. They believed the war had significantly damaged Europe's traditional balance of power, and that maintaining the new world order would fall to the United States, the United Kingdom, and the Soviet Union. They believed that America should, and could, in this world maintain its leading position by using the United Nations collective security apparatus to organize and sustain a great power balance. In the period immediately following the war, Roosevelt's inherently appealing globalism and idealism were the basic principles of American foreign policy. By early 1946, the outlines of the post-war world and

American attitudes toward the Soviet Union had taken shape. In mainstream American opinion, the Soviet Union had ceased to be a war ally and a partner in cooperation, and became a rival for world dominance that needed to be contained.

America's grand strategy developed along a track that kept abreast with the times. This is a strategy that went from the independence of an isolationist foreign policy, to the continental hegemony of the Monroe Doctrine, to the imperialism of a sea power beyond the Americas, to the globalism of a world hegemon, where it finally reached its peak. Throughout the process, America's grand strategy adapted to the needs of the rising nation and guided the implementation of America's rise. America's successful rise was the success of its strategy.

## American Culture Is a Strategic Culture

Noted strategy expert Niu Xianzhong said in his *Strategy Research* that Americans prioritize technology over thinking, and management over strategy, which is why America's is a non-strategic culture of strategy. He cites the unique environment in which America's strategic culture formed: First, it was geographically isolated from the outside world, which is the root of isolationism. Second, as America expanded its territory, it faced pressing problems of survival, causing it to develop an appreciation for instantaneous payoffs and quick success. Third, the United States is a country without long-standing historical traditions, so the society lacks a universal awareness of history. Fourth, the United States is a highly industrialized society, so Americans are essentially all engineers, and they seek technical solutions to every problem; however, this understanding doesn't match with the facts of American strategic history.

A nation's strategic culture is a reflection of its present strategic pursuits. America's goals have deep strategic significance. The first colonists in what would become the United States wanted to establish a new nation in the New World different from the nations of the old world. They wanted to obey the will of God and build a City on a Hill, and set a new example for the world. The knowledge the earliest Americans sought was twofold: one was a transcendent faith that allowed them to approach God; the other was experience and rational insight into the profound mysteries of the material world. Those strategic groupings and goals shaped the strategic culture they created and aspired to.

The strategic culture of the United States after it was founded had a deep impact on the shape of the world today: the strategies of the American Revolution, the American Civil War, Franklin D. Roosevelt's New Deal, and America's design for the world after World War II. In both domestic policy and foreign relations, Americans have set many historical precedents and put forth many of the world's best strategies. The course of America's strategies and its grand strategy through history are proof that the United States is a powerhouse of strategy. The proof of the nation's strategic culture and the nature of strategy in a nation's

wider culture are best seen in how a nation puts its strategy into practice, its strategic thinking, and how it solves major strategic problems. Nations that can't form good strategies are
nations that can't possibly rise. America's rise may have been the fastest rise in world history, but its journey to prosperity was a brilliant one. America may be a culture that worships
technology and utilitarianism, but it's also a country with a mature strategic culture. America may have a deficiency in its love of instantaneous solutions, but they have the advantage
of deep and far-reaching consideration of problems. American culture is most certainly not
a "non-strategic" culture.

## America's Art of the Cheapest Rise

America's rise is remarkable for its speed, its low starting costs, and the low costs incurred in the process. Compared to the incredible price some nations pay to attempt to
rise, only to fail, America's was the cheapest price paid by any great nation to rise. America's
unique geographical attributes are one reason it was able to rise so cheaply. The sheer scale
is enough to impress anyone who goes to the United States. Located between the world's
two largest oceans, the United States has 9.3 million square kilometers of territory containing continent-long rivers, fertile plains, lakes, rich mineral resources, and marine resources
from two coastlines. It is the very definition of geographical advantage. Lenin once said
the United States had the safest location in the world. No great nation in history has been
able to invest so little in national defense after independence, or avoid external threats to
its safety over such a long period of time. The war between north and south that concluded
in 1865 was the last large-scale war to occur on the North American mainland. From the
end of the War of 1812 to the bombing of Pearl Harbor, for 120 years, America's sovereignty
and territory were never threatened. It was only after nuclear weapons made long-distance
mass slaughter possible that America's geographical advantage of distance lessened, and it
took terror attacks to finally shake the Americans from their sense of being in a safe harbor.

But while America's geographical advantages contributed to the low cost of its rise,
America's rise was more importantly a prudent rise, an artful rise, and an intelligent rise.
Obviously, America's rise was also a cunning rise, and in some respects it was even contemptible and cruel. As to whether its rise was artful or deceitful, those who wish to make
a case for either will find evidence.

## America Is Good at Rising and Curbing

The rise of great nations is almost always a process of containment and breaking
through containment. In modern history's struggle among champion nations, there are
three classic examples of nations that broke through the containment of old champion nations and rose to become new ones: the Dutch Republic broke out of Spain's containment

and established a commercial empire, England broke out of the containment by European mainland countries (including the Netherlands, France, and Spain) and established an industrial empire, and the United States broke out of British containment and established the world's strongest empire.

During America's rise, Britain didn't have the overwhelming superiority the United States has today. Britain couldn't stop America from breaking away and declaring independence, and then couldn't reoccupy the United States in the War of 1812 (due to fear of reigniting war in Europe), and following that, couldn't crush the American economy. But that doesn't mean Great Britain and the other European powers recognized or admitted America's rise. They tried to find ways to stop it. The process of containment and resisting containment is continuous during a great country's rise, and America's rise was a process of continuously breaking through British containment.

In America's rise among containment, we can see American wisdom, American cleverness, American cunning, and American dishonor. Since the moment the United States began competing on a global scale, it has paid the lowest cost to compete—it paid the lowest cost to rise (the cost paid to take hegemony) and the lowest cost to maintain hegemony (its wars to protect hegemony). On the surface, World War II appears to be a contest between reigning world hegemon Great Britain and new challenger Germany, but the end result was that the United States took over hegemony from Britain. America gained without a struggle, or gained much with a minor struggle. This was sheer brilliance! From 1898 to 1920, America not only won leadership in the Americas, it realized a historic peaceful handoff of global hegemony, and bound the former hegemon and the future hegemon in an alliance. And after the Second World War, the United States took its place as world hegemon, and then fought a half-century war with the Soviet Union to protect its hegemony. The essence of the Cold War, to America, was a fight to protect its hegemony. Sun Tzu called it "breaking the enemy's resistance without fighting." The United States broke the enemy's country without fighting, with a Cold War. This was one of the most miraculous outcomes of grand strategy in modern history.

America had two great strategic successes: first, it rose to become a great power; second, it effectively contained other rising great powers that challenged its place as hegemon. The United States is a country both skilled at rising and containing; in both rising to become a great power and in containing the rise of great powers, it provides a model to study. But no matter whether we're researching how America rose from under a strong power, or how it uses its own power to contain the rise of other nations, both have significance for China's own rise. China needs to draw on the wisdom and artfulness of an American rise, while suppressing the deceitfulness, dishonor, and cruelty of an American-style rise, and create a new, more civilized way for great nations to rise—a non-hegemonic rise, a morally upright rise, a peaceful rise, and an artful rise.

## Reducing the Cost: Avoiding Self-Inflicted Setbacks

The rise of great nations takes strategic resources, and no matter how large or powerful a country is, there are limits to the resources it can use and gamble. The largest consumers of a nation's strategic resources are internal struggle and external conflict. In both internal struggle and external conflict, the United States effectively reduced the amount of strategic resources consumed, saving them a huge amount. Their secret to saving these resources is that, in both international relations and internally, they choose battles effectively. Alex de Tocqueville said, "After sixty years, all the peoples of Europe have either been ruined by war, or fallen due to internal conflict. Only the American people remain safe and at peace. While almost the whole of Europe has been overturned by revolution, America has not suffered this turmoil."

Warren I. Cohen also said, "In other countries, or at least in most other countries, political changes produce class struggles and resistance to economic allocation, which results in what Americans see as non-republican turmoil. These tensions also exist in the United States, but they are most often eased. Americans don't understand how nations like the Third and Fourth French Republic can still struggle, while the same United States hurries toward the future." Compared to other great nations, the United States spent the least time during its rise engaged in war, and the most time engaged in peaceful construction. This is in stark contrast with England, which spent almost half of the 75 years between 1688 and 1763 at war. The fact that America enjoyed such a long period of peace during its rise owes in part to its unique geographical environment, which gave it a singular guarantee of safety. But it also owes to the isolationist foreign policy held by the United States for so long after it was founded. Staying out of Europe's struggles gave it time to focus on the future while the powers of Europe exhausted their strength fighting one another. That difference predicted the fall of Europe and the rise of America. Avoiding trouble, lowering the cost of internal political trouble, and the cost of international conflict was an important tool in America's low-cost rise.

## The Snipe Grapples with the Clam

America's rise was built on the ruins of conflict between other great nations. America's rise to hegemony was cheap for the United States, but the rest of the world paid a terribly high price. In this process, America's competitive tactics were vicious, brutal, dark, poisonous, and treacherous. In 1941 when Hitler invaded the Soviet Union, Missouri senator (and later US president) Harry Truman pointed out that in the conflict between Germany and the Soviet Union, American policy should be, "If we see Germany winning the war, we should help Russia; if we see the Russia winning the war, we should help Germany; and this way use their strength against each other."

An American politician described US political trickery like this: the United States is the backup player in the football game of world politics. It sits on the bench and waits for both sides to exhaust themselves, then comes onto the field to mop up. In both world wars the United States entered the fighting last. The only contribution of the last one onto the field is to be the straw that breaks the camel's back, but his spoils are always the whole camel.

Looking at the final results and the long-term significance of the 20th century's two world wars, it seems as though they were fought for America. While on the surface the two world wars were Germany's attempts to seize world hegemony and Britain defending its position as hegemon, the actual result was that the United States took over Britain's role. Victory in both wars was a British victory, but they were victories of a declining power, and victories earned by hastening its decline, Pyrrhic victories. Britain won the war and beat Germany, but it lost its position to the United States. The real victor in both wars was America. Britain defeated Germany for America, and Germany brought Britain to its knees for America. The way America took over from Britain was cunning and brilliant. Britain paid the strategic bill for America to take over as world hegemon. England won two global wars, but lost an empire and its position as the world's leading nation, instead giving up the seat to America. Two dogs fought over a bone, and a third ran away with it. The third dog was America.

America took over Britain's place while the two were in alliance. America and Britain's strategic competition and strategic handoff occurred through their strategic cooperation and alliance. This was America's strategic fortune, strategic brilliance, and strategic miracle.

## War Preparation

The United States, guided by the knowledge that there are no permanent friends or enemies, only permanent national interests, was thoroughly ready for war during its dealings with both friends and enemies as it rose, even with its ally the United Kingdom in the First World War.

During World War I America faced competition for control of the oceans from the UK and Japan. In 1919 America's Joint Army and Navy Board met with the War Department to discuss possible British attitudes. The Joint Army and Navy Board believed that the possibility for conflict existed between the US and the UK, and that if the UK launched a war against the US, Japan would not hesitate to join on the side of the UK. In March 1920 the United States produced two war plans: one was the Orange Plan for war in the Pacific against Japan, the second revision of 1911's Orange Plan; the other was the Red-Orange Plan, a plan for a war in the Atlantic against the UK and in the Pacific against Japan. In the war plan, it's clear the board believed a Britain-Japan alliance would not just directly influence US strength in the Pacific region, but also influence America's strategic position globally. America would have to distribute its fleet over both oceans.

From 1922 to 1924 the United States Navy made this judgment regarding its war plans in its annual reports: Japan and the United Kingdom are still countries capable of competing with the United States for naval supremacy, and the risk of an evenly matched contest with one or both still exists. The United States Navy should first prepare for war against Japan, and second for a war against Britain or an Anglo-Japanese alliance.

In the interwar world of the 1920s and 1930s the nation most likely to go to war with the United States was Japan. We believe that is the most likely war to happen, and the Orange Plan was America's most important military plan. The plan was kept in place for more than ten years, and although it was modified several times, the core strategy of preparing to conduct a unilateral Pacific offensive against Japan never changed.

In the later interwar period, the United States began to alter its strategic war plans. In the 1938 revision to the Orange Plan, beyond maintaining the original plan for an offensive war in the Pacific against Japan, the plan began to include a possible Atlantic threat from Italy and Germany. In February 1939 Roosevelt proposed strengthening 16 foreign naval bases to Congress, and of these 16, there were three times more in the Pacific region than the Caribbean. This showed that American strategy was still focused on the Pacific theater. It was only after Germany occupied Czechoslovakia in March 1939 and then made territorial claims against Poland in April 1939 that the Joint Chiefs of Staff issued a report pointing out the threat from the Atlantic. The report suggested taking a defensive posture in the Pacific and using Hawaii as a base, holding the strategic triangle (Hawaii – Alaska – Panama). This meant that the offensive strategy against Japan in the Pacific at the core of the Orange Plan had been abandoned. It was a turning point for American military thinking. In June 1939 the Joint Chiefs of Staff produced a new war plan: the Rainbow Plan, which envisioned five scenarios for war on both coasts. Rainbow Plan No. 5 imagined an alliance between America, Britain, and France, and imagined dispatching American troops to the eastern Atlantic theater while maintaining a defensive posture in the Western Hemisphere to assist in a British and French attack on Italy and Germany. It had America maintaining its defensive position in the Pacific until the Axis powers of Europe were defeated, after which a counteroffensive strategy against Japan would begin. Rainbow Plan No. 5 was the war plan closest to America's actual conduct in World War II, and marked the formation of a "Europe first" strategy. The "Europe first" strategy was confirmed as the ASC-1 Plan at a meeting between US and British intelligence services in January 1941.

America's strategic leadership shows in its leadership on military strategy. It showed strong military foresight and decisive war readiness, and an ability to change its military target and strategy based on changes in the international situation, and from these take the strategic initiative. The success of American military strategy was an especially important factor of America's rise.

## *The Secret to a Slow Rise: Hiding Power and Biding Time*

One of the skills demonstrated in America's rise is a special American ability to bide its time. Even with the capacity to lead the world, America does not rush to take the lead. 1913–1945 was a turning point in world history, and in the history of America's global role. Europe, once the center of international relations whose influence swayed even America, lost its global hegemony after World War I. All signs after 1917 pointed to the rise of America as the world's new leader, and even when it didn't use its full military strength (during the 1920s), it provided economic and cultural resources that defined and maintained the world order. The period in the 1930s when the United States shirked its power as leader at every level, withdrew from the international order, and retreated into nationalism and unilateralism was truly an exception, but even then, in the words of Joseph Nye, it was obvious that the United States was 'doomed to leadership.' On the eve of victory in World War II, Roosevelt and his colleagues expected the United States to rise from the war and enter the world as the most powerful nation. And unlike after the First World War, they were determined to lead the world after this war. This time, they would create a world order that promoted American interests, and they would use it not only to increase American wealth and power, but also to spread American values to every corner of the world. America could never again avoid the responsibilities of a great nation. It had to create a liberal international economic order; one based on free trade and stable currencies; so it had to take on leadership, and create untold prosperity for every nation. America had to lead the world to prevent the resurrection of German and Japanese power, and to stop fascism and Japanese militarism from arising elsewhere.

This special American ability to bide its time is rooted deep in its isolationist past. The strength of this tradition is such that even when America had the strength to lead the world, and when some of America's most brilliant men called for it to take a more active role in the international community, when it did, the attempt was aborted. The tragedy of Wilson after the First World War was a classic example.

After America became the world's champion nation with the largest economy, it bided its time for half a century before it took over as leader of the world. The Spanish-American War of 1898 was an important turning point in America's path from isolationist to globalist international relations. America's Open Door Policy toward China in 1899 and Theodore Roosevelt's "Corollary" to the Monroe Doctrine in 1904 strengthened the transition. In early 1918, when Woodrow Wilson raised his Fourteen Points on how to preserve the peace following the war, he was actually announcing a plan to take world hegemony, a plan for America to guide and lead the world. The Fourteen Points contained three important conditions for America's seizure of world hegemony: first was forbidding secret treaties, which would have prevented Europe from partitioning the world without America's permission; second was national self-determination, which would dissolve the European colonial system; and the third was establishing a League of Nations, which was an attempt to control the international security apparatus after the war. This plan for hegemony failed, because even though the United States possessed the military and economic power to wield such control, it was weak in international politics and foreign relations. The other major powers weren't ready to accept American leadership. It also failed because the idea that America should lead the world hadn't gained mainstream acceptance domestically. This is why Wilson lost the peace despite winning the war; even though he designed a perfect blueprint for the world, he didn't get to see it built.

After the Second World War, Roosevelt's anti-Fascist alliance allowed him to establish the international security organization Wilson couldn't—the United Nations. The five permanent members of the Security Council and their veto power ensured America's dominance over the United Nations. Every sector of America's economy expanded rapidly during World War II, especially the military-industrial sector. By 1945, American per capita income was double its 1939 level; the US controlled a 57 million-tonnage merchant fleet, two-thirds of the world's total; the US had 59% of the world's gold and precious metals, and the US dollar was the world's only true hard currency; America also had a monopoly on world trade. America's military strength reached deep into Europe, and they controlled bases at key locations all around the globe. Their monopoly on nuclear weapons made them an even more imposing foe. America's massive economic, military, and political strength defined its role on the stage of world politics, and gave it the qualifications it needed to fill the position left vacant by Europe. But the strength to lead the world also requires the strategic policy and ambition to lead, and that would depend on whether the United States could leave its isolationist policies and traditions behind. In view of what happened after World War I, when Wilson's globalism utterly failed, Roosevelt decided to avoid the same mistakes, so his administration made the necessary preparations in policy and public opinion while World War II was ongoing. After the attack on Pearl Harbor, the US government established the Advisory Committee on Postwar Foreign Policy, chaired by Secretary of State Cordell Hull, with Under Secretary of State Sumner Welles as vice chairman, to plan policies that would shape the postwar world order. At the wartime meetings of the Big Three, Roosevelt turned these policies into specific plans to bring the Allies together in a postwar cooperative organization led by America. Secretary of State Hull and his colleagues tried to persuade the American public that joining the international economic order after the war and reviving the multilateral free trade system were necessary for continued American prosperity after the war. Treasury Secretary Henry Morgenthau explained to the Senate that America needed to establish a global system that would allow entrepreneurs to conduct international trade and investment according to the principles of commerce. But when the war ended, there were still people in America insisting that America not involve itself in Europe's affairs, and the American government considered withdrawing its forces from Europe; but the fall of the Western European nations convinced American policy-makers that their choices were: either allow serious economic turmoil in Western Europe to threaten the global capitalist system, or face large-scale European involvement. America's strength and global strategic interests caused it to choose the latter, so it signed the Anglo-American Loan Agreement with the United Kingdom in December 1945 and other aid agreements with Europe.

## How Can America Remain Vigilant Against Strategic Traps?

One of America's most distinctive traits is its high degree of strategic vigilance against foreign threats, a strategic tradition that began with the nation's founder, George Washington. George Washington warned the American people to keep vigilant against foreign dirty tricks. In 1796 he warned the American people in his parting address, "Nothing is more essential than that permanent, inveterate antipathy against particular nations, and passionate attachments for others, should be excluded [. . .] Against the insidious wiles of foreign influence [. . .] the jealousy of a free people ought to be constantly awake." This advice from Washington was an earnest warning to the American people, filled with a sense of caution and the wisdom of America's founding fathers, and was the summary of Washington's experiences during a life of struggle.

To Washington, a free people ought to be vigilant against foreign conspiracies and plots, and he especially chose the word *vigilant*. A free people must maintain an awareness of the threat at all times. There can be no numbness or relaxation of caution. Of course, the conspiracy theory lens cannot only be used to view foreign power and international problems, but it cannot be entirely put aside either. Conspiracies exist in our world, so we need to be on guard against them, as Washington asked the American people to do.

## The Bismarck Trap and Charles de Gaulle Statistics

In the strategic competition between great nations, the insidious wiles of foreign influence Washington described are always present. The Bismarck trap seen in the 19th century struggle between France and Germany is the classic example. In the Franco-Prussian War of 1870–1871 Prussia defeated France, and the French emperor was taken captive. Then a serious split developed in Germany over what policy to take toward France. Germany's chief ambassador to France, Harry von Arnim, supported restoring the French emperor, but Bismarck's strategic goal was an independent, chaotic, weak France that could no longer compete with Germany, so he supported restoring the French Republic. Bismarck thought an unstable republic would be ostracized and isolated by the monarchic continent of Europe. In 1872 Bismarck wrote, "To a Europe united in monarchy, the Parisian volcano (the unstable politics of a republic) poses no threat at all. It will burn itself out." Bismarck believed that the French Republic was like a volcano spouting nonstop democracy, forever caught in turmoil and instability, and this was exactly how Germany wanted it. Harry von Arnim maintained his opinion, for which he was removed from his position and charged with treason.

Bismarck's conspiracy was revealed in full 70 years later by Charles de Gaulle's numbers. He believed one of the most important reasons for the defeat of French strategy was weakness caused by the divisive struggles of French political parties before the war and the high cabinet turnover. The parliamentary nature of the French Third Republic led to "102 changes of government in France over the 65 years from 1875–1940, while in the same period the UK changed government only 20 times and the United States had only 14 presidents." Time and again Charles de Gaulle watched a new prime minister take office only to be met with relentless demands and criticism, "and though they spent all their strength countering them, it was never enough, let alone to lead the nation. The legislature would not support him, and tasks were given to him only to lead him into the dark, where he was forsaken. His ministers were his political enemies. Public opinion, the newspapers, and party interests made him the natural subject of their complaints. Everyone knew he would only be in office a short time, and he himself was the first to know it."

The harm of the Bismarck trap lasted well into the 1950s. In the French Fourth Republic, established in 1947, cabinet turnover was abysmal. From 1947 to 1958 there were 24 new cabinets, and each cabinet only lasted an average of five months. Two cabinets only lasted a day: the Binuo government of February 17–18, 1955, and the Binei government of October 17–18, 1957. De Gaulle asked the Constituent Assembly for a constitution in which the legislature had the right to draft laws and supervise the government in power, but could not replace it. Government should have tenure, power, and stability. Charles de Gaulle resigned in anger on January 20, 1946, due to constraints from the Constituent Assembly. When a constitution that drastically strengthened presidential power was passed in September 1958, the new French Fifth Republic chose Charles de Gaulle as its first president, and finally put down its political baggage.

Actively promoting the construction of democracy with Chinese characteristics is an important job. But those abroad shouting for China to adopt American-style democracy simply hope to use democracy to cause China to sink into turmoil and chaos, and are laying a trap for China. This is a conspiracy. China also needs to remember the words of George Washington, and remain on guard against the insidious wiles of foreign influence.

# CHAPTER 6

# LEARNING FROM MISTAKES

# MADE ABROAD

The first strategic issue for Chinese people in the world during the 21st century involves facing America. China must cooperate with and alert America. America not only alerts mechanisms of foreign forces, but is also clever at use of intrigue and setting strategic traps. America had confronted the Soviet Union with a strategic trap and it is a veteran of the Cold War. The Cold War, in fact, is a battle of trap, intrigue, and deception. China must keep both eyes open upon America.

America can set a lot of traps to oppose China, such as political traps in the form of exporting and investing great democracy to stir internal issues in China; economic traps in the form of engaging in financial crisis and the financial war to sweep away the Chinese people's significant hard-earned money from hard work; military traps in the form of inciting conflict in neighboring hot spots; and diplomacy traps in the form of instigating relationships, creating conflicts, and forming a coalition against China. In January 2007 Mark Leonard, of the UK think tank Centre for European Reform believed that the year of 2020 will be a watershed of the 21st century. China will overtake America and become the world's largest economic entity and global politics will be changed from unipolar to multipolar politics. The so-called "balance of power" policy implemented by America has two latitudes: maintaining a leading position of America and maintaining the balance of power in the region by supporting democratic regimes in each region. For example, in Europe, America regards the European Union as a balancing force to curb Russia. In Asia, America has entered into an alliance with Australia, India, and Japan to curb China. An international public figure believed that China's most important achievement in soft power transmission will be if Beijing can prevent the formation of any international coalition to curb its rise. There will be no anti-America alliance in the future, but, what about anti-China alliance?

China should remember George Washington's advice: to deal with the machinations of foreign forces, a free people should always maintain a vigilant heart. China should always maintain the policy of cooperation, friendly and partner theories for cohesion of more social consensus internationally. But China should also not fail to hear the wake-up call of containment theories, conspiracy theory, and trap theory while maintaining a heart of vigilance against the machinations of foreign forces. Expectations of America cannot be divorced from reality, and on Sino-American relations they cannot be idealized. Enhancing strategic mutual trust is of great significance for the maintenance and development of Sino-America relations, but it needs to prevent strategic fantasy while enhancing strategic mutual trust.

Americans have the American Dream, which has two major meanings: in respect to the struggle of the individual citizen, the American Dream is the successful entrepreneurial dream for citizens and families; in respect of the struggle of the entire American people and the country, the American Dream is one of dominating and leading the world. America has never wavered to defend and maintain the status of world leader; America has never given ground in the game of defending leadership. The most important issue in China's grand strategy is not to have illusions about America in the 21st century.

## I. Strategic Fantasy Is Tantamount to Suicide

Strategic fantasy is an error politicians typically commit, but should not commit. For the potential champion nation in the competition against the champion nation, how can we prevent dissemination of misleading information regarding the champion nation? How can we avoid strategic fantasy? In this regard, the founding leaders of America showed great wisdom and sober spirit in the strategic competition with the British Empire, but the politicians' appeasement policy in Europe before World War II brought disaster to the world. Sun Yat-sen's strategy was informed by that of America, Japan, and Russia—but was this justified?

### John Adams's Warning

John Adams, who once served as the first America's ambassador to Britain and later served as America's second president, predicted in 1816: "Britain will never be our friend until we become their master." Adams's prophecy was a warning that America should not have illusions about the UK—the anti-British heart cannot be abandoned. In two world wars, the British were American allies, but only to the extent that they needed to be rescued from America. It was only after World War II ended that America, the UK's lifesaving bene-factor, became the clear master in the relationship.

Today, if someone shared the prophecy of America's statesman John Adams, "America will never be a friend of China until China becomes the master of America so far," Amer-icans would not accept, but Chinese people would also not agree, because China does not want to be the master of others. However, when China's overall national strength, national status, and international influence are beyond that of America, America will certainly be a very sincere friend. This will usher in the best Sino-America relations of any period in history.

The UK became America's friend after America became the master of UK and Ameri-ca will become China's friend after China overtakes America. American-UK relations were transformed fundamentally after America became stronger than the UK. Sino-America re-lations will also be transformed fundamentally when China is stronger than America. John Adams's prophecy reflects a clear American strategy and strategic intelligence, and serves as a warning against strategic fantasy for today's China.

## Adolf Hitler's Fear

Before World War II, when most Western politicians in power (in addition to Louis Barthou, Winston Churchill, and Duff Cooper Alfred, etc.) had an unclear understanding of the nature of Hitler, they believed that peace could be exchanged through compromise and believed Nazi Germany was a strong bulwark against the spread of communism in Western Europe, and therefore save the green light for all the actions of Hitler. When Hit-ler pushed forward on his rearmament policy, he told his generals apprehensively: "the moment for building national defense forces is our most vulnerable moment, no politician in France can be aware of this. If any do, they will not give us time and impinge upon us."

Unfortunately, neither French nor British politicians evaluated Germany's rearma-ment with a sober strategic brain, resulting in appeasement in the 1930s gradually becom-ing a basic national policy in Western countries. European politicians were caught in the strategic fantasy that appeasement can prevent disaster and almost suffered an ignominious death due to insufficient understanding of the nature of fascism. In today's international community, peace, development, and cooperation are the mainstream, but hegemonic dan-gers still exist, so hegemony cannot be ignored.

## Sun Yat-sen's Dream

In order to achieve the ideal of the founding through revolution, Sun Yat-sen had three major political dreams regarding China that he learned from Japan, America, and Russia: Japanese Dream—create common prosperity in China and Japan by upholding the fraternal friendship and mutual help. American Dream—to help China create an Oriental Republic of China like America by friendship between America and China. Russian Dream—resist the forces of Western capitalism and realize the good wishes of a completely separated China by learning from China. Three major dreams eventually became fantasy, because Japan, America, and Russia regarded China's revival as a threat and did not want a powerful China competing with them.

In fact, in recent history, China's elites constantly held unrealistic fantasies and expectations of America, including royalists Kang Youwei and Liang Qichao, the leader of China's bloodless revolution, and revolutionary Sun Yat-sen's dream in this regard was really a regret. Almost all great powers will be unaccommodating of the rise of other great powers. In international relations, especially in the relations among major great powers, it seems there is no great power that wants others to become as powerful or see more powerful than itself.

If there are expectations of the pupil outdoing the master in the relationship between people, then in state relations, especially in the relations among major great powers, the master will stifle the pupil. The powerful country will never willingly allow such phenomen in relationships with other countries. So it will only be a fantasy for a great power to become powerful through fraternal friendship and friendship between the student and teacher. The final result, as seen with Japan, Russia, and America, were countries threatening China's national security through various brands of imperialism. In the era of Sun Yat-sen, Japan, Russia, and America did not want a strong China. In the 21st century, do they want a stronger China?

On August 14, 1949, Mao Zedong wrote an article entitled "Cast Away Illusions, Prepare for Revolution," exposing the imperialist nature of America's policy toward China and criticizing some people's fantasy of America. In respect to today's Sino-America relations, cooperation should be strengthened, but fantasies of America should be resolutely cast away and the preparation for revolution should be wholehearted.

## II. The Potential Champion Rivals the Reigning Champion

In the history of the modern world, the potential champion nation is always the natural rival of the current champion on the world stage. There will be cooperation and partnership between them to deal with common specific international issues, but it will not change nor dilute their competition at the national level. While there are several potential champion nations, in order to divide and rule them and cope with the challenges of the largest poten-

tial champion nation, the current champion nation will establish an alliance with other potential champion. As long as there is only one potential champion nation on the world stage,
the strategic competition between the champion nation and potential champion nation will
be intensified and the relationships among opponents will be highlighted.

With China's rapid rise and America's relative decline in the financial crisis, the constructive strategic partnership between America and China established to address and solve
global problems will become increasingly tight-knit. However, the competition between the
two countries will intensify.

## China and America Are Destined for Fierce Competition

A natural relationship exists between the two rivals in a competition between countries, particularly in the competition between a champion nation and potential champion
nation. Of course, the runner-up, with its natural rival of the champion nation, must have
the determination and ability to win the championship; it will not be the rival of champion
nations without ambition, ability, and potential. Similarly, a second runner-up can be regarded as the biggest competitor by the runner-up in terms of their potential to raise their
strength above that of the runner-up.

It is historical destiny that China must strive to become a champion nation, and so
must America. Thus a championship battle cannot be avoided as long as both America and
China are on the playing field.

## America's Anti-Chinese Prophecy in 1942

A comprehensive historical survey of the United States' prevention of the rise of China
is a task for specialists. However, China was regarded as America's target in the world arena
before the Cold War. The written record presented this clearly during the Japanese War of
Aggression Against China in the 1940s. This reflects both the quick success and forethought
of America.

Shortly after the outbreak of the Pacific war, the famous American expert on international issues Nicholas John Spykman pointed out in his famous book *American Strategy in
World Politics: US and the Balance of Power*: "America's postwar policy should be formulated
under the strategic guidance to maintain the power balance between Europe and Asia [. . .]
America's interest is not the unified power, but balanced power [. . .] China will become a
major post-war issue rather than Japan [. . .] a modern, vibrant and militarized China with
400 million population will not only be a threat against the status of Japan, but also the
status of the Western powers in Asia [. . .] If the power is balanced now and in the future in
the Far East, America will take the same Japan defending policies."[1] This was written after
the Pearl Harbor attack in 1941, when Americans shared unanimous animosity against

Japan. This book not only had huge repercussions in America, but also became a necessary reference book for studying America's national strategy.

China arose as a new competitor in America's mind just after the Cold War and collapse of the Soviet Union. In an article titled "Awakening Dragon: The Real Danger in Asia Is Coming from China" in the fall 1992 issue of *Policy Review*, Ross H. Munro stated, "Finally, after almost a century of false starts, China seems firmly embarked on a course of explosive economic growth and military assertiveness that will indeed reverberate throughout Asia and the world. The implications for the economic and security interests of the United States are enormous. China is the only major country in the world whose military now is expanding rapidly. And it is the first example of a Communist political system on its way to meeting the economic aspirations of its people."[2] Since then, the "China Threat Theory" has become highly publicized. Advocates of this argument believe that China suffered humiliation in modern times, thus it must be vengeful.

After 1992, with the rapid development of China's economy, America began paying more attention to the so-called threat to America's dominance brought on by China. In 1995, some senior officials from the United States Department of Defense said: "We are most worried about China becoming strong; if China's economic development speed lasts, by the end of the decade our biggest strategic concern will be the rise of China."

From America's strategic prediction in 1942 that "the major postwar issue is China rather than Japan," to the strategic declaration in the late 20th century by the United States Department of Defense that the biggest strategic concern is the rise of China, China finally became the biggest concern in respect to the US strategy. China is honored to be the biggest competitor of America and is ready to compete.

## China Is the Inevitable Rival of the US

Many Chinese people believe Americans don't regard them as a rival. Some people say that China pursues a Four Don'ts policy: Don't challenge America's hegemony, challenge the world order, regard America as a rival and adversary, or threaten America. China regards America as a constructive strategic partner and friend. It wants to cooperate with America, and these aspirations and expectations are sincere, rare, and precious. Unfortunately, China cannot escape its fate as America's rival.

The truth that China will become America's strategic competitor was not decided by China. Some American strategists have pointed out that whether the United States is to take precautions against a country does not depend on the intention of the country, but on the strength. Kissinger also said that from a geopolitical perspective, the United States is a very vast country with many resources and is far more than an island off the coast of Eurasia. The emergence of a dominant big country in Europe or Asia constitutes a strategic threat to the

United States, because it would have the ability to overtake America in terms of economy and military. The United States must fight this danger, even if the big dominant country seems very friendly, because once its intention changes, the United States will find its own ability to effectively resist and reverse the situation greatly diminished.

To Americans, the state will is unreliable. An important feature of America's strategic thinking is that power determines a nation's status, nature, and relationships. Relations between two countries are decided by power rather than state will. America's strategic adversary is chosen depending on power rather than ideology and goodwill. One American expert said that only due to their rapid development has China embarked on a path conflicting with the United States—this is the strategic concept and thinking of the United States. In this world, the United States is the only leader, the country with the fastest development pace and the shortest distance to the United States will inevitably and historically become America's rival. If a nation is fast-growing and near the United States in terms of the playing field of comprehensive national strength, opponent status will give to that nation by America. Unless a nation gives up or is curbed by the United States, it will never escape the destiny of being classified as America's adversary. China in the 21st century has already been honorably selected as America's rival. The result will not be changed regardless of the Cold War, even if the big dominant country seems very friendly.

## The Fundamental Contradiction Between China and the United States

The United States is the world's largest developed country, and China is the world's largest developing country, so what is the fundamental divide between the two countries? Harvard professor Ezra Vogel summarized ten major disagreements between the two countries: Taiwan, Tibet, South China Sea, economy, multilateral and international organizations, views on potential threat in Asia, strategic alliance, weapon proliferation, human rights, and environmental issues. However, the fundamental contradiction between the two countries is a champion nation and potential champion nation.

Brzezinski has pointed out that the United States is the first global power, but also the last global superpower. America's strategic goal is to be ranked first in the world, while China's strategic goal is to overtake the champion. As a result, the two countries will inevitably collide.

The United States is the world's largest capitalist country; China is the world's largest socialist country. Different social systems and ideologies are important sources of contradictions between these two great powers, but the United States doesn't care whether China is socialist and capitalist, but rather whether it is strong or weak. The United States is not afraid of a socialist China, it is afraid of a strong China. For the United States, it would rather like a poor socialist China than a powerful capitalist China. As long as China does not catch up with and surpass the United States and does not replace the US as the leader of the world, the United States will tolerate, cooperate with, and assist China in building socialism. As long as China desires the status of number one and champion in the world, the US will be resolutely curbed by it.

America's goal is not to Westernize China in ideology, but to weaken China in national strength, dwarf China in national status, and delay China in its national renaissance. The so-called Westernization, division, and tarnishing are all strategic means to weaken China and delay the rise and revival of China, so that China does not catch up and surpass the United States in the 21st century. The 21st century would remain the American century rather than Chinese century.

## China-US Relations in the 21st Century: Competition, Cooperation, and Transformation

China-US relations in the 21st century are the most complex relations between big powers in the history of global powers: there is the strategic competitive relationship in international status; strategic partnership in common interests; and strategic transformation relationships in ideology. This is a trinitarian relationship system and its main theme is strategic competition. Strategic competition plays a leading role in the China-US relations system. These above three aspects also reveal central form of China-US relations: strategic competition at the center and strategic cooperation and strategic transformation as two related points.

A strategic competition between China and the US dominates the international position, namely a strategic adversary relationship. The difference and opposition in strategic interests between China and the US will inevitably lead to strategic competition. Now the United States is not only the world champion, but also a global hegemonic country; it is afraid of the impact from China's rise. The fundamental problem brought on by China's rise in the world is the issue of who will lead the world in the 21st century. This is a strategic competition between China and the United States in fundamental national strategic positioning.

There is also strategic cooperation between the two countries in common interests; this is a strategic partnership. China and the United States are the biggest competitors in the 21st century and also the largest trade partners. Since all national economies share a common destiny in economic globalization and global governance becomes the basis and prerequisite for the development of a nationstate, as world powers both China and the United States need cooperation. The Asia "miracle" and the rise of China as a manufacturing superpower has been a good return on investment, and we should not forget that in the past 10 years, the Asian economy has played a vital role in our economic growth. Among the core countries, there is no one country that can do everything independently; the relationship between us all is becoming more and more closely knit.

The strategic transformation relationship between China and US is in their ideologies, namely the relationship of mutual influence. In the process of competition and cooperation between China and the US, American culture can influence China and Chinese culture can transform America. China learns from the world by opening up, including learning and referring to useful characteristics of the United States. The transformative role of Chinese in the United States will help America evolve from a domestic-type democratic state to a non-hegemonic country internationally. Applying international constraining force is an important cause of rampant American hegemony. Using the strongly non-hegemonic China to restrict US hegemony and using China's harmonious culture to transform American cultural hegemony can lead the United States to becoming a democratized and civilized international community member.

China-US strategic competition and cooperation should be constructive. Constructive competition is healthy competition, which rules out war and conflict. Constructive cooperation means cooperation without sacrificing international equity and justice and without prejudice to the interests of singular parties. Constructive competition and cooperation must be limited competition, not indefinite competition; cooperation must comply with principle—cooperation cannot be inconsistent with its principles. Constructive competition and cooperation relation between China and US must meet China's interests, America's interests, and the interests of world peace and development.

## *The Most Important Concern for the President of the United States*

Since the United States took the leadership role in the Western world, defending its leadership has become its core national interest. The Cold War lasted more than 40 years as the United States and Soviet Union contended for world "leadership." After the Cold War, ensuring US leadership in the world has been the primary goal of the United States as reflected in national security strategy, Quadrennial Defense Review reports, defense reports, presidential State of the Union speeches, and other strategic documents issued by the US over the years. So-called American security means above all the security of US hegemony and leadership in the world. The core strengths of American national interests are American hegemony and maintaining the leading position in the world.

John Mearsheimer, a political science professor from University of Chicago, said in an interview with China Central Television: "As president, the basic US strategy includes first to dominate the Western world [. . .] and second to ensure that there is no US competitor worldwide, which means that no other countries can take the lead in their own region through the same dominating methods in the Western world. In the 20th century, the United States strived to ensure that Japan, Germany, and the Soviet Union had no ability to dominate Asia or Europe, because the United States did not want a competitor. The present situation is that the United States has clearly become the world's most powerful country, and there are no competitors or potential competitors, which can not be changed in a period of time."

Currently, the commanding height of America's national strategy is to prevent the emergence of a strategic competitor, hegemonic challenger, peer, or replacer. The US president is busy all year round trying to resolve various contradictions. But the most fundamental strategic issue is maintaining hegemony in the world, with no potential competitors worldwide. We can say that America's strategy is to defend its strategic hegemony.

## *Enhancing the Competitive Spirit to Build a Harmonious World*

China has an opportunity to start a new round of competition to lead the world with the United States in the 21st century. China currently has a strategic opportunity; if it is missed, it will be difficult to get a second chance. The default American mechanism is competition, including both domestic competition and international competition. In international competition, America is a master of hegemony. Domestic competition includes competition between the two political parties, between the various government departments, between the continents, between the military and local governments, between military services, between land capital and financial capital, between new and old businesses, between corporations, and between individuals. Under the influence of Social Darwinism, America advocates the value of competition and regards competitiveness as a necessary quality for an individual worthy of praise. Competition in all aspects of the United States results in a balance of mutual restraint, which achieves a combination of competition and balance mechanisms and ensures the viability and stability of the United States.

A harmonious world cannot exist under jungle principles in the international order and under hegemony. Only depending on harmony will not build a democratic domestic state or international community. Harmony is both a means and a result. Whether in a peaceful world, harmonious world, or democratic world, it is a kind of competition and a balance of power. In past historical periods, because the Chinese lacked the spirit of competition and competitive forces, they blindly advocated that harmony is most precious and peace is to be cherished. As a result, China not only lacked domestic power and vitality, but also didn't play its due role in creating a balance in the world. Thus in Lu Xun's book, *The Discussion on Chinese Character*, he not only laments his misfortune but rages against his servility, which is not respected. He believes that China's servility is an important cause of national misfortune and sorrow. New China was created through fighting by the Chinese revolution led by Mao over decades of war. The rise of China was incited through fighting by reform led by Deng Xiaoping and other party leaders in a complex struggle while keeping a low profile. In the 21st century, China will finally achieve great rejuvenation from the competition with champion nations.

## III. How the United States Curbed Japan's Competition

America defended its champion status twice in the second half of the 20th century: the United States successfully curbed competition against Japan, a country with a similar capitalist ideology, and against the Soviet Union, a country under a contrary communist system. In the 21st century, the United States began its third international championship, namely a comprehensive response to the rise of China. These are three battles between champion countries and potential champion countries—three strategic but very different battles for world dominance and leadership. The United States prevailed in two of the three battles, successfully suppressing Japan and containing the Soviet Union. Can the United States win the third battle, in response to China?

*Squandering of US Strategic Resources Accelerated the Coming of Japanese Hegemony*

Continued hegemony brings costs any hegemon must pay. Continued hegemony will result in squandering and wasting strategic resources, and thus weaken the hegemony over time. After World War II, the United States was at a peak of hegemony. The United States paid a terrible strategic cost in the Korean and Vietnam wars, resulting in a considerable waste of US strategic resources and general power decline, which created the conditions and opportunities for the economic rise of Japan and the major European industrial countries. Kong Huarun said: "After their defeat in World War II, Germany and Japan were deprived of the opportunity to participate in the military competition among large countries, and thus became the main beneficiary of the decline of the United States. 99% of R&D budgets were put into civilian production by Japan, while over 50% of R&D budgets were put into weapons and military equipment by Americans. Although the focus of trading in countries such as Japan and Germany was not voluntary, these countries acquired wealth and power through economic development. Because of the irrational Vietnam War, the United States accelerated the coming of 'Japanese hegemony' and a new and post-hegemonic leadership opportunity was created while America's wealth and power was squandered."

In the 1980s, Japan, Europe, and China's political forces grew continuously and began fiercely competing with the United States in the energy sector, as well as in other markets; a wave of European autonomy and Japanese hegemony challenged the US ally system. Japan's economic success had an almost subversive impact on the United States. America's leading economic role seemed in jeopardy in the wave of Japan's hegemony.

*Japan's Economic Achievements Shook the United States*

With Japan's postwar economic development, trade friction occurred between Japan and the United States beginning in the late 1950s and evolved into comprehensive friction in the 1980s. The scope of Japan-US trade friction was not limited to individual products, but extended to cutting-edge technology, financial sectors, and industrial structure. Semiconductors in the field of cutting-edge technology became a central industry to both countries; a typical case of a high-tech trade war between Japan and the United States was the semiconductor war. Since the semiconductor was invented by an American, the United States had an absolute advantage in the beginning. In 1977 US semiconductor products accounted for 3% in the Japanese market while Japanese products in the US market accounted for only 1.6%. But in the 1980s Japan came from behind over the United States, resulting in nearly full use of Japanese storage chips in supercomputers and full use of Japan's semiconductor parts in sophisticated weapons. According to statistics of the US Semiconductor Industry Association, in 1984 the US semiconductor market turnover reached $11.6 billion; by 1987, it increased to $18.1 billion, of which the Japanese percentage rose from 14% to 20%. During this period, Japan's share in the world semiconductor market increased from 38% to 43%. From cutting-edge technology products, the Japanese computer market share in the United States increased from less than 1% in 1980 to 7.2% in 1984, communication machinery rose from 1.8% to 3.6%, electronic components rose from 3.2% to 7.2%, and audio and video equipment rose from 27.1% to 40.2%. Due to a sharp increase in exports of Japanese electronics to the US, criticism of Japan in the United States increased sharply. In July 1987 protestors smashed radios produced by the Capitol Toshiba Corporation in front of the US Senate, demanding a total ban on Toshiba products into the United States. In the late 1980s the Japanese continued to dabble in international industries and purchased a large number of US assets, including Rockefeller Center, a symbol of the United States, and Columbia Pictures, America's soul. As Japan's creditor position with the United States grew, regardless of the exchange rate between US dollars and the Japanese yen, it was difficult to improve the huge US trade deficit with Japan. In the mid-1980s Japan had become the world's largest creditor nation, while the United States became the world's largest debtor nation.

A huge contrast between the Japanese economy and the US economy was significantly reflected in in four areas. The first is that a significant change occurred between the US and Japan in their global economic positions in regards to gross national product; Japan's proportion increased from 2.2% in 1955 to 12% in 1986, while that of the United States dropped from 36.3% to 25.7% in the same period. The second is that the technological gap between the two sides became smaller. Japan continued to challenge the United States in science and research, and the export share of Japan's high-tech products in the world nearly doubled in the years leading to 1980, while the US share dropped by 16.67%. Among 83 technological fields, Japan had caught up or surpassed the United States in 35 fields and had their own merits in 18 fields. The third is that Japanese foreign economic activity was highlighted around the world. During the years from 1970 to 1986, Japan's export scale expanded by 10 times, but the United States' export scale only doubled. Japan's trade surplus with the United States in 1980 was $9.9 billion and increased to $58.6 billion in 1986. Japan's foreign investment grew rapidly and the annual growth rate between 1980 and 1986 reached 19.45%, while US growth was only 3.2%. The fourth is that the international financial position between Japan and the US was reversed. In the 1980s, Japan became the world's largest "net creditor," and the United States became the world's largest "net debtor." In 1986, Japan's foreign net assets reached $180.4 billion, while the US debt reached $263.6 billion.

In the 1980s Japan had started making a global impact. At the end of 1985 Japan's overseas net assets were more than Britain or West Germany; it had become the world's largest bond country. By 1988, Japan had become the largest investor, creditor, and financial country. In 1987 Japan's GDP accounted for 15% of world GDP, of which 56% was held by the United States. In 1988, Japan's per capita GDP was more than Sweden and ranked first in the world.

Japan's international influence rapidly expanded with the rise of the Japanese economy. In the early 1980s the West would set off a craze to learn Japanese. US Secretary of Labor Ray Marshall said after a visit to Japan: "Japan's labor productivity has been improved year after year and it has the advantage in terms of labor relations and business that the United States does not have; it is necessary to study this business management from Japan." British Ambassador to Japan Sir Michael Wilford pointed out in a report to the government: "if the British industry does not further develop the independent technology or introduce new technologies from Japan and other foreign countries, the UK will become a small industry country in this century." He suggested that the government send permanent representatives responsible for this issue to Japan in order to better learn from the Japanese. Some of the European community ridiculed the Japanese in the past as leeches of global productivity, but this mindset had changed. One European economist said: "As Japan learned from us in the past, we should also strive to catch up and learn from Japanese in advanced fields." France has always stressed autonomy and it also put forward the suggestion to learn from Japan and not Europe. Many international seminars were held on Japanese "secrets of success"; various government and industry groups flocked to Japan; Japan's labor productivity headquarters received more than 20 groups from April to August in 1980. In 1988 Japan paid 10.84% of total contributions to the UN for UN membership dues; it surpassed the Soviet Union and ranked second overall behind the US. In the 1980s, Japan had not only become the world's largest trade surplus country and the largest creditor country; it also challenged American enterprises' leading advantage in many high-tech industries. For a time, the possibility that the Japanese economy would overtake the United States and become the world's leader was widely discussed.

Japan is a key US ally, but also a powerful economic competitor. Friction between Japan and the United States was ongoing throughout the 1980s and has since continued to increase. The US trade deficit with Japan was $7 billion in 1982, $19 billion in 1983, $37 billion in 1984, and $50 billion every year after 1984. Previous trade friction between the US and Japan often ended in concessions by Japan. In 1988 the US Congress passed the Comprehensive Trade Act, requiring retaliation for "unfair trade partners." In May 1989 the United States declared Japan an "unfair trading partner" under section 301 of this act; the two sides began negotiations. In the late 1980s rising trade frictions caused growing nationalist sentiment between Japan and the US; Japan had accumulated a huge trade surplus, and Japanese capital "made a massive invasion into" the US, making large acquisitions of American capital. US businesses and real estate became Japan's priority and the momentum of its acquisitions was very fierce, causing concern with the American public. Especially in 1989 the Japanese companies Sony Corporation and Mitsubishi Land Corporation acquired Columbia Pictures and Rockefeller Center in New York. Columbia Pictures Entertainment is a symbol of American film culture and Rockefeller Center, an American landmark. The two acquisitions greatly stimulated the American public's mood. Japan's economic aggressiveness stirred a psychological sense of menace in the United States; a strong voice called, inside and outside Congress to beat Japan, seek revenge on Japan, and curb Japan. "Japan's economic power was more dangerous than the Soviet military to United States security," and "If a blind eye is turned to Japan's economic aggression, the United States won't be able to grasp their own destiny." The "economic friction" between Japan and the US has gone beyond the scope of the economy and increased substantially to national, emotional friction; it is now a social psychological struggle and has become a national struggle between Japan and the United States.

## Japan Wants to Be the Pillar of the World

In 1989 Sony's chairman, Akio Morita, and Shintaro Ishihara, the Liberal Democratic Party congressman, jointly wrote the book *The Japan That Can Say No*, which was highly critical of the economic and trade policies rooted in racial prejudice that were implemented by the US for Japan. They encouraged Japan to abandon the small-country consciousness formed after World War II as well as the consciousness of succumbing to America, and instead take a road of independence, assume the mainstay responsibility of a new era, and become the leading actor in the creation of a new world history. Publication of the book shook US-Japan relations. America's perception of the book was that it made Japanese anger and pride public to the world. This relationship between the United States and Japan lasted into the 1990s.

Japan wants to start the third voyage, and Japan wants to become the world's leading flower. These were sentiments announced by Prime Minister Suzuki at a grand banquet in New York held when he visited the United States in 1981. Later, this declaration was called the third founding or the third new starting point. Japan's first founding refers to the events in 1853 in which the US fleet forced the Tokugawa shogun to found a state, and later after the Meiji Restoration, Japan became one of the world's great powers; the second founding refers to after the Second World War and the later revival, where Japan quickly became the Western world's second-largest economy and completed the mission of catching up with developed countries such as Europe and America; the third founding refers to a time beginning in the 1980s, when Japan strived to become an active creator rather than passive beneficiary in order to gain political power from economic power. The book *The Japanese Model of Mature Society* was published by Japan's Nomura Research Institute, and it clearly stated that: Japan is facing a major turning point in history. So far, over the last 100 years, Japan has been dedicated to becoming an advanced country and an axis of economic development. Japan's development will not be focused on economic development of a singular axis, but will maintain emphasis on multiple aspects and a multi-axes model. In the course of moving toward the 21st century, Japan will increase its status as an advanced country. The Japanese government officially announced in its Economic Survey in the early 1980s that the Japanese mission to catch up with developed countries such as in Europe and America was basically completed. The issue raised in *MITI Policy Future Prospect in the '80s* was that in the future, Japan will move from imitating and following the civilized nations toward creating and leading civilization. In 1981, Prime Minister Suzuki expressed more clearly during his visit to the United States that the past passive attitude must be changed: Japan must perform with a spirit of initiative and play a role commensurate with its strength and status and in a way most proportionate to Japan's talent and ability. In 1982 Prime Minister Nakasone published his speech in the monthly magazine *Upright Statement* a few days before taking office: so far, we have been striving to catch up with a cloud on the slope and now this cloud has disappeared; we need to create a new cloud. Japan should transform from following, catching up, and imitating to innovating, pioneering, and leading national transformation, to reflect Japanese national ambition.

## Japan Becomes America's Rival

Japan, the US ally, had become America's strategic archrival. In the 1980s the United States not only fought against the Soviet Union, but also curbed Japan's progress; it faced two strategic rivals simultaneously. Due to Japan's momentum in competition for global economic supremacy, the sense of crisis in the United States regarding Japan became more intense. Americans' disdain for Japan was mainly reflected in the following four areas:

1. A Japanese threat mentality spread in the United States. According to a public opinion survey in January 1989, 63% of Americans believed that compared with the Soviet military, Japan's economic power was more dangerous to United States security. It was also reported that a document circulated in the US Congress pointing out that the United States is facing two world wars: the military struggle with the Soviet Union and economic, technological

struggle with Japan; the nuclear weapons owned by the United States are enough to prevent a military offensive launched by the Soviet Union, but there is no sufficient economic means to prevent Japanese attack. If Japan marches forward, the United States will ultimately become Japan's economic colony. The document sounded the alarm that Japan had begun to threaten the existence of the United States.

**2.** America was very worried about Japan's strategic ambition. Politically, the United States was worried that Japan would occupy the leading position in the world because of its economic power and beat the United States. When the United States became the first net debtor in the world, many Americans were very worried about challenges from the Japanese and believed the US global leadership was in jeopardy. Economically, the United States feared being subject to Japan. In the late 1980s Japanese investment in the United States increased sharply; Japan had begun to directly invest in US factories and enterprises and investment in this area reached $30.9 billion in 1987, increasing by one-third compared with that in 1986. The Japanese also acquired US companies, such as the famous Firestone Tire & Rubber Company, which was purchased by the Japanese at a price of $2.6 billion. As of 1987, US stocks, bonds, and Treasury bills held by the Japanese had reached $110 billion, and many Americans were worried that the invasion of Japanese capital could cause the US to become Japan's economic colony.

**3.** In terms of military, the Pentagon was worried that Japan would endanger US security. More and more Americans believed that the Soviet's military threat to the United States would no longer be the most serious challenge. Japan was more dangerous to US security than the Soviet Union. Japan, which who nearly surpassed the United States in economic strength, was more dangerous to US, especially if its military became more powerful. An important figure responsible for the development of US security policy, General Brent Scowcroft, published an article that said Japan should not be required to increase its ratio of defense spending in the future. Undersecretary of State Lawrence Eagleburger published an article that pointed out that the increase in Japan's defense forces could damage the interests of the United States. Kissinger sounded the alarm bell that Japan could become a military power.

**4.** Japan's confidence to ask the United States to share power was boosted. When the United States' sense of crisis against Japan was deepening, Japan accelerated its attemtps to gain political power and more right to speak of the redistribution of powers in the West. The first attempt was to implement autonomous diplomacy. Japan publicly proposed to play a role as "one of the major countries to maintain international order. In September 1989, Prime Minister Kaifu visited the United States and publicly declared that Japan was no longer a pupil taking orders from the American teacher, but a cooperative and sometimes competitive partner. He also suggested that the US should reduce its obligations undertaken in the world so that the Japanese could make commensurate international contributions. Due to the decrease in economic strength, the United States had to ask Japan to help with US obligations. Japan's foreign aid was rapidly increased, and Japan became the world's number-one country for providing foreign aid. The true reason Prime Minister Kaifu stressed sharing obligations with the US was to share powers with the United States. Japan's special adviser Kuroda of MITI said: "The United States must consider the power-sharing issues accompanying burden-sharing." Former Japanese foreign minister Saburo Okita also said that the United States must now change its mentality and way of thinking. If the United States wants other countries to help deal with the world economic problems, it must agree to share decision-making rights or obligation rights. In the past, friction between the US and Japan was mostly eased with Japanese concessions; now Japan had the courage to say no to the United States.

## America Stimulates the Awareness of Unexpected Development

In 1979 the famous Harvard University scholar Ezra Vogel published *Japan as Number One*, causing great repercussions around the world. It became a best-selling book in the United States and Japan. In 1987 professor of history Paul Kennedy at Yale University published *The Rise and Fall of the Great Powers*, which became a world-famous bestseller.

If *Japan as Number One* indicated that the US was left behind from the rise of Japan, then *The Rise and Fall of the Great Powers* directly revealed the decline of the United States. Kennedy comprehensively pointed out the signs of US decline in the book and claimed that the relative decline of America is even more than that of the Soviet Union. He reported that the situation that the United States faced is not whether or not to decline, but how to decline decently, just like the British Empire. For a time, US recession became a hot topic in the whole nation.

*Japan as Number One* and *The Rise and Fall of the Great Powers* reflected the American elite's awareness of unexpected developments. There were large groups shouting American decline theories to the American people, not just several scholars. The elite's awareness of unexpected development was further promoted and impelled by the hardship of the whole United States. Many Americans believed that the United States could prevail in Cold War competition but would lose in the economic race with Japan and Europe, and even lose its superpower status. A strong awareness of unexpected development became the most important driving force for the United States to meet the challenges of power.

## Strategic Counterattack: The Financial Atomic Bomb

In the case of the rapid rise of Japan, the basic objective of US government policy against Japan was to ensure US leadership yet still allow the Japanese to share responsibilities. Specifically, in respect to bilateral trade, it allowed Japan to make concessions to the United States to help reduce the US trade deficit; in respect to economy, it required Japan to make more contributions, but prohibited Japan to use aid and investment to impact the US strategically; in respect to politics, it allowed Japan to play a greater role, but did not allow it to replace the US; in respect to military, under the premise of maintaining the absolute leadership of the United States, it allowed Japan to improve defense capabilities and share security costs with the United States. During the Cold War, US global strategy had two pillars: the Atlantic Alliance and the US-Japan alliance. Relations between the US and Japan had traditionally been seen as a cornerstone of US policy in Asia. However, for a long time, the United States and Japan have been in disagreement on security and defense issues. The United States complained that Japan fully developed its economy but refused to spend more money on defense, getting a free ride in national security and profiting at the United States' expense; the US asked Japan to share more defense responsibilities as a result. However, Japan had become a major economic power, and is pursuing the status of a political power, so Japan can no longer be absolutely controlled by the United States. The United States wanted Japan to share burdens and responsibilities, while Japan wanted to share rights with the United States.

The United States' strategic counterattack against Japan could fundamentally seize strategic initiative and mainly depends on two trump cards: one is to implement a financial war against Japan, tantamount to using financial nuclear weapons against Japan, and another is to create new economy with information technology and globalization as the basic features.

Regarding the deadly consequences of the use of financial weapons against the Japanese economy by the US, history professor Qi Shirong at the Chinese Capital Normal University pointed out: in 1999 the United States used 85% of the world's working capital and 72% of the world reserves with 4.5% of world population, indicating the US still dominated the world in the area of currency. The special status of the US dollar in the world economy can pass economic issues to other countries through exchange rates of US dollars alone—namely by substantial devaluation. After the United States reached the Plaza Accord with Germany and Japan in 1985, the exchange rate of the yen doubled in two years and Japan's economic bubble burst, leading to 10 years of economic recession for Japan. This illustrates how the United States can use the US dollar to beat opponents and get benefits. The so-called Plaza Accord was named for a meeting held at the Plaza hotel in New York in September 1985, by finance ministers from the United States, Britain, West Germany, France, and Japan, in hopes that the exchange rate of major currencies to the US dollar would be improved. Japan was forced to increase the value of the yen; after a year's time, the foreign exchange rate of yen was increased by 60%, resulting in the continued downturn of the Japanese economy over more than 10 years, into the late 1990s. Only in 2005 did it begin a slow recovery. The Plaza Accord forced Japan into the appreciation of the yen, which collapsed its economic bubble. During the period from 1993–2000, seven prime ministers were replaced, each with an average tenure of less than one year.

When Japan suffered a crushing defeat due to financial weapons used by the United States, they launched a new global economy. Japan's inadequate response to its bursting economic bubble led to a prolonged trend of economic stagnation. By the mid-1990s, the US economy had strongly recovered and regained a superior competitive edge thanks to the information technology revolution.

At the beginning of the 1990s Americans were widely worried about the decline in US economic competitiveness and the decline of US hegemony. By the end of the 1990s, the decline they were worried about had seemingly disappeared. After the United States experienced a mild recession in late 1990 and early 1991 (according to statistics by the US Department of Commerce, economic growth rate in the fourth quarter of 1990 was -1.6% and -2.8% in the first quarter of 1991), the economy entered into a sustained and rapid period of expansion. By the end of 1999 the US economy had achieved growth for 105 consecutive months (this round of economic expansion finally ended in the fourth quarter of 2000, totaling continuous growth for 114 months). This was the longest period of peaceful growth for the US economy since the mid-19th century. At that time, Western European countries were plagued by high unemployment and sluggish economic growth; in addition, Japan's economic bubble had burst. While the US economy appeared to achieve miraculous growth and remained sound in the developed world, the US economy's share in the world economy also rebounded. In 1990, the United States, Europe, and Japan's GDP ratio was 1.88:2.07:1; the US gross domestic product accounted for 25.29% of global output. By 2000, the US GDP share in world GDP was raised to 27.07%, reaching $7.898 trillion. The GDP ratio of the United States, the European Community, and Japan was 2.2:2.2:1.

All the basic indicators of the US economy were improved, which not only was rare in the modern American economic cycle, but did not conform to mainstream Western economics theories. This new economic phenomenon had three main manifestations: For one, during his tenure, Clinton completely wiped out more than $200 billion in federal budget deficit; fiscal deficit was transformed to fiscal surplus by 1998, while an average annual economic growth of 3% was achieved. US deficit reduction and adoption of tightening fiscal policy avoided a depression. Then, in the process of economic growth in the 1990s the US maintained an unemployment rate below 5%, while the inflation rate had been curbed to 2% or less. Traditional economic theory holds that below the natural rate of unemployment one gets high inflation, but this theory failed to predict American performance. Furthermore, labor productivity was significantly improved, while return on capital was maintained at a high level and the stock market was soaring. Dominance of the US economy was consolidated and strengthened relying on the sudden emergence of this new economic phenomenon: information technology. In the 1990s the contribution rate of the information industry to economic growth in the US was 35%. Information industry employment (in the broad sense, including communications, media, etc.) accounted for about 60% of the total labor force, and its percentage of GDP for computer and communication industries reached 8.2% as early as 1988. Information technology became the first major industry, more so than the automotive and construction industries. The information industry can greatly improve labor productivity, reduce energy and material consumption, and enhance the ability to continue to grow not only through its own development but also through transformation of traditional industries. The United States occupied the leading role in international competitiveness rankings from the mid-1990s for 20 consecutive years. America changed its backward situation in electronic components, engineering technology, materials technology, and processing technology and made new progress. It also established its role as the head of the development of information infrastructure and other key new technologies through its seizure of the initiative. It also strengthened its position in traditional advantageous areas such as biology, environment, and engineering design.

## How Did the United States Curb Japan's Competition?

**1.** In the competition between champion nation (the United States) and potential champion (Japan), the factors of ideology and social systems will always rank second, while national interests and statehood always rank first. When Japan's economy threatened the United States' status of world leader, the United States put its quarrel with the Soviet Union behind it and regarded Japan as the new opponent.

**2.** In the strategic competition between countries and in competition for the fundamental lead competitive position in the world among countries, at a crucial moment in the strategic game, tools of conspiracy and trapping will be used. The Plaza Accord was orchestrated by the United States to deal with Japan; it was a financial conspiracy, a financial trap, and a financial war. In this case, a conspiracy theory or trap theory in the international arena was not groundless.

**3.** In strategic competition among large countries, to gain the strategic initiative fundamentally and truly be a winner, one cannot only depend on principle, conspiracy, or traps. Development cannot only depend on curbing opponents. The key questions and factors involve how to effectively develop so as to form a powerful advantage over rivals in innovation and development. In the 1990s, the United States put Japan far behind with its information-based new economy, which played an important role in winning.

## IV. How Did America Curb the Soviet Union's Competition?

If the containment of the United States against Japan was containment within the camp of capitalism, then the containment of United States against the Soviet Union was containment outside the camp and containment of foreign opponents outside a league of alliance. This battle was a marathon campaign lasting for nearly half a century.

### America's Strategic Invention in the Cold War

The concept of the Cold War was created and put forward by Americans. US senator Bernard Baruch first proposed the concept of Cold War in a speech on April 16, 1947. The famous American columnist Walter Lippmann wrote a series of articles on it. Since then, the Cold War concept has been widely spread and used, and the Cold War has become common terminology in US postwar policy and particularly the policy against the Soviet Union. Furthermore, it has been widely recognized and widely accepted by the international community.

What is the Cold War? What is the meaning of the Cold War? There are three meanings. The first is the Soviet Union's definition. The Soviet Union believed the Cold War was a policy adopted by the United States and other imperialist countries to deal with socialist states (firstly the Soviet Union) after World War II from the late 1940s to the 1960s. It aimed at ruining the victorious results of World War II and depriving the Soviet people and the world of peace by democratic forces. The Cold War reflected interests of the West's most reactionary monopoly bourgeoisie, especially the US monopoly bourgeoisie. The Cold War was a confrontation between two major military and political groups for geopolitical interests. Contradictions between the two were reflected in many aspects, for instance, discriminating against the Soviet Union and its allies in economic, trade, and technological fields by the Western group in an attempt to control these countries. The second is America's definition of Cold War. American scholars believed that the Cold War was an all-out confrontation in addition to the direct military conflicts among countries with conflicting interests and it reflected the East and the West's grand confrontation. The third is China scholars' definition of Cold War. Chinese scholars believed that the Cold War was a comprehensive confrontation after World War II between the socialist camp headed by the Soviet Union and the Western camp led by US. In addition to direct military confrontation, this conflict also involved political, economic, and ideological fields; it was a war expressed in peaceful form.

When did the Cold War begin? On this issue, the two protagonists of the Cold War have different statements. The former Soviet Union and Russia held three major perspectives: First, the October Revolution was taken as a starting point. The atomic bombs dropped by United States on Japan were also taken as a starting point; this shocked the

Soviet Union and threatened the entire world. It not only made for final victory of the war against Japan, but also successfully showed off US strength to the Soviet Union, thus leading to the outbreak of the Cold War. Third, the emergence of the Truman Doctrine in 1947 was taken as a starting point. In the United States, there are five perspectives:

**1.** The Cold War was the basic model of the relationship between the United States and the Soviet Union and the Cold War began after World War II. According to wartime agreements, the United States and the Soviet Union arranged their political influence geographically. The period from 1947 to 1948 was a critical moment, mainly marked by the establishment of the Intelligence Bureau, the Berlin crisis, Victorious February in the Czech Republic, and the Korean War.

**2.** The Cold War was an ideological confrontation and competition and began in the period from 1917 to 1920,with the October Revolution, with the armed intervention and establishment of the nationally recognized communist leadership.

**3.** The Cold War began between the two world wars.

**4.** The Cold War began during World War II.

**5.** The Cold War began in August 1945, when the United States used atomic bombs against Japan. Chinese experts and scholars believed that the containment theory proposed by Kennan provided ideological and theoretical foundation for the Cold War mentality in the United States; Churchill's "Iron Curtain Speech" kicked off the Cold War; and the beginning of Cold War was marked by the official start of the Truman Doctrine. The main battlefield of the Cold War was in Europe and it gradually extended to the entire world. The leading players in the Cold War were United States and its Western allies, as well as the Soviet Union and Warsaw Pact states. China and many developing countries were also involved to varying degrees.

## The Meaning of "Cold" in Cold War

A Cold War has no artillery smoke, nor swords. What is the meaning of "cold" in Cold War? In fact, the most fundamental element of the Cold War relies on cold thinking. Cold War thinking is a mental war, without bloodshed. Therefore, the key to understand the cold in Cold War is to reveal the nature of the Cold War mentality.

The so-called Cold War mentality is the fundamental strategic concept, strategic principle, and strategic way which that be followed in the game between the United States and the Soviet Union for world hegemony and is the guiding ideology of the Cold War between the US and Soviet Union. Cold War mentality was in essence a hegemonic mindset. For both sides, the struggle for world hegemony and mindset was the source of competition. The Cold War mentality has six main characteristics.

1. The jungle mentality that one mountain cannot accommodate two tigers is predominant. Cold War thinking is the jungle principle. If one takes the international community as a jungle, the strongest country is the king, and does not allow for the emergence of challengers and competitors, and is constantly looking for ways to suppress and contain opponents. Cold War mentality is afraid of a multipolar world and obstructs the formation of a democratic world.

2. The privileged mindset, with hegemonic interests as national interests: each sovereign country in the international community has its own national interests. However, national interests are not arbitrary; national interests are also bound to circumstance, like national territory. For the country struggling for hegemony, an important feature and content of its Cold War mentality is that it grabs global hegemony as its own national interest so as to put a cloak of "national interest" on the struggle for world hegemony. Taking the pursuit of hegemony as an interest and maintaining hegemonic interests as national interests is to flex national and ethnic privilege while damaging the interests of the entire international community.

3. The absolute thinking of achieving absolute safety by absolute risk of others: the Cold War mentality includes hegemonic security theory, which believes that the safety and security of a country depends on global hegemony. To be safe requires hegemony, and without it there is no security. As a result, desperate expansion of armaments and implementation of arms races, along with the pursuit of absolute military superiority and threatening opponents with absolute danger, could achieve and guard absolute security of a country. This consequently results in a global arms race, exacerbating tensions in the world and perpetuating insecurity within each competing nation. Hegemony is not absolute security protection. The reason for basing absolute security on someone else's absolute insecurity rather than on the establishment of common security stems from a lack of trust that forms a universal "security dilemma."

4. Competition cannot achieve mutual benefit, or zero-sum thinking: the Cold War mentality started a vicious competition in accordance with a zero-sum game principle, both sides believing one's achievement is another's loss. In the relationship, and in each other's competition, the result is winning or falling, gain or loss, achievement or defeat. There is no win-win and no common interest.

5. The rejection mentality, that two systems cannot coexist in the world. In March 1947, President Harry Truman stated: "the whole world should adopt the American system, for we can survive only by adopting the American system." According to Truman's thinking, there should be only one system in the world, namely the American system, and other systems have no right to exist. Differing social systems and ideologies were sentenced to death by Cold War thinking. American ideological hegemony believed its human rights, democracy, and Christian civilization were seriously threatened by the socialist state planned economy. This system was viewed as despotism and atheism, and Americans believed that these two political and economic systems were not compatible—like fire and water. The resulting confrontation and struggle between them could only be black or white. The mission of the Soviet Union was to act as the gravedigger of the United States' capitalism; that of the United States is to sweep the Soviet system into the dustbin of history. Cold War mentality does not allow for the emergence and existence of models such as "one world, two systems" or "one world, many systems"; it is the murder of the world's diversity.

6. The Cold War mentality of "friend or foe" thinking perpetuates the phenomena: the Cold War mentality is strictly in accordance with ideological lines; each of the parties builds its own camp, implements a strategic alliance, seeks geopolitical advantages, carries on bloc confrontation, and attempts to segment the whole world into a Cold War mentality, resulting in the whole world being shrouded in a haze of Cold War competition.

## The Reason for the Cold War

Americans once thought that the Cold War was a fight for world leadership. American history professor Kong Huarui once said: "Why did the United States and the Soviet Union take the attitude of mutual threat in the late 1940s and why was this situation continued until the late 1980s? Three cross-study methods can be used to get three answers. Firstly, American leaders accepted major power responsibility and determination to lead the world and create a new world order. Secondly, the characteristics of the US and the USSR highlighted the excesses of one civil society (America's strong country and weak government model), while another country had no such civil society (highly totalitarian Stalinist political system). The third was the security dilemma.

"If the United States had no determination to lead the world, it would be difficult to imagine the emergence of the Cold War, if the United States chose continental ideas proposed by some intellectuals in the 1930s (the policy tending to cooperate with other countries on their continent in political and economic aspects, while excluding other continents) that praised self-sufficiency. This move was once again advocated by intellectuals in the 1960s, and the notion's momentum was very different in the post-war world, but a generation of American leaders have drawn the following conclusion: It is America's escape of responsibility to lead the world after the first World War that caused Adolf Hitler and the Japanese militarists' rise, and the realities of Great Depression and World War II were the consequences. American poet and philosopher George Santayana once said that 'those who cannot remember the past are condemned to repeat it', they learned a lesson from historians and began to apply it in practice in the mid-1940s. [...] Their goal is to create a world order to promote US interests, in the world order and America's wealth and power will continue to grow, and the values that Americans hold will be extended to the whole world."

For Americans, the reason for Adolf Hitler and the Japanese militarists' rise was due to the Great Depression and realities after World War II. The lesson was that the United States evaded responsibility to lead the world after World War I and did not promptly take up the position as world leader. It was one of America's historic and strategic mistakes and biggest regrets. Out of this came the mentality for America not to repeat this mistake. As a result, it was accepted that the United States must embark on a leadership position in the world after World War II. This began the Cold War with the Soviet Union, to maintain a position of leadership. So, for the Americans, the Cold War was a fight for world leadership in order to maintain security.

The essence of the Cold War between the United States and the Soviet Union is competition and contest around global hegemony, whether it is the struggle and conflict between capitalism and Marxism-Leninism at the ideological level, the fight between political and economic systems of capitalism and political and economic systems of socialism at the societal system level, or an arms race at the military level—in order to maintain military superiority, especially in the nuclear arms race.

The Cold War was a protracted battle for supremacy between two powers in the world, the United States and the Soviet Union, at the end of World War II. They both wanted to compete in the world, and both wanted their ideologies to dominate the world. Nuclear weapons became strategic tokens in this competition among great nations, with global hegemony as the goal, military strength as backing, ideology as banner, and party and union as the organization form. The Cold War was a containment and an anti-containment struggle carried out between the champion United States and the runner-up Soviet Union. The Cold War was an international system with a combination of confrontation and dialogue, competition and cooperation, containment and collusion, as well as struggle and compromise. The Cold War was a special war with peace at its core. The main means of the Cold War included arms races, diplomatic struggles, economic and technological pressures, ideological antagonism, espionage, and so on. The root of the Cold War was the pursuit of hegemony. The Cold War between the United States and the Soviet Union was a fight for supremacy.

## The Role of Development in the Cold War

The world is always progressing; participating in the Cold War is to seek world hegemony, and the referee of the Cold War is development. The logic of historical progress is
to change the Cold War between the US and the USSR into an inevitable and independent
competition for development to be the fittest.

Development competition decided the success of the Cold War. In the process of competing for global hegemony, America and the Soviet Union attacked and demonized each
other in terms of ideologies and social systems and competed in economic and social development. America advertised competition between the US and the USSR as a struggle
between two lifestyles and a struggle between the free world and the totalitarian world. The
United States propagated its material civilization, excellent living conditions, and freedom
of lifestyle with unparalleled appeal. The Soviet Union attacked the United States for its
decadent and moribund capitalism. The development comparison between American and
Soviet systems determined the competitive situation between the two sides and decided the
rise and fall of the two countries during the competition.

Although the United States was the world's leading country in comprehensive national
strength, during the competition between the US and the USSR, there were points where its
supremacy was threatened. In the 1970s the US economy continued to decline, the number
of unemployed people reached 8 million and the government lost the confidence of the
American people, who were more and more pessimistic about their future. Polls showed
that in 1978, compared with 1958, American attitudes had changed significantly: the people
who believed that the US government was working for the wealthy few increased from 18%
to 74%; the people who believed the government could not make the right judgments increased from 25% to 70%; the people who believed the US government was ruled by people
who didn't know how to perform their jobs properly increased from 28% to 56%. Reagan
admitted in the first article of his State of the Union address that there were six people pessimistic about their future in every 10 respondents. Reagan said at the Republican primary
election in New Hampshire in February 1980, without emotion: "Some older Americans
might remember that before World War II, Americans all over the world could go to everywhere with an American flag as their badge. Today, a crisis of trust and confidence has
emerged in the United States, we have lost the respect of friends and enemies, it is really a
sad thing. Development is hard truth; if development is in trouble, we will lose initiative in
the competition."

Reagan came to power when the United States was in trouble. Reagan's efforts to revive
America's prestige were mainly to focus on domestic problems, accelerating development,
economic revitalization, and expansion of armaments. He took a series of strategic measures to achieve these goals; particularly on August 13, 1981, he signed a substantial tax cut
bill that would reduce income tax by 25% within three years, which became the catalyst for

the US economic recovery and prosperity. From the beginning of the second half of 1982, the Reagan administration launched the "three-high" policy of high deficit, high interest rates, and high dollar currency rates, stimulating US economic recovery and development. The US economy bottomed out in December 1982. In 1983, US real GDP had grown by 3.6%; in 1984, the economic growth rate reached 6.5%, which was the highest growth rate in the last 30 years; the inflation rate fell to 3.9% in these three years, which was the lowest in the past 17 years; within these two years, it also provided 7.3 million jobs. Reagan's national strategy was to revitalize national prestige, revitalize the armed forces, and seek peace with strength. America's military spending was increased from $171 billion in 1981 to $376 billion in 1986.

People say that the Reagan era was one of a general offensive against the Soviet Union launched under the neoconservative banner. The basis and the backing for the implementation of this offensive strategy by the US was economic development. In the United States, liberalism and conservatism rise and fall continuously. From the 1940s to 1960s liberalism prevailed, and America had a prosperous economy and strong strategic position. During this time it was the leader of the Western world and stronger in US-Soviet competition, but it also accumulated a variety of contradictions. Beginning in the 1970s neoconservatism rose in the capitalist world and gradually became the mainstream trend. The main features of the neoconservatism are: right deviation in politics, strong anticommunism in ideology, and the proposition of implementing war against irreconcilable systems such as communism. In the economic field, it pursues supply-side theory, performs operations against social welfare policies, adheres to the strategic vision of bipolar confrontation, actively implements power diplomacy, and carries out arms races to safeguard national interests. Reagan's basic tenets included curtailing government, lowering taxes, cutting welfare, and strengthening national defense. He worshipped strength, was obsessed with the Cold War, and firmly opposed the Soviet Union and communism. Reagan's advisers argued that the Soviet communist leaders must make a choice to abandon their communism in accordance with the direction of the Western world peacefully or through war; there was no other alternative or compromise. Into the 1980s the Soviet Union's strategic goal against the United States was not to coexist, but to change the Soviet system and achieve the goal of victory without fighting. Under the guidance of neoconservatism, the Reagan administration established a trinitarian comprehensive policy against the Soviet Union, namely an arms race, economic sanctions, and the space race. He comprehensively challenged the Soviet Union in military, economic, and technological aspects. The reason that Reagan was able to launch offensive operations against the Soviet Union at this stage and implement tough, comprehensive policy was the development of the US economy. Comprehensive policy could not be exerted without the support of economic power.

Reagan's offensive era and high-development era for the US economy was precisely an era of stagnation in the Soviet Union. In the late 1970s the Soviet Union's stagnation was mainly reflected in a traditional political and economic system that became increasingly rigid, which severely restricted social and economic development; dogmatism and bureaucracy prevailed and power was highly centralized; democracy remained in name only; economic growth was slow; social and ethnic conflicts were revealed; in comparison and competition with the forces of United States, it was more disadvantaged; a huge bureaucracy and cadres created by the Soviet Union had become inflated during the term of Brezhnev. According to statistics in 1982, there were 110 units at the ministry level (the Ministry and the Commission) and subordinate units to the Council of Ministers. During the years 1975–1983 regulatory agency personnel in the Soviet Union had a net increase of 3 million forming cadres composed of 2,100 people. Management departments and agencies were interlaced from the central to local governments. Soviet manufacturing and construction industries established more than 40 ministries throughout the republic's with more than 700 general management authorities established, which managed more than 50 thousand businesses through various programs. In the Soviet Union, 6 million leading cadres manipulated the economic activity of the country. Furthermore, the number of agricultural management sectors was as many as 3 million, even more than the total number of US farmers.

Soviet cadres had an annual appointment system and life tenure, so cadres were generally aging. In 1981, 25 people were elected from the 26th conference as members of the Political Bureau of the Central Committee, with an average age of 70.1, and an average age of 68 years for secretary offices. Cadres were responsible for their leaders, leading to a decrease in leadership with political institutions implementing reverse natural selection. Some mediocre, incompetent, and dishonest people were promoted, but those with the abilities and the courage to put forward their views were abandoned by the government. Bureaucracy and corruption prevailed; many inherited leadership and then extorted money, which not only formed a privileged aristocracy—the transfer of privileges to their offspring formed a renewing privilege inheritance system. Brezhnev appreciated praises; in 1976 the Soviet Union publication *Pravda* first published a column to celebrate his seventieth birthday. The articles were filled with nauseating flattery. Soviet politicians called Brezhnev the greatest man of our time and demanded that the people of the Soviet Union read, reread, and study avidly Brezhnev's work, because it was filled with endless sources of wisdom.

By 1975, Brezhnev was gravely ill while he controlled the Soviet Union. In *The Rise and Fall of Gorbachev* Dmitry Mikheyev describes that Brezhnev was unable to continue to lead the party and the state, and the interval between the meetings of the Political Bureau of the Central Committee became shorter and shorter. Brezhnev would sit there blankly, and was not very clear where he was, who was in the conference room, or what should be done. These situations happened often. He would sit and read a brief speech in large letters typed by aides and would sometimes read the wrong line. His speech was incoherent, but he seemed to be aware of it and often looked at people with sad eyes. Participants were often rushed to pass a variety of resolutions in order to end this excruciating situation and would leave the venue restless.[3] Yuri Andropov ruled the country for 14 months, but when his illness is taken into account, his ruling term was only six months. Konstantin Chernenko, his predecessor, was a typical office worker in the Soviet regime with conservative thinking, and when he was in power, he was unable to work and achieved little success in his tenure of one year.

Without development, there is no attraction or competition. The Soviet model of socialism came to an end and the collapse of the Soviet camp was inevitable. The escape of citizens from the German Democratic Republic (East Germany) was one of the classic scenes of Soviet failure. West Berlin was a showcase of the capitalist world and a mirror showing the Western lifestyle. According to statistics, during 1948–1960, 2.5 million people from the German Democratic Republic escaped to Federal Germany, a figure equivalent to about 20% of the total population of the GDR. In 1961, 200,000 people from the German Democratic Republic escaped to Federal Germany. Most of them fled from East Berlin to West Berlin. In 1989 a large number of residents in East Germany began to leave their homes. On November 4, 1989, a 500,000-person demonstration in East Berlin broke out; within 24 hours from November 11 to 12, a total of 540,000 in East Germany escaped to the Federal Republic of Germany; by November 13, the police office of the GDR had issued 518,000 tourist visas. According to the person responsible for Customs Authority of the German Democratic Republic, from November 9 to 27, about 1.6 million people and 240,000 vehicles passed through the border stations. A large number of GDR citizens were abandoning a lifestyle that was not attractive to them.

An important condition for a Cold War to be maintained is the balance of power. The United States and the Soviet Union, for a time, had the balanced strength to compete with each other, which was the material basis and the material condition of the Cold War. Horrific forces such as a nuclear threat formed a balance and peace was established on the basis of military competition; this was a close game of strategic tug-of-war. When the development gap between them widened and the balance of power broke, the Cold War ended.

## An Evaluation of the Cold War

In terms of merits and demerits of the Cold War, a historical position of the Cold War should be objective. In modern world history, competition for hegemony among major powers has never stopped. Comparatively speaking, the Cold War is still the most civilized competition. The Cold War can be regarded as a war of civilization, which is mainly reflected in four aspects.

1. The goal of the Cold War was more civilized. The competition between the Soviet Union and the United States was for the world's three powers: cultural dominance of rights, leadership, and hegemony. This cannot be compared with previous competitions for occupying

rights, dominion, and colonial rights among world powers. This conflict is quite different, with a relatively civilized strategic objective.

**2.** The means of the Cold War were more civilized. Although there were various means used in the Cold War and there were many crises, there was no direct military conflicts, no world wars, and no nuclear war between the United States and the Soviet Union. The case of drastic competition without war was unprecedented. This illustrated the restraint and reason between the two sides and was indicative of global civilization's progress, as well as the evolution of national politics.

**3.** The end of the Cold War was more civilized. Compared with the treatments and arrangements on the defeated party by the victors after World War I and World War II, the Cold War showed a degree of restraint.

**4.** The Cold War was relatively inexpensive. Although the cost of the Cold War was certainly heavy in terms of material expenses, it was a competition among great powers without fighting. When considering human life, the Cold War was relatively inexpensive compared to other wars among large countries in history.

The Cold War was a product of its era; in that era, humans still could not bear the cost of World War II, and certainly could not afford a nuclear war. As a result, global powers of the world could only launch the Cold War. The Cold War mentality is now an outdated product; today, the Cold War seems to only have a place in the museums and history books. Although this mentality is no longer extant, strategic competition among powers will continue in a non–Cold War form.

## Revelations of the Cold War

The Cold War was a period of strategic competition among the world powers, which is a model of competition strategy under specific historical conditions. The great powers surely benefited from the Cold War.

## Inevitability and Contingency of the Cold War

The Cold War was inevitable, but accidental in a way. People said that if Roosevelt had lived for another five years, the relationship between the United States and the Soviet Union would have been quite different. The United States is a country that pays attention to public opinion. Before the Cold War, what was the public opinion in America? By the end of the Second World War, although some United States officials had regarded the Soviet Union as an enemy, only one-third of Americans predicted a war in the next quarter century and regarded the Soviet as a threat to the US in a survey in December 1945. In September 1946, the poll showed only 8% Americans were willing to give up reconciling with Moscow and 74% people thought that both United States and the Soviet Union were responsible for the growing gap. Obviously, awareness of the Cold War was not a mainstream among the United States public opinion at the time, but America's elite had begun its program of propaganda and incitement. If America's elite were not Cold War hawks and kept an friendly opinion, it would have been a different situation.

America's mainstream public opinion was not in support, or even aware of, the Cold War; it seems officials within the United States government preferred to introduce a Cold War mentality. There were definitely some internal differences among the US government. Some of America's politicians who were against the Cold War were quite vocal. After World War II, Truman's tough policy toward the Soviet Union resulted in what came to be Cold War policy. There were opponents, such as Henry Wallace, Truman's commerce secretary. He advocated pursuing Roosevelt's policy of cooperation and coexistence on the basis of strategic alliance and global balance, continuing the two powers' wartime relationship. He advocated guaranteeing Soviet security in Eastern Europe, in order to fairly compete with Soviet political understanding over capitalism and communism on the basis of friendship. In order to open trade doors all over the world, he denounced the United States government's tough policy toward the Soviet Union, arguing that the Truman Doctrine was equal to declaring war on the Soviet Union, and was a reckless adventure that would bring the world into a century of terror. Truman declared that pacifists about the Soviet Bloc were more dangerous than the Nazi supporters in the buildup to World War II. R Wallace ultimately lost his job. Truman's policy of containment replaced Roosevelt's great power cooperation and collective security policy, and thus ended peacetime United States isolationism.

Obviously, the differences between Roosevelt's cooperative policy and Truman's containment policy had huge effects on the United States and the postwar world order. History cannot be undone, but the future can be created. The inevitability and contingency of the Cold War limited people's roles in taking initiative and flexing creativity. China, in its policy toward America, adheres to enhancing mutual trust, broadening common ground, developing cooperation, and avoiding confrontation, which is a new concept in the history of great power rivalries. China's efforts contribute not only to creating a new phase of Sino-US relations, but also to global patterns that will form positive strategic implications.

## The Competition of Models

World domination was the goal of the Cold War between the United States and the Soviet Union, while the outcome depended on the development of competition. Thus, in practice, the Cold War was a comparison of two development models as well as the Soviet and United States models of competition. The results of the competition were that American capitalism triumphed over Soviet socialism. The Soviet model was a great creation of mankind, but this system crystallized after the 1930s, which undid half a century of progress and consistency and created years of stagnation and fossilization. The system ultimately lost momentum and vitality. However, the United States model of capitalism after Roosevelt's New Deal reform had profound evolutionary effects following the economic crisis of the 1930s. After adjustment, the US model found greater vitality and potential for development than the Soviet mode; this fundamentally determined the outcomes for both American and Soviet competition and destiny.

National ideals can only be realized through changing ideology. With rigid patterns of development, no matter what kind of "-ism," there is no vitality, cohesion, or competitiveness. National development models must evolve. A model of development that surpasses others in international comparisons will take precedence over an opponent's development model. The rise of China is the rise of socialism with Chinese characteristics, and this model of development is unmatched by any other model in the world, and is still in constant innovation. Its pace of growth has shocked the world, and shows great potential for the future.

## The Competition of Ideology in the Cold War

The competition between United States and the Soviet Union always occurred under the banner of ideology. The so-called competition for development was not only regarding economic development, but also ideological development. Marxism criticized capitalism and informed socialism, and socialist ideology originally had a powerful advantage; however, it was slow to develop and lost ground due to stagnation and fossilization. It is regrettable that after the Second World War, and especially after the death of Stalin, the Soviet Union was unable to continue exciting and inspiring world ideology and did not formulate its ideological advantages in a timely fashion. As a result it not only failed to achieve its material goals but was also not widely recognized spiritually or culturally. Some of the ideology proposed by the Soviet Union was difficult to rally around and could not win over moral initiative in the world, and even led the country to become more isolated to the world. The Soviet Union was chauvinistic in its the relationship with China, which caused a logical ally to become an enemy. The limited sovereignty and international dictatorship proposed by the Soviet Union and their aggressive border behavior grew more and more unpopular. The resolution condemning the Soviet invasion of Afghanistan in 1980 attracted many nations; by 1986, it was endorsed by 122 countries and only opposed by 19. The Soviet Union's support for Vietnam's occupation of Cambodia was also widely opposed; in 1986 the condemnation resolution on Vietnam was supported by 114 countries, and only 21 nations opposed it.

The United States did well to occupy the moral high ground internationally. From

Wilson's idealistic diplomacy to Roosevelt's Four Freedoms and to Carter's human rights diplomacy, the United States had a strategic competitiveness in terms of ideological soft power at home and abroad. During World War I, America's foreign policy included human rights considerations—President Wilson created his idealistic diplomacy and declared the United States was not to pursue selfish interests, but to defend human rights. This set a precedent for so-called human rights and the dignity of nations as an important basis for policy. President Wilson's diplomacy had an important influence on Roosevelt. On January 6, 1941, Roosevelt's State of the Union address proposed the establishment of security and the search for the world of four fundamental human freedoms: freedom of expression, freedom of opinion, freedom to worship God in any way, and freedom from fear or want. On August 9, 1941, Roosevelt and Churchill signed the Atlantic Charter, which reaffirmed these principles: in the aftermath of the defeat of the Fascist powers, peace was to be cherished in the world, and these two nations would strive to allow people to live freely, without fear of privation. In the later declarations of the United States and the United Nations Charter, as well as other international documents, they all reiterated the principles and provisions relating to fundamental human rights. The United States government remains concerned over human rights issues as they relate to US values and the image and status of the United States as the world's leader. In the mid-1970s the United States government was not tied together on human rights and foreign policy. Jimmy Carter wanted to lead the civil rights movement in the world, and he thought that the promotion of human rights would become the wave of the future. Since the United States wanted to stand at the crest of this movement, emphasis on human rights became the essence of foreign policy for the United States; it became the important factor in identifying diplomatic relations with other countries. Proclamation of human rights was regarded as United States foreign policy's cornerstone. Human rights became the United States' flag to the world and the commanding height of ideology in its universal value system. The United States used human rights to restrict sovereignty, operate global hegemony, and enhance capabilities for strategic competition with the Soviet Union and other challengers.

Development does not only refer to economy, but also the development of ideas, spirit, and culture. An important field of strategic competition between China and the United States is competition between Chinese and American values. Chinese ideology must have its own defined vantage point, Chinese values must have universal appeal, and Chinese values must have universal spread. China can most certainly be a country that can lead the world and become the world's soul.

## The Cold War Era and Post-Cold War Era

The Cold War was a strategic competition among great powers, and the cost was difficult to bear. The Cold War between the Soviet Union and the United States was not only a gamble for the fates of these two countries, but also a gamble for the fate of humanity.

The Cold War had a heavy political cost, which not only expanded the class struggle in the international community, but also within countries. America's Cold War policy not only curbed the Soviet Union abroad, but also encouraged a domestic loyalty oath movement. Truman issued Order No. 9835 on March 21, 1947, calling for a new safety review of 2.5 million civil servants. The investigation expanded to 3 million members of the armed forces and 3 million employees of defense contractors. Thus, at last 8 million people in the United States were ordered to prove their loyalty. If coupled with their families, there were 20 million people in the United States facing imminent threat of censorship. Eventually, even the loyalty of the president himself was in question—Truman faced a charge from the Department of Justice on the November 6, 1953, of intentionally harboring a Soviet spy. Communists had to apply and register in the court, or otherwise were sentenced to two years in prison.

An enormous economic cost was paid in the Cold War. In the mid-1920s some progress was made in the economic relationship between the United States and the Soviet Union; private trade organizations emerged in succession. The US became one of the largest equipment suppliers for Soviet construction and started investing in the Soviet Union and technological cooperation. By 1931 about 40 large US companies signed 134 technical cooperation agreements with the Soviet Union. There were about 1,000 US engineers working in the Soviet Union and 842 Soviet engineers were trained in the United States. The United States and the Soviet Union established official diplomatic relations in 1933. In 1937 the United States provided Most Favored Nation (MFN) status for the Soviet Union. But in 1953, after the Cold War began, East-West trade volume accounted for only 1.3% of total world trade and still only 2.6% in 1956. Economic and trade relations between the US and the Soviet Union were left undeveloped for a long time.

Maintaining Cold War camps were costly. Organization camps and alliances were established during the Cold War. A heavy burden was put upon the Soviet Union in order to maintain them. According to Western estimates, in 1986 the Soviet Union offered $13 million to Cuba a day (and as much as $5 billion a year), $12 million to Afghanistan a day, $8 million to Vietnam, and more than $3 million to Ethiopia. Other statistics report that during the period from 1986 to 1990, the Soviet Union provided Vietnam annually with $2.5 billion in aid, as well as $1 billion as military aid. In these five years, the Soviet Union provided $3 billion to Mongolia. The Soviet Union paid over $3.5 billion to Cuba as economic and military aid, which excluded indirect assistance and physical deals.

The Cold War's half a century was a test, a sentence, and also an education. Cold War–style, cutthroat competition is a human disaster, and the end of the Cold War is history's verdict. Afterward, there was an international consensus to create a world not dominated by a Cold War mentality.

## V. How Will the United States Curb China?

In the battle for the global supremacy, the United States is skillful in curbing opponents. During containment, the US is good at playing short-term war and talented at protracted war. Japan was curbed through effective short-term warfare while containment of the Soviet Union was a protracted war. Now the United States will start its third war—an attempt to curb China.

### Four Distinctive Characteristics for Curbing China

1. It is inevitable in essence: the US was blunt to curb Japan and ruthless to curb the Soviet Union; now the US will attempt to curb China unblinkingly and without hesitation. President Obama declared that the United States does not seek to curb China, but in fact, the United States has been containing China—it does not recognize China as a democratic state, which functions as political containment against China. Likewise, the US does not recognize China's market economy status, which is a form of economic containment against China. The United States trumpeted a Chinese military threat theory, and in turn applied pressure and an arms embargo against China and restricted exports of high-tech and military technology to China jointly with Europe while regularly selling advanced weapons to Taiwan—a clear example of military containment against China. The US often interferes in the Taiwan issue and obstructs the reunification of China. This not only curbs China, but also meddles with China's internal affairs. In response to the issue of China's rise, the United States will not "give up containment and become a Buddha immediately."

2. If we say that America's containment of Japan was mainly economic containment, while containment against the Soviet Union involved a sharply divided camp with clear demarcation lines, then America's containment against China is containment in close contact and cooperation, a combination of cooperation and containment that requires more artful execution. For example, some Chinese scholars have suggested that China employs a freeloader strategy in its relations with the United States, benefiting from America's road to recovery with the aid of US hegemony. Hillary Clinton, former US secretary of state, called for the United States and China to help each other. The two sides are very intelligent, but also very artful. However, it cannot be denied that America has a clear upper hand in terms of control and power with China. China can be promoted to copilot to help the United States to cope with risks, but this will only help America maintain its position as pilot. America allows opponents to board its plane, which is ultimately a higher degree of control and containment.

3. It will be a long-term competition. Although the United States employed some intensive strategy, to curb Japan's first sprint to global control, it only took about ten years. This de-

cade consisted of a few years in critical period and several key actions, To contain the Soviet Union, the United States paid a much greater expense. While the Cold War only lasted half a century, both sides went through several rounds as if it were a boxing match. The competition between the United States and China will be a marathon competition, rather than a sprint or boxing match.

**4.** Unprecedented strategic creativity is required. To contain China, the United States needs innovation and creativity; it must keep pace with the times, because this post–Cold War era is different from the Cold War era. America's experience curbing Japan and the Soviet is useful for dealing with China, but limited. In November 2009, Obama visited China and gave a Go game set as gift to President Hu Jintao. Chinese grandmaster Nie Weiping published an article on his blog that this gift was meaningful: Go is a game of wisdom and intelligence both sides may be brothers sometimes, but they are still competitors in the game. If Obama applies the same methods in the game with China as against Japan and the Soviet Union, it will be clearly not enough. America is a country of innovation, in the years since the Nobel Prize began being awarded in 1901, more than 200 people in the United States have received it. America is the most innovative country in the modern world. How to effectively curb China is a major and difficult innovation task that will be a priority for 21st century America. Will the US have enough intelligence to curb China?

## Difficulties for the United States in Its Response to China's Rise

In the latter half of the 20th century, the United States won against Japan and the Soviet Union, two potential champion nations, and accumulated rich experience dealing with potential champion nations, but in the 21st century, it is facing a completely new rival in China, and the United States cannot help but feel helpless. China is America's third type of rival encountered after World War II and quite different from Japan and the Soviet Union; it is a country that cannot be effectively dealt with using short-term and outdated methods. If the United States wants to defeat China, it will have to overcome the following difficulties:

**1.** China is practicing a discreet rise to power; it is very difficult to determine the nature of China. Chinese are so artful that China cannot be simply defined as America's enemies even by the most conservative political forces in the United States. President George W. Bush, who was known as a champion of neoconservatism, applied the concept of not enemy, but friend—he also said that the relationship between the United States and China is one of the most complex bilateral relations; neither friend nor foe. Kissinger argued that we do not have permanent enemies; we will determine our relationship with other countries based on their actions rather than ideologies, especially the People's Republic of China. Both President George W. Bush and former secretary of state Henry Kissinger thought China was difficult to define, showing that America's strategy against China will require innovation. In dealing with such a peaceful and civilized opponent, the United States is really inexperienced.

**2.** China adheres to a policy of soft rise—like flowing water and streaming clouds, it is hard to be blocked. Haruo Ozaki, the senior principal scientist of the Asian Research Department of the Japanese Center for Economic Research, pointed out in *China's Power Strategy* that China is most vigilant to collapse the US super system in respect to strategy, thus it strengthens economic interdependence in order to avoid substantial opposition in East Asia security, Taiwan, and other issues. But America's policy against China has always vacillated, leading to deepening doubts between the two countries, which objectively supports the idea of increasing an Asian army against the United States. China stresses coordination, multilateralism, and regional cooperation to create a favorable external environment and build interdependence, cooperation, and a mutual-win system in strategy. The view of Japanese experts is insightful. They depict the United States as a country advocating strength and force, while China is a country advocating strategy and conquering the unyielding with the yielding. China implements a soft, strategic, civilized, and peaceful rise so that America's use of force is like a stone hitting water or a sword stabbing cotton.

**3.** China has always been rising within the system, and it is difficult to exclude China. From the beginning of China's reform and opening up, China has been blended into the world and geared to international standards; it has developed in the same system with the United States and rose on the same platform instead of establishing a separate system. Utilizing an existing platform allowed for a small expense to build the system, and also can save on maintenance fees. It also doesn't challenge the world system, so it becomes difficult to find an excuse for the US to contain China.

**4.** China's mutual benefit rise combines the rise of China with the interests of the prosperity of United States. In China's eyes, both countries are in the same boat; it would be difficult for the United States to harm China to benefit itself, and the damage against China will not benefit the United States. A mutually beneficial, interconnected rise has formed because of the conditions provided by economic globalization. Competition and cooperation with China, America's new strategic rival, can serve the most strategic interest of the United States. China's rise has become America's welfare and provides opportunities for the United States to maintain prosperity—in a sense, the United States can gain from China's rise. Therefore, compared to the rise of other nations, China's rise is most favorable to the United States. China implements a mutual benefit principle, which includes competitors in a community of shared interest, rather than as interest antibodies. In particular, resolving political conflicts through the business sector can often receive surprising results. For example, the US Chamber of Commerce and US-China Business Council often actively promote Sino-US relations. In the years after 1989 these groups played a vital role in the annual debate on China's MFN status and in the 1999–2000 debate on permanent normal trade treatment of China. Economic and trade relations have become an important basis for the development and a stabilizer of Sino-US relations, as well as the field with the minimum variables and widest development prospect in Sino-US relations. In June 1991, some companies in the United States lobbied on the issue of MFN for China in succession and tens of thousands of Americans wrote to Congress and asked not to abolish China's MFN status. On May 12, 1993, 298 large companies and 37 trade groups in US jointly wrote to President Bill Clinton and asked him to give an unconditional extension of China's MFN status. In early May 1994, 800 American companies, trade associations, agricultural organizations, and consumer organizations sent a letter to President Clinton jointly. They strongly urged him to support continued trade between the United States and China, extend MFN status, and separate human rights issues from the trade sanctions. Executives from Boeing, Du-Pont, McDonnell Douglas, Coca-Cola, and other large companies made speeches to exert influence on the government, which forced President Clinton to extend MFN status to China on May 26, 1993 and unhook human rights issues from China's annual MFN renewal.

These four aspects reflect the characteristics of China's rise, but also the difficulties in US strategic choices. After World War II the United States formed a grand strategy against the Soviet Union within two years. In 1947 George Kennan proposed containment strategy against the Soviet Union in "The Sources of Soviet Conduct." US senator Bernard Baruch proposed the core strategic concept of Cold War in a speech on April 16, 1947. The grand strategic competition between the US and the Soviet Union was the Cold War strategy and containment strategy. It has been 20 years since the Cold War, so what is America's grand strategy against China? China has put forward a grand strategy of peaceful rise and development. What about the United States? As of now, it seems a grand competition strategy against China has not yet formed in the United States.

## How to Lead and Manage the Rise of China

America's grand strategy for leading, managing embracing the rise of China is worthy of concern. These three aspects are an important manifestation of America's grand strategic thinking against China.

Regarding leading theory, one US think tank believes that China's rise is sending waves much like a tsunami into the world. The United States must deal with the rise of China and build strategy against China. This strategy is to lead the rise of China, and as long as the United States leads China, there will be no threat. To this end, the US must continue to adhere to Nixon's first contact strategy. Former Pentagon adviser Thomas Barnett pointed out in an article published on August 6, 2007: "If we are wise, we should face China's rise cooperatively, like how the British treated us in the last century, we should not try to contain China. On the contrary, we should guide its rise in order to meet our strategic goals."

Regarding management theory, Kissinger said that the existing international system is undergoing fundamental changes and the focus of the world is shifting from the Atlantic Ocean toward the Pacific Ocean. The key countries of the world are primarily in Asia and mainly will be Asian countries in the future. We must manage their rise, and they will counter and complement our management. James Steinberg said: "America's goal should be not to hinder and contain China, but to manage China's rise."

Regarding embracing theory, in September 2005 Undersecretary of State Robert Zoellick proposed to allow China to become a responsible stakeholder; he noted that China was a part of the US-led international system of the past 30 years, and both countries therefore benefited. China would maintain the system and bear responsibility as a stakeholder. In July 2009 Undersecretary James Steinberg, proposed the concept of strategic reassurance between China and the US. He said, "As stated by us and our allies, we have been ready to welcome China as a prosperous and successful country, and China also must promise to the world and other countries that its development and growing global role will not hinder the safety and well-being of other countries," and stressed that "'strategic reassurance must highlight and emphasize the common interests." This strategic reassurance proposed by Americans is actually one of the strategic limits against China in the US-led world system. Strategic reassurance can guarantee US world dominance as long as it ensures that China will not break through the limitations of the US and become the champion nation.

America's leading theory, managing theory, and embracing theory in response to China's rise are all much more civilized than America's containment theories against the Soviet Union, but the US is still under the shadow of a Cold War mentality. The rise of China is viewed as an object led and managed by America. Sino-US relations are defined as a leading-and-led and managing-and-managed relationship; although this relationship is realized in contact, friendship, and cooperation, it is still a smiling curbing of handshakes and hugs.

The right of development is the same as the right to exist; it is the right of a sovereign country. China's rise is China's national sovereignty and an independent step that does not require leading and management by the United States. If China's development is led and managed by America, the rise will not be truly realized. Therefore, the leading and management theories are actually replicas of containment strategy affixed with a more civilized label.

## From the Cold War to a Semi-Cold War

The so-called warm war means that in strategic competition the United States applies a Cold War mentality while China does not. This has led to difficulties for the United States in fully applying Cold War thinking, resulting in competitive state of semi-Cold War; the two sides are engaged in competition not only in a state of relaxation, but also in a mild state of war.

"Warm war" is not so cruel as "hot war" and not so terrible as "Cold War"; it is a game of wrestling and plying in cooperation. The salient features of warm war are curbing in contact, competition in cooperation, melding in globalization, and control through management. It is a competition model more civilized than Cold War, but still somewhat in it's shadow. For competition among great powers and strategic competition between champion nations and potential champion nations, it is a historical process of ending world hegemony through forceful competition and represents an inevitable transition from long-term strategic competition between United States (the last hegemony in the world) and China (the first non-hegemonic leader in the world).

America's customary strategy and tactics is that "if you cannot beat him, you should hug them and tie them up." Since the Nixon administration, Washington has always adopted a two-pronged strategy in dealing with the issue of China's rise: on the one hand, America tries to include China and allow China to become a responsible participant in international affairs; on the other hand, America uses a divide-and-conquer strategy and continued support for Japan, India, Australia, and other great powers to balance and curb China. US strategic experts made the Sino-US alliance, two groups and "Chimerica" to tame the Chinese dragon and absorb China into their existing hegemonic system.

Warm war is proposed to summarize the fundamental characteristics of Sino-US strategic competition, reveal the basic features of the American grand strategy to deal with China, and create core concepts that can express the essence of Sino-US relations. In the 20th century, the core concept of strategic competition between the United States and the Soviet Union was Cold War. In the 21st century the game between United States and China—leading and managing China by the United States and America's friendly containment and co-containment against China—is actually a type of warm war with the same nature as a semi-Cold War.

America's grand strategy to deal with China is not to start a new Cold War but engage in a semi-Cold War because the times are different. American hegemony differs from former British hegemony in occupation and domination, and is a relatively civilized hegemony rather than direct rule. Strategic competition between China and the United States is not only different from the two world wars, but also different from the Cold War competition between the United States and the Soviet Union that lasted for nearly half a century; it is a new competition combining peaceful rise and peaceful containment as well as strategic competition and strategic cooperation.

From the Cold War to warm war: this is a progression of the grand strategy of the United States and a new development of international relations. China-US strategic competition in the 21st century cannot be started on the orbit of the Cold War, because this would not meet the trend of the times. However, Sino-US strategic competition in the 21st century cannot completely get rid of Cold War thinking and cannot go beyond the limitations of this day and age.

In the 21st century China will become the world leader. International structure and behavior rules mainly established by the United States in the Cold War still lead the development of international relations and operation of international politics. The current international political and economic order mainly represents the values and national interests of Western countries, especially America. As an antagonist, the Soviet Union had to fight against it by not participating in the game according to the rules established by the West. After the Cold War, countries had to adapt to the rules established by the United States. China and some other developing countries set out to establish a new international political and economic order, which will be a long-term task. Now the United States continues to use international mechanisms to control and manage the world according to its own will and interests and achieve its global strategic objectives. America's salvation mission, imperial superiority, and fear of being surpassed by the new powers have had a serious impact on US foreign policy. The US will not weed out intervention and effective Cold War weapons; there are still remaining conditions and attitudes from the Cold War.

## America's Fate to Encounter China

America has a record of good luck. Kong Huarui said: "America's success can hardly be attributed just to achievements it has made in foreign relations in many ways. Germany's Iron Chancellor Otto von Bismarck once said that God seems to have special place for wine bibbers, idiots, and the Americans in His heart. The young republic does seem to turn in good luck. European disaster is often the United States' chance [. . .] of course, European disaster may also be spread. Look at 1812: even at that time, the Americans were spared, to a large extent, because the British put all their resources into the war against Napoleon [. . .] European factors became the main reason for America's success; its promotion is different from others, but remains ongoing. No matter whether God prefers Americans, they are still lucky, they often open a half-opened door and then lock the door too tightly, so they do not need to mobilize a large military to engage in large-scale expansion of conquest, nor do they need to maintain a standing army to defend the Empire [. . .] Before the 1840s, the armed forces in peacetime have been never more than twenty thousand people, and there were still no more than 30,000 after civil war."

In the 21st century the United States has met good luck; now, the United States has encountered one of the best rivals and partners on the world stage—the kind-hearted Chinese. The following three factors characterize China at this stage:

**1.** China is the world's most civilized country without extension and invasion since ancient times. A country without extension or invasion over thousands of years is unique in the world. Of all the strategic rivals in the history of the United States, China is the most civilized and charitable opponent. For the United States, it only has a few hundred years of history, but even the Americans themselves do not dare flaunt in this regard. America's success is attributed to their courage and ambition—and sometimes, their cruelty and brutality.

2. China has never harmed America. Deng Xiaoping pointed out in an important conversation that on December 10, 1989 Sino-US relations will become better eventually: China cannot threaten the United States and the United States should not regard China as an opponent or threat. China has never harmed America. Among the world powers, only China has never harmed the United States.

3. China has no enemy countries in the world. In today's world, no country is declared as China's enemy, and no country can regard China as its enemy. At the national level, China has no enemies. China has no enemy countries in the international community, and in national relations, China has achieved an invincible status. China has won an invincible position and a lot of friends through an attitude of peace, friendship, kindness, and integrity to the world, which forms a stark contrast with America's use of strength and force and its crusade against its enemies all over the world.

Who can regard China as an enemy? Kind and angelic China subverts the traditional American strategic mindset—always looking for large countries to declare as strategic enemies. The United States was caught in strategic confusion on how to interpret China and define Sino-US relations. The United States has never faced the recognition of China as an enemy so that it is difficult for it to draw a definitive conclusion even after 20 years of developing a national, long-term grand strategy to deal with the rise of China. It is America's good luck that encounters China and this good luck can be caught or missed out on by China.

## America Is Neither Demon nor Angel

Brzezinski said: "For historical and political reasons, 'Greater China' should regard the United States as a natural ally. Different from Japan and Russia, the United States has never had territorial claims against China, and different from the United Kingdom, America has never humiliated China." Distinguished American history professor Kong Huarun said: "US officials are always excellent with a cosmopolitan foresight; they are not shortsighted businessmen who are only interested in figures on the books at the end of the day."

With this cosmopolitan foresight, Americans are different from the British, the Russians, and the Japanese. In the history of relations with China, there are some remarkable events that have left a number of generations of Chinese people with a good impression of the United States. Therefore, the United States is considered as beautiful imperialists and virtuous robbers.

There is ambivalence toward the United States in China, which is just a reflection of the contradictory United States. Although from the mid-19th century, the United States has joined the ranks among the Western powers and invaded China, the United States implemented an open-door policy, democratic spirit, multiculturalism, and material assistance. It made friendly decisions in some key moments to make Chinese people look toward the future. The Chinese government, including the Qing government, the Northern Warlords government, the Kuomintang government, and even the revolutionary regime in Yan'an, was always expected to get support and help from the United States in difficult times. Their friendship in World War II deepened the Chinese-American complex. The foresight of the United States included deep-seated seeking of long-term strategic interests, and the moral generosity of the United States always showed America's shrewd calculation of American interests: the fundamental purpose of open-door policy and the preservation of China was to protect America's market in Asia; training of overseas students was to expand the influence of American culture in China; material assistance was required not only for politics, but also for the long-term economic benefits; America was the first country that recognized the Republic of China, and they took the lead to abandon agreements, tariff rights, and consular jurisdiction.

We should admit that it is rational for the Americans to handle Sino-US relations with their national interests as the yardstick. Their cleverness, foresight, vision, and strategy made them combine national interests and the global situation at that time with due consideration of China's national interests, so they could win more relative favor from the Chinese government and people. This shows that the United States is a country skilled at investment in human relationships and image cultivation, which is one aspect of American soft power, a feature of American strategic culture, and an important reason the United States became a world power—especially the world's first superpower.

The United States is a national paradox: it is far-sighted and also shortsighted, it has a great power's generosity and also selfish failures and turpitudes. The United States did a lot of things in violation of global trends, harming Chinese interests and prohibiting Chinese people in dealing with Sino-US relations due to the limitations of its imperial interests and ideological biases. For example, at the Paris Peace Conference after World War I, the US government decided to sell China's Shandong in order to avoid conflict with Japan; after World War II, in order to reduce US military casualties, it made a deal with the Soviet Union in the Yalta Agreement at the expense of Chinese national interests; in China's liberation war, as an anti-Soviet, anticommunist gesture, the United States desperately supported the Kuomintang regime without popular support.

US imperialism is different. Since the Opium War in 1840, among the world's great powers with strategic stakes in China, the United States is special. In the century between 1840 and 1949, China experienced only aggression, occupation, oppression, and exploitation in its relations with Britain, Russia, and Japan on the world stage for competition among countries. These countries committed aggression against China unscrupulously; they acquisitively occupied China's vast territory and even conquered China's holdings; they plundered China's resources, enslaved and oppressed the Chinese people, and had no sympathy, respect, or desire to help the Chinese people. The United States was different, and in 100 years of Sino-US relations, it did not invade, oppress, or interfere with China as imperialists and also built a general alliance with China for strategic cooperation against the common enemies and in the name of promoting world civilization.

On February 2, 1959, *People's Daily* reprinted the letter sent by American Communist Party Honorary Chairman William Z. Foster to Chairman Mao Zedong on December 19, 1958, published in *Red Flag* magazine, as well as Mao's reply on January 17, 1959, addressed to him. Chairman Mao said in the letter that the Chinese people know the US imperialists have caused a lot of mischief in China and a lot of mischief in the world, but this is only due to the US ruling group; the American people are friendly.

US imperialism has certainly caused mischief in China: after 1840, it participated in the invasion and oppression against China by Western powers and basically enslaved the Chinese people; the United States proposed an open-door policy in the 19th century and seized opportunities and benefits in invading and exploiting the Chinese people along with other Western countries; they participated in the war launched by the allied forces of eight powers against China; and supported Chiang Kai-shek in the Chinese civil war. All these indicate imperialist aggression, bullying, and intervention in modern US policy against China. However, when handling the relationship between the United States and China, America is different from Britain, Russia, and Japan—it is more intelligent, civilized, enlightened, and far-sighted.

Over the last century certain events have shaped Sino-US relations. The US has not separately waged aggressive war against China. The US has not directly entrenched China's territory. The US was against monopoly of China by any great power when the great powers intended to carve up China, advocated the existence of China as a country, and ultimately objected to carving up China. No matter how selfish the motive was or how complicated the reasons were, objectively it helped to avoid the crisis of national subjugation and genocide of China. Furthermore, the US returned nearly half of the "Boxer indemnities" to China for overseas education, which contained the strategic conspiracy of long-range culture investment, which was a good deed that did more good than harm to China's talent cultivation and national interests from the perspective of long-range strategic effects.

The scale of education of the US in China was the largest of any Western presence. Mao Zedong said in "Friendship or Aggression?," published on the eve of victory of the Chinese revolution in 1949: "For a very long period, U.S. imperialism laid greater stress than other imperialist countries on activities in the sphere of spiritual aggression, extending from religious to 'philanthropic' and cultural undertakings. According to certain statistics, the investments of U.S. missionary and 'philanthropic' organizations in China totaled $41,900,000, and 14.7 percent of the assets of the missionary organizations were in medical service, 38.2 percent in education and 47.1 per cent in religious activities. Many well-known educational institutions in China, such as Yenching University, Peking Union Medical College, the Huei Wen Academies, St. John's University, the University of Nanking, Soochow University, Hangchow Christian College, Hsiangya Medical School, West China Union University and Lingnan University, were established by Americans."[4] The remarks of Mao Zedong criticized and revealed the spiritual aggression of Americans, but they served as a critical affirmation of what Americans did in China's cultural education.

As for Japan's war to dominate China, the US first supported China morally, and then in materiel after outbreak of the Pacific war. Americans fought together with the Chinese army and people in some regions and aspects and entered into an anti-Fascist alliance with China. These are the differences between US imperialism and other imperialist countries toward China. Objectively knowing and admitting such differences has a positive effect on treating Sino-US relation in a comprehensive and fair way, and correctly knowing and dealing with history, status quo, and the future of Sino-US relations.

The tensest stage of Sino-US relation was from the 1950s to the early 1970s, after the new China was founded. The US isolated, blockaded, and contained China, and waged ideological war against China. However, US imperialism was rational in aggression while not expanding aggression without limit, and was temperate in crises. Moreover, from the late 1960s to the early 1970s, the US hierarchy kept pace with the times with an active attitude toward improving Sino-US relations. After China and the US established diplomatic relations, the US took advantage of, restricted, and guarded against China; on the other hand, it improved and developed relations and sought cooperation. The US attitude toward China was containment and cooperation. Since the founding of new China, particularly establishment of diplomatic relations between China and the US, Sino-US relations were antagonistic, tortuous, and even retrogressive, but the general trend was improvement and cooperation. The US is neither a demon nor an angel; China should help it evolve into an angel and prevent it from becoming a demon in strategic competition.

## VI. "If There Is No Great Enemy, There Is No Great US"

There is a motto in the US: "If there is no great enemy, there is no great US." The US needs enemies. The US strategic culture is a culture of creating enemies. The US must keep searching for enemies and rendering crisis. Why does the US need enemies? What is the standard of the US for choosing enemies? How does the US effectively take advantage of enemies? How does the US defeat enemies?

## The American Art of Using Enemies

On January 20, 1981, Republican president Reagan clearly positioned the Soviet Union as an enemy rather than simply a strategic competitor after taking the oath of the office. According to Reagan, the Soviet Union was the focus of evil and archenemy of the US. He declared strategic offence must be taken to contain expansion of the Soviet Union and ensure US security. The US won and benefited by turning against Soviet Union.

At the end of 1993 President Clinton blurted out: "Ah! I miss the Cold War." Missing the Cold War means missing enemies and the era with enemies. After the Cold War, the US had no enemy, which made President Clinton feel lost. Charles Krauthammer said when the Cold War was over: "Our country needs enemies. We will find another one when the enemy is gone." According to the famous US historian Arthur M. Schlesinger, "The US needs an enemy to bring focus and continuity to diplomatic policy. It turned against Germany in the two world wars and against the Soviet Union in the Cold War. It will announce the existence of other potential enemies in due time." US statesmen and experts are keen on looking for enemies like a treasure hunt. What does *enemy* mean to the US?

1. Enemy means a challenge and competition, and thus a motive for power. In the Cold War's half a century, the powerful Soviet enemy provided a great motivating power and stimulus for US development. They gave full play to their potential death match, forcing them to develop and progress at full speed. Before the collapse of the Soviet Union, some authorities of the US fully affirmed the feats of Cold War and contributions of the Soviet Union to the US: "The Soviet Union was a useful enemy. The US believed that it should compete with Soviet Union in both military force and achievements. Now it seems to be a fantastical notion. Many Americans positioned the competition of two systems as a competition of superiority in the 1950s and 1960s. Without the space program of the Soviet Union, the Americans would not have landed on the moon." The continuity of Cold War bordering on war stimulated the national defense industry and created sophisticated technology in the US.

2. With an enemy, the US can effectively unite and cohere itself. On the eve of collapse of the Soviet Union in September 1991, the US sighed with feeling for the Cold War: for a country with diversity like the US, only external challenges can unite it. By making an archenemy and creating the situation of being confronted with a formidable enemy, the US can call on the people to create the national atmosphere of sharing a bitter hatred of the enemy to effectively unite and cohere parties, and keep and enhance authority and the appeal of US leadership. The US looks for external enemies to cohere itself. Looking for and making enemies becomes a strategy of administering state affairs and ensuring the national security of the US.

**3.** Enemies support the special interests of the defense industry. US strategist Thomas Barnett said, "I mean, all this sexy, high-tech military capability that we were buying across the nineties really needed a sexy, high-tech enemy to fight against, right? Absolutely, said the Cold Worriers, and if Russia looked more feeble as the decade unfolded, then, damn it, we would make do with China."[5] Barnett pointed out that after 9/11, China fell off the radar overnight, replaced by a worldwide terrorist organization and any rogue state suspected of supporting it. "The U.S. military has always done well in respondin gto defeats. It has never done as well responding to victories. America won a huge victory across the Cold War: we stood down the world's only other military superpower while simultaneously setting in motion globalization's great advance around the planet. A new era was born with the collapse of the Soviet Union, but our being present at its creation was not nearly enough. America needed to embrace the new security environment in which it faced no peers, through its clear redefinition of both an enemy worth fighting and a future military building. The Pentagon failed dramatically on both counts, and it did so primarily out of fear for its own institutional standing within the U.S. political system—or, to put it more bluntly, its share of the federal budget. That fear drove the military to cling to the dream of a 'near-peer' which would justify its desire to retain a military fashioned primarily for great-power war, when the new era not only did not generate such a threat but instead challenged America's defintion of a 'New World Order' by producing its exact opposite: the rise of the so-called lesser includeds."[6] It is thus clear that the US needs enemies because the Pentagon needs status in the US political system and needs to keep its share of military expenditures in the federal budget, and only making a powerful enemy can justify the army aimed at a war of superpowers. Jokingly, without enemies, what can the US armed forces and military industry groups eat and earn? Enemies mean powerful interests will be met.

**4.** Only with enemies can the US call the shots and maintain its dominance. Containing and crusading against rising powers that affect dominance of the US by positioning them as enemies can be justified to maintain the hegemony and interests of the US in the world by effectively containing the rising countries. Furthermore, the US categorizes enemies of the US as common enemies of the Western world, takes the lead, organizes and strengthens alliances, calls the shots, and involves Western countries in war. Some authoritative analysts of the US argue when evaluating the role of Cold War that the Eisenhower, Kennedy, and Johnson administrations challenged by the Soviet Union found reasons for boosting the national security of the oppressed. This promoted development of the US national defense industry, particularly sophisticated technology, and above all, provided good opportunity for the US to rope in capitalist allies. Thus, the US organizes anti-enemy alliances and creates a unified front in the world, controlling Western countries and containing rising countries to guarantee its status and interests as a hegemonic power.

## US Standards for Choosing Enemies

The US standard for choosing enemies is comprehensive, but focuses on two aspects. The standard of ideology is the first. For the US, the ideal enemy is antagonist in ideology, different in race and culture, and militarily powerful enough to pose a credible threat to US security. The main issue in foreign policy debate since the 1990s is which country can be such an enemy.

The US adhered to the standard of ideology in positioning against Germany, Japan, and the Soviet Union. The basis of war against Germany, Japan, and the Soviet Union in the 20th century was that the three rivals objected to main principles of the American creed. Due to their objection to individualistic values of the US, they became enemies of the US. This was a near consensus of the American people. In 1945 the question of the Gallup poll was: do you think that one who is a communist and can be loyal to the US? Five percent answered "yes" while 87% answered "no." At the end of 1989 47% said they would rather get involved in a comprehensive nuclear war than live under the rule of communism.

Dividing friends or foes by values was doubtful among some statesmen, and discussion beyond ideology appeared even during the Cold War, but it failed to fundamentally shake the adherence to this standard of the US. Discussion beyond ideology in a specific period and case can even be the expression of pragmatism and power tactics of American politicians. For example, in the late 1960s some American decision-makers believed that the traditional criteria of right and wrong should be reviewed. Nixon said: "Nowadays, 'ism' has lost vitality…our goal is to remove all sensitive and emotional things in diplomatic policies." "Countries with different ideologies may have common goals in specific conditions and situations, while countries with the same ideology may be antagonists." Kissinger also said that we have no permanent enemies, but "we will judge other countries by their actions rather than ideology, particularly the People's Republic of China."

The second is the standard of force. The US seeks countries that develop rapidly and with the greatest strength and potential to challenge the US, and copes with them as enemies. Such countries are the rising ones. In the strategic thinking of the US, rising nations are competitors, challengers, and antagonists. At the end of and after the Cold War, Japan was at the top of the list of "rivals" of the US. American scholars and statesmen wrote dozens of books and hundreds of articles with rigorous arguments to describe the upcoming conflict between Japan and the US. But later, as the Japanese economy lost growth momentum, the US removed Japan from the list of potential enemies. According to report of National Security Institute in 1997, "Only Russia and China can be potential regional rivals. India may become an important regional military power in the future decade." Later, the US regarded Russia as a candidate for archenemy again, but due to its "terrible economic situation, turmoil at home, and disorderly social structure," as Owen Harris, chief editor of the *National Interest* put it, Russia is "just a wounded beast, a former superpower striving to become a democratic country," and would pose no threat to the US in the short term. After 1997, the US finally targeted China as the archenemy. According to public opinion in the US, the long-range goal of China was to challenge the global dominance of the US, and the US must be hostile to China; otherwise it would be appeasement or indulgence.

According to the US standard for choosing enemies, China is eligible. As China is different from the US in ideology and has the most potential among rising powers, it is at the top of the list for choosing enemies in the US.

## Huntington Felt Sad for the Lonely US

The US thinking of choosing enemies and creating enemies sets others against itself around the world and makes it the loneliest country in the world. Samuel Huntington pointed out that American officials praise the US as a beneficent hegemony, and parade the US as the first non-imperialist superpower. In fact, the US is a rogue superpower, and finds itself more and more isolated in the world. The American leaders have been claiming the US represents the international community. But which countries do they think they represent? China? Russia? India? Pakistan? Iran? Or the Arab world? ASEAN? Or Africa? Latin America? France? Do these countries or regions regard the US as representative of their society? In most issues, what the US represents is, at best, its Anglo-Saxon brothers (Britain, Canada, Australia, and New Zealand); in many issues, it represents Germany and some small democratic countries in Europe; in the Middle East issues, Israel; in implementation of UN resolutions, Japan. Although these are important countries, they are far from the global international community. Through issues one after another, the US finds itself more and more isolated with few allies, antagonistic to the majority of countries and peoples in the world. The countries regarding interests complementary to interests of the US are on the decrease. At least this is true among core permanent member states of the UN Security Council. In the first decade of Cold War, the pattern was 4:1 with the US, Britain, France, and China jointly against the Soviet Union. After the Chinese government led by Mao Zedong recovered its lawful seat in the UN, the pattern was 3:1 with China in a middle position. Now it is 2:1:2, it is US and Britain vs. China and Russia with France in the middle position. At a meeting at Harvard University in 1997, some scholars pointed out that countries with at least two-thirds of world population—China, Russia, India, Arab, Muslim, and African countries—regard the US as the largest unique external threat to their society. The public of Japan listed the US as a threat only second to North Korea in 1997. The US has become amazingly good at creating great enemies and has become a lonely nation. The greatness of the US cannot be realized and maintained by creating great enemies.

## *The Sino-US Alliance*

More and more Americans realize that the US should promote national development by making friends instead of keeping hegemony by making enemies. People of insight have even proposed a Sino-US alliance. On June 26, 2006, famous US strategic expert Thomas Barnett put forward in a speech at the China Foundation for International Strategic Studies the goal of establishing a Sino-US strategic alliance in the 21st century, a very creative idea.

Barnett said that a Sino-US alliance would be extremely beneficial to both parties. Like Britain in the early 20th century, the US is faced with an important choice as for China's rise. They can regard it as a rising power and calmly accept it like Britain looked at the US in early 20th century, or regard it as Germany in the last century, i.e. a source of global war. Britain kept and developed its national power by establishing a strategic alliance with the US. The US is in a period of gradual economic weakness, though its military strength is still powerful. The US should establish a strategic alliance with China to make up for economic strength with military strength. Such a strategic alliance will be very beneficial to China, so China should also support such an alliance. But the Pentagon will not approve of the Sino-US strategic alliance, as they need to keep China as an excuse for expanding military spending. In the three years after 9/11, the Pentagon paid less attention to China. As during this period, the US focused on terrorism in the Middle East. But in 2005, the China issue came on the agenda again. In fact, this was the strategy for the US Navy, Air Force, and Army to scramble for a defense budget. Therefore, more exactly, the US Navy and Air Force needed the imaginary enemy of China more than ever. Sino-US relations are extremely important in the 21st century. As long as China and the US cooperate, globalization can never be destroyed; but if they are at war, globalization will be devastated in a day. The US will keep the right to exist in globalization during war, but China will not. I believe that leaders of both China and the US haven't foreseen that a Sino-US strategic alliance is inevitable. My advice for US leaders is this: the fifth generation of Chinese leaders will be completely different from the fourth generation. The fourth generation of leaders stayed at home under the influence of the Cultural Revolution, while the fifth generation will mainly stem from students studying in the US in the 1980s. My prediction is that the fifth generation of Chinese leaders will be wiser, more familiar with globalization, and friendlier towards the US. Therefore, US leaders must be more open to cooperating with China. Bush had no diplomatic experience. His diplomatic policy mainly came from diplomatic advisers and diplomatic legacies of the Republican Party. This limits US policy towards China to a Cold War mentality, firmly believing that China is a threat to the US. The reason that I'm optimistic about a Sino-US strategic alliance is that leaders of both China and the US will be updated. I can say that the change China is undergoing is the epitome of the change of the US in the last 125 years. In diplomatic policy, China is very similar to the US in early 20th century. China's space program is similar to that of the US in the 1960s. The prosperity of

China's stock market and large-scale expansion of infrastructure is basically similar to that of the US in the 1920s. In sports, China is very similar to the US in the 1950s. China's film industry reminds me of Hollywood in the 1930s. Some labor conflicts and farmer problems in China are also similar to the situation of American Federation of Labor in those years. Therefore, China is very similar to the US in the past 125 years in all aspects.

Barnett believed that threat of China should not be exaggerated. By 2020, the majority of the population of China will live in cities, which will be the largest population migration in human history. In fact, China has grown old before getting powerful and posing a threat to the US. Twenty percent of the population of China will be above 65 years old in 2036. It will take 60 years for the population of the US above 65 to increase from 10% to 20%, but it will only take 19 years in China. Aging will be the fastest in China in the next 30 years. In the next 30 years, China will be a potential challenger of the US. The hope or threat China brings to the world is larger than any country in history. Therefore, I hope that the US and China can establish strategic alliance, and strive to reach an agreement as soon as possible. With China becoming more and more confident, the cost of Sino-US strategic alliance will be increasingly higher.

Barnett pointed out that in regard to a Sino-US strategic alliance, we know well the price. The US first should cancel the promise to unconditionally safeguard Taiwan. Such a promise is very dangerous. It may allow Taipei to drag China and the US into war. It is extremely unwise to let Taiwan shape the future destiny of the US. Britain returned Hong Kong to China as early as in 1997. Many trade clauses of China come from Hong Kong. The change Hong Kong brings to mainland China is bigger than what the mainland brings to Hong Kong. It is very unwise for the US not to establish strategic alliance with China.

The reason that a Sino-US alliance is possible and even inevitable is that both China and the US are changing. According to Barnett, in the 20th century, the US observed the world from the following perspective. Americans believed that if a country was similar to the US politically, it was the friend of the US. The US was a democratic country, so was France. They were certainly friends. Similarly, Americans also believed that if the US and another were different in politics, they were enemies. Such a practice was feasible in the Cold War, as international politics was separate from international economics. But now there are some new ideas about friends and foes in American society. The new ideas mainly come from the generation following the baby boom, born in the 1980s, children of baby boomers after World War II. This is the generation with the largest population in American history, accounting for about 83 million Americans. They have grown up with the Internet and their concept of friendship is completely different from the last generation. Their idea about alliance is out of economic factors rather than political factors. The future ideal of Americans is that the best allies of the US are countries economically related to the US. In the current international community, China is more capitalist than the US. I predict that the Sino-US relation will be closer than that between the US and Japan. No matter how the Sino-US strategic alliance proposed by Thomas Barnett is supported in mainstream American society or feasible in reality, it is a pioneering voice from American society and a positive expression of ideological emancipation in American strategy.

## Washington's Thoughts on China

Before 1830, almost no books about East Asia had been published in the US and Canada. There were few even into the 1880s. Such publications increased in the US only from the 1890s. After the 1940s, publications about China in the US exceeded those in Europe. The outlook of Americans regarding China was actually that of Europeans for a very long time.

Four days after the Wuchang uprising in 1911, in an article titled "Ignorance of Americans and Oriental Chinese," an American sighed with emotion: China is a miraculously awakening country with one-fourth of the world population. It is absurd for nobody to be proficient in its language in the newsroom of American newspapers, or make contact with this country to get the firsthand knowledge and know the ideas of the people of this great nation, and only depend on relevant reports in publications in Shanghai and Hong Kong.

George Washington was astonished to learn in 1785 that the Chinese were not white. The US started to study China in 1902. In 1863 there were only three translators in eight US consulates in China. Strengthening communication between groups helps to resolve conflicts of civilization. Misunderstanding gives rise to enemies; exchange and understanding makes for friends. Americans need to have a correct Chinese outlook, and the Chinese need to have a correct American outlook. Cultivating statesmen knowing each other in China and the US makes for sound and friendly Sino-US relations.

## Enemies and Rivals

Enemies can keep a country vigilant and vibrant. When enemies disappear, without rivals and alarm, competition and challenge, enthusiasm tends to become slack, decline, and even perish. Such a phenomenon is not rare in history. Liu Zongyuan, a well-known litterateur and philosopher in the Tang Dynasty, wrote "The Law About Enemy," profoundly expounding on this point. Everybody knows that enemies are antagonistic, but everyone doesn't necessarily know that they are beneficial; everybody knows that enemies are harmful, but not necessarily that they are favorable.

The Qin State turned against the six states, thus it could be cautious and conscientious to make the state powerful and prosperous; after the six states were destroyed, the Qin State became conceited and soon perished. The army of the State of Jin defeated the State of Chu in Yanling County. Fan Wenzi, a senior official of the State of Jin, was worried. Turning a deaf ear to the Fan's suggestion of keeping watch, Duke Li of Jin got more overbearing, made the people boil with resentment, and finally was killed. Meng Sunsu, a senior official of the State of Lu, hated his counterpart Zang Sunhe. Zang was worried after Meng died; Zang condoled at Meng's home and cried sadly, saying that the hatred of Meng was good medicine for him, and he would die soon without medicine since Meng had died.

The wise men may be endangered, although they know this point; some people dismiss it nowadays! Enemies keep forces scared; otherwise they become highly conceited, stand down, and get complacent, which leads to greater disaster. Enemies can raise one's vigilance and avoid disaster; lack of enemies makes one slack to cause mistakes. The one that knows this will have good virtues and popularity. The one that can prevent diseases is able to live long; the one that boasts of strength tends to die from sudden illnesses; the one that indulges oneself and stands down is a fool. Those that can think about the arguments in "The Law About Enemy" can avoid mistakes and disasters.

The short essay "The Law About Enemy" is composed of 144 words, brilliantly expounding the relationship between opposites. The article points out that the existence of enemies is harmful, but in case of having strong alertness to the presence of the enemy, keeping alert and making efforts, the harm can be turned into good. Getting a swelled head after losing opposites will cause endless disasters. The author emphasizes awareness of unexpected developments.

"The Law About Enemy" of Liu Zongyuan reveals political dialectics. That is to say, with enemy states, remain vigilant at all times, but when enemy states disappear, don't forget to remain strong no matter whether there are enemies or not. "The Law About Enemy" of Liu Zongyuan is completely different from Americans' enemy addiction. The Americans' enemy addiction is a kind of pragmatism that deliberately and artificially makes enemies to stimulate themselves. It positions, treats, and uses countries that are not enemies as enemy states to serve its own political needs.

## A Great US Without Great Enemies

The US is a country that cannot develop without enemies, and cannot be great without great enemies. Therefore, looking for and creating great enemies becomes the primary strategic task for the US. Once there are no great enemies, the US will suffer from strategic panic and its enemy deficiency disease will be aggravated. Therefore, the US must target an enemy state in the world, and make it play a role in contributing to the greatness of the US as an "enemy."

During the Cold War, the global strategy of the US was centered on containing the Soviet Union. The collapse of the Soviet Union stripped the US of its strategic rival, while the strategy, thinking, and interests of hegemony of the US remained. The US needed to cohere internal forces, mobilize and control forces of allies, maintain momentum of arms expansion and war preparation, and protect interests of arms merchants by creating enemies. Therefore, the collapse of Soviet Union made Americans happy for a while, but soon they suffered from a deep sense of loss and melancholy for lacking enemies. The policies and works of the US lost direction in all aspects. The aggressiveness of elites dropped and the vitality of the US declined. The US had to find an enemy in the world as soon as possible. Terrorism became its enemy, but this failed to fill in the gap in Americans' strategic thinking. Americans felt that they must find a potential enemy state as a long-term potential enemy to maintain their power. The US, the largest power in the world, must have a rival power that can match it to meet America's strategic demand for enemies. But times are different. The US must change its traditional strategic thinking of "no enemy, no motive power."

A country must have awareness of unexpected development, but that is not necessarily artificially making enemies. A country must have alertness to the presence of the enemy and see its enemy, but the presence of the enemy must be real rather than imaginary, and the enemy must be objective rather than subjective. If the presence of the enemy is imaginary, and the enemy is not objective but designated according to subjective needs, the final consequence of such thinking and behavior of replacing objective enemies with subjective enemies, artificially creating enemies, and forcibly turning friends into enemies will be harm to oneself, others, and the world.

In international politics, there is an important relationship that should be figured out about the enemy, that is, the relationship between enemies of countries and enemies of times. Hegemonic power always lists countries and things inconsistent with interests of their hegemony as enemies, but the hegemony itself is an enemy of times and the world. Hegemony is unpopular in the world, and hegemonic powers are unpopular in the international community and antagonistic to global development.

In an era with peace, development, and cooperation as the mainstream, there is still a competitive relationship between countries, especially great powers, and thus there are rivals. There is no need for reticence of rivals. However, rivals are not equal to enemies, and strategic competitors are not equal to opponents and enemies.

The attitude of no great enemy meaning no great US may have been true in the past. However, this road to success of maintaining a great US with great enemies has come to an end. Continuing to take this road will lead to a lonely and declining US rather than a great US. The development of American history is at a turning point. The US should learn to build a great US without great enemies. This is a major and new subject in strategic innovation of the US.

## VII. The US Is Only Half Democratic

To dispel illusions about the US, we must know its nature. What is the US like? According to Americans, the US is a model democratic country in the world. This positioning is only half right. The US is not a complete democratic country, but a semi-democratic country, or half a democratic country.

## *Definition of a Democratic Country*

The substantive characteristic of a democratic country has two aspects: The first, democratic domestic policies without totalitarianism in domestic society, and the second, democratic international policies without hegemony in the international community. A truly democratic country is a country that has no monarch at home and no hegemony abroad. If a country is only democratic at home and hegemonic and autocratic in the world, it is at most half a democratic country. Therefore, Americans overrate themselves and evaluate themselves untruthfully by saying that they are a democratic country. The US is half a democratic country, which is a scientific positioning of its nature. To judge whether a country is democratic one needs to see whether it adopts democratic systems at home and in international diplomacy. In other words, only those countries that build a democratic country at home and a democratic world internationally are truly democratic countries.

## *"One Country, Two Systems"*

The US has been contradictory since its founding. Its prominent contradiction is "One Country, Two Systems"—represented by contradiction and conflict between slavery in the South and the capitalist system in the North from the founding until the American Civil War. This contradiction was solved by the American Civil War. From the end of World War II until today, "One Country, Two Systems" has been represented by contradiction between a democratic system at home and hegemonic system abroad.

"One Country, Two Systems" in the first stage lasted nearly a hundred years from its founding until the end of the American Civil War. The American Civil War defended the unity of the US, abolished slavery, and solved contradictions between the domestic democratic system and slavery. The predecessors of the bourgeoisie, driven by the huge profits of the slave trade, created a peculiar malformed slave plantation in half of the US. Dominated by industry and commerce, states in the North adopted a free, laissez-faire capitalist system, while states in the South, dominated by the agriculture industry, kept black slavery controlled by farmers. After independence, the US first established a confederation system and then a federal system, in which the bourgeoisie and slave owners of plantations jointly held power. This regime was a temporary coalition between two systems and forces. In the first census in 1790, one in every six Americans was a slave; and the ratio was 1:8 when the Civil War broke out. Jefferson had over 200 slaves in his plantation when he wrote the Declaration of Independence. When he proposed that all men are created equal, he may not have included black slaves, but equality and human rights would become ideological weapons for black slaves to strive for freedom and emancipation later. Washington let his slaves choose their own road when he died in 1799. Jefferson also gave the slaves freedom when he died in 1826. In 1860, there was a population of 9 million in the South, of which there were 4 million black slaves. Collision, contradiction, and conflict between the two social systems in the South and North led to the American Civil War. Marx once pointed out that the struggle between South and North was a struggle between two social systems: slavery and the free labor system. The two systems could not be at peace in North America.

American secession during the Civil War was caused by conflicts of the "One Nation, Two Systems" and the reason for the United States winning the war of national unity was that the Civil War emancipation of slaves was included in the goal of safeguarding national unity, which made the war more sacred. At the beginning of the war, the northern population was 21 million while the southern population was 9 million. On the morning of January 1, 1863, Lincoln signed the Emancipation Proclamation, giving tremendous moral values and strength to the Civil War. The war was both for national unity and human freedom and dignity. This proclamation created a new era in American history, and also shocked the world, so that any wavering European powers dared not to bear the unjust accusation to support the South. Millions of slaves became free men, and in the northern army, there were 210,000 black soldiers. Half a million slaves escaped from the plantations.

The second phase of the "One Nation, Two Systems" started when the United States became the world's hegemon after the victory of World War II, showing two faces: domestic democracy and foreign overlordship.

So, we can say that the United States has always implemented the "One Nation, Two Systems" dichotomy. Before the abolition of slavery, the United States was a country of semi-slavery, and semi-democracy. After World War II, the United States was a country of semi-democracy, and a semi-hegemonic system. The "One Nation, Two Systems" model with American characteristics determines that the United States only belongs to a "half-democratic country." The United States, in order to become a true democratic state, must solve the contradiction between internal democracy and international tyranny.

## The US is Semi-Democracy, Semi-Hegemon

On June 16, 1858, Lincoln, in his first speech for his Illinois senatorial campaign, pointed out that a split house is untenable. He believed that a government cannot forever remain half-slave and half-free. America in the 21st century cannot be internally democratic and externally hegemonic.

Today, it can be said that the split United States is also untenable. America cannot always keep a semi-democratic, semi-dominant state. The semi-democratic, semi-dominant state, promoting democracy internally and hegemony internationally, cannot continue. Changing from a country of semi-democracy, semi-slavery to a country dominated by democracy, America realized its first rebirth, and resolving the contradiction between the domestic democracy and international hegemony will be America's second rebirth. As democracy and slavery coexisted, the US was a semi-democratic county; as internal democracy and external hegemony coexist, the US is still a semi-democratic country. The United States can become a real democratic country only by achieving a second rebirth. Constructing a new United States and becoming a thoroughly democratic country, the United States must eradicate the two systems. First was slavery in domestic relations; second will be the hegemonic system in international relations. Obviously, this will be a revolution with far-reaching significance for both the United States and the world.

If the American War for Independence was the first revolution, a national revolution that overthrew the British colonial rule and fought for independence, and the Civil War was America's second revolution, a democratic revolution that maintained the federal unity and abolished the slavery, then the third revolution would be a diplomatic revolution that changes the foreign policy of American hegemony, a revolution that changes the United States from a hegemonic country into a non-hegemonic country.

Americans raised the banner of advancing democratization in the world, and international democracy and domestic democracy are two aspects in promoting democratization of the world. Realizing America's third revolution and the ensuing significant changes in US policy are important to promoting the democratization of the world.

Where there are competition and counterbalance, there will be democracy. America without counterbalance will be an imperious country. Democratic America must be counterbalanced by a democratic world. If a superpower exclusively dominates the global stage without constraints, international tyranny will appear. Only a multinational competition mechanism can form global democratic politics. Since the Cold War, America intensified hegemony, barbarization, and unilateralism, because it had no competitors. To prevent tyranny and corruption of the superpower and to prevent the evolution from powerfulness to power politics, we must create a situation with great powers taking part in benign international competition.

# CHAPTER 7

# THE REASON FOR MILITARY

# DEVELOPMENT

In the 21st century, China will rise and confront the threat of United States. China must have huge armies to guarantee that there will be no war between China and America. This is a safe investment in development and quite necessary for China. China must transfer part of its productive forces into combat and a portion of its wealth into military capabilities.

## I. Great Rejuvenation Calls for a Martial Spirit

For a century, from the autumn of 1894, when Sun Yat-sen founded the Revive China Society in Honolulu and proposed the slogan "Rejuvenating the Chinese Nation," to the end of 20th century, when leaders of the Communist Party of China set out to achieve the great rejuvenation of the Chinese nation, the Chinese nation has been on a journey of revitalization and rejuvenation. Now China is on the rise and rejuvenation is being achieved, but it still needs to make more efforts. To achieving the great rejuvenation of the Chinese nation, China must revive its martial spirit.

Martial spirit in different historical eras has different meanings. In the 21st century, Chinese martial spirit, in the process of a strong rise and great rejuvenation, is a kind of spirit that dares to risk its life for the survival of the nation—a kind of spirit that dares to strengthen armies for the great rejuvenation of the our country, and it is also a kind of spirit that dares to fight for peace and development.

## A Heroic China in the Han and Tang Dynasties

On June 23, 1924, Sun Yat-sen, in a conversation with the labor representatives of the Philippines, said, "Two thousand years ago, China was very strong, not just dominating the East, but also overawing the Europe." China dominated the East two thousand years ago, and the cornerstone of such domination was its martial spirit. The martial spirit of the Chinese nation, at different times, has different representatives and manifestations. In the era of its foundation and peak times, three heroes played iconic roles in the formation of the Chinese nation and the creation of the martial spirit culture.

The first figure was the first Qin Emperor. He concentrated long-term martial traditions from the Five Hegemons of the Spring and Autumn Period and Seven Powers in the Warring State Period, engulfed six countries in China's war for unification, and realized China's unification. As the first emperor that realized the unification of China by force, his successful practice of unification illustrated a truth: without martial spirit, China cannot realize unification. The first Qin Emperor's martial spirit is most conspicuous in his advocating of unification, that is, he advocated national unity to achieve world domination.

The second figure is Emperor Wu of the Han Dynasty. The national character of Emperor Wu was peace-loving as well as not afraid of war. In the aspects of the political, diplomatic, and military culture, Emperor Wu not only made peace with rulers of minority nationalities in border areas by marriage, but also upheld a warrior culture, and advocated defensive as well as offensive culture. If he was only peace-loving and did not dare to wage war, and if he only made peace by marriage with invaders of minority nationalities and relied on defense, then the result would have been defeat by the Xiongnu, and the Central Plains would have been enslaved. The success of Emperor Wu defeating the Xiongnu by force and eradicating national suffering proved a truth: without an offensive spirit, it would be difficult to fundamentally eliminate suffering for national survival, and it would also be difficult to make a country win strategic initiative for long-lasting national survival and stable development. The most prominent martial spirit for Emperor Wu was his offensive spirit and spirit of expedition. After the Song Dynasty, due to the lack of such offensive spirit and a spirit of the expedition, China suffered from invasions at its border. Ultimately, China moved toward failure and destruction in the endless debate between advocating peace and war, endless constraints and delays, passive compromises, too much patience, and helplessness.

The third figure is Li Shimin, Emperor Taizong of the Tang. The Tang Dynasty, in Chinese history, is known as the Great Tang. The greatness of Tang Dynasty was not only its large territory, large scale of the wealth, and large degree of openness to the world, but also its unrivaled power in the world. A host of lesser states paying tribute to China in the flourishing Tang Dynasty showed that Tang Dynasty's Kindness (soft power) and Deterrence (hard power) had reached a pinnacle level. The brilliance of the Great Tang in the history of China proves a truth: advocating martial spirit must advocate power, and a martial nation must be a nation advocating power, not just a nation advocating wealth. If a country only advocates wealth, and cannot combine richness with powerfulness, it will be more affluent, yet more insecure.

Emperor Qin's unification and the Han and Tang Dynasties' power and grandeur not only make great contributions to contemporary times but also remain a foundation for future generations. All flourishing ages in Chinese history are created with blades, and are built based on the martial spirit and strong military. Emperor Qin's overwhelming momentum in containing competitors and sweeping down six countries, Emperor Wu's boldness in taking on offensive and defensive roles and sending expeditions to Xiongnu, and Emperor Taizong of Tang Dynasty's generosity in creating a situation of a host of lesser states paying tribute to China with unrivaled military accomplishments all reflect the Chinese' precious fighting character. This is the martial spirit of the Chinese nation. Later generations, due to the weakening of the ancestral fighting character, were often beaten and humiliated. The variation of the Chinese fighting character led to a number of historical tragedies. Only since the Chinese Communist Party has entered Chinese history has the fighting character of Chinese nation flourished again.

We can say that the martial spirit of the Chinese nation is fully embodied in the national unity of Emperor Qin, the expedition and offensive spirit of the Emperor Wu, Emperor Taizong's spirit of furthering the country with military force, and Mao Zedong's spirit of saving and defending the country with just war.

A joke goes that China should change the Chinese totem from a dragon to a panda. The reason is that China's dragon is a monster full of aggressiveness and domineering in English. The existence of dragons in the world may make others feel threatened, worried, and anxious. The dragon represents ancient China, and now the panda should be the totem of a modern China, because the panda is docile and cute, without aggressiveness.

The panda represents auspiciousness but does not mean safety. As an endangered animal, the Chinese panda can grow and reproduce only with the special protection of the state. However, the security and the rise of a big country cannot be protected by anyone else. Martial spirit is a country's cultural and spiritual pillar and spine. The culture without weapons and martial spirit is just cultural fat and scraps. Achieving the great rejuvenation of the Chinese nation is to revive the martial spirit, and revive the domination of the Han and Tang Dynasties.

## A Weak China in the Song Dynasty

The Chinese nation advocated martial spirit and was good at fighting before the Tang Dynasty, but later generations became diluted and the martial spirit weakened. The word "gentlemen" having the meaning of "warrior" during the pre-Qin period became fully synonymous with "frail-looking scholar." Rulers mostly gave up the sword for the pen; the entire nation buried itself in the promotion of economy; the elite groups engaged in research of the classics, and devoted themselves to the Confucian books. Externally, they compromised, and advocating peace prevailed. Most of these groups were leading groups or mainstream groups. As a result, foreign enemies ravaged China's land, and their civilization and wealth became prey of the strong nations. In the anti-Japanese war period, Tan Kah Kee, an overseas patriotic Chinese leader, said to peace groups that the one who advocates peace before driving enemies out is a traitor. When Cai Yuanpei held the presidency of Peking University, he also particularly stressed to the students the need to foster a martial spirit to reverse the weak aspects in Chinese culture. The martial spirit of the Chinese nation weakened from the Song Dynasty. The weakening was embodied in five aspects.

**1.** Basic national policy of valuing literary talent above martial arts. The founding of the Song Dynasty was different from that of Han and Tang Dynasties. Through Military Mutiny at Chenqiao, and draped with the imperial yellow robe, Zhao Kuangyin implemented a national policy of valuing literary talent above martial arts against the wisdom of his advisors. The Song Dynasty followed the principle of "literati managing soldiers," and government respected and gave special treatment to civil officers and held disdain for military officers. In the Southern Song Dynasty, Liu Kezhuang's poem read: "the late emperor governs the country with the literati, and the most advisors stubbornly adhere to books." Even though the Song Dynasty was barely able to unify the Central Plains, it still did not create a country as powerful and prosperous as the Sui and Tang Dynasties. Without a large empire's style and magnanimity, it was always content in exercising sovereignty over a part of the country, and could not solve nor defend against foreign aggression—a sharp contrast between the strong and weak Song form.

**2.** Errors in strategic thinking. This was embodied in the unification policy of first south and then north and choosing Kaifeng as the capital. Upon the founding of the country, Zhao Kuangyin didn't continue to adopt the northern expedition policy of Emperor Shizong of the Later Zhou Dynasty. Instead, he took Zhao Pu's advice and made an important yet unwise decision: he changed the original expedition strategy, and adopted the combat plan of first south and then north. At that time, the southern states were relatively small and weak, while the Liao in the north was powerful. He chose the easier way. This was the wrong decision, and its military strength had already become a spent arrow after it pacified the southern states. The favorable strategic opportunity had already been missed. Therefore, the Song Dynasty lost the opportunity to unify the North, and its regime over only a part of the country had become a foregone conclusion. Song Taizu, after pacifying the south, started the northern expedition, but during his lifetime, three expeditions were fruitless. A politician should defeat enemies upon the founding of the country when both the morale and national prestige are highest. From beginning to end, the Song Dynasty can only exercise sovereignty over a part. The important fault in strategic decision-making was attempting to first deal with the south and then the north. What's more, geographically, choosing Kaifeng as the capital of the Song Dynasty was an inappropriate decision. At that time, cavalrymen could directly cross to the north shore of the Yellow River within three or four days. Kaifeng, located at the south bank of the Yellow River, was flat in terrain and had no steep place favorable for defense. The Song Dynasty chose Kaifeng as the capital just because the Five Dynasties chose Kaifeng as the capital, Kaifeng had convenient water transportation, and Chang'an and Luoyang were severely damaged in the war. But the pursuit of short-term interests and temporary comfort left hidden troubles.

3. Defects in strategic system. The outstanding reflection in the Song Dynasty was to strengthen the central forces and weaken the local ones and implement checks and balances. The Song Dynasty adopted a system of centralization of state power and weakening local institutions. Local counties had neither self-defense forces nor financial resources for construction. In terms of military service, soldiers were mainly recruited. The people who responded to the call for recruits were mostly vagrants, so soldier quality was bad. The better military strength was concentrated in the capital and called imperial guards. The inferior soldiers were distributed to localities and called the Xiang army; they had no fighting experience and they ate grains. Moreover, even the criminals were sent to the army as soldiers. The word in Chinese for banished comes from this. In this regard, many of these soldiers have been described in *Water Margin*. Song implemented the principle of decentralization and counterbalance, but excessive counterbalance became a constraint. The emperor, prime minister, and imperial censors were counterbalanced but actually not balanced, which led to political paralysis. The authority of the prime minister in the Song Dynasty was far less than that of the Tang Dynasty, who was not authorized to involve themselves in military politics. The right of military orders was managed by the Privy Council (similar to Imperial Army General Staff Office). Three ministries administrated finance (the Ministry of Revenue, the Ministry of Salt and Iron, and the Ministry of Statistics and Auditing), none of which were controlled by the prime minister. The imperial censor had great authority, and could criticize any problems. Kuangyin had a pledge, hidden in the Imperial Ancestral Temple: do not kill the ministers and imperial censors. Therefore, they were fearless and dared to provoke heated debate, which made it difficult for the government to make decisions. The Chinese saying "the Song had not yet made a decision when Jin soldiers had

already crossed the Yellow River" reflects this indecision's lasting cultural relevance.

**4.** Detaching military science from the military practice. Although Song was cumulatively weak and not prosperous and ultimately perished from foreign aggression, strangely, the Northern Song made amazing developments setting up military schools and issuing military books. Later, military schools were set up in various counties, and military teachers were sent to spread this knowledge. The emperor also ordered a revision of Master Sun's *Art of War* and six other military books as standard textbooks, which became the *Seven Military Classics* handed down for posterity. In the Northern Song Dynasty, literati discussing military affairs became a trend, and such trend still prevailed after moving the capital to the south. Unfortunately, the Song Dynasty had many talents adept at paper wars, but less talents adept at real fighting. Weak and ineffective, the Song still left more military books than any previous dynasty. On one hand, this showed signifies the invention of printing. In 1045, Bi Sheng invented movable type, which allowed military books of the Song to be handed down; on the other hand, it highlighted Song's issue: strong in military theory, poor in military practice.

**5.** The contrast between the number of troops and military quality. Song was a dynasty that was extremely rich in the world, but it was not a rich country with powerful military, instead, it was rich yet weak in military. Song's army was huge and bloated, large in quantity but poor in quality.

Within one hundred years, from Song Taizu to Emperor Renzong, the number of soldiers increased by more than six times. The main reasons were the high rate of escape of mercenary troops; large war consumption; freeloading of government structures; and recruiting famine refugees as soldiers, which made people use military service as a form of unemployment relief. Recruited soldiers would serve from 20 to 60 years old. In truth, most served for 20 years and freeloaded for the other 20 years. Xiang military could freeload until they died even though they had no fighting capacity. Among one million of soldiers, at last 400,000 were Xiang Army; among 600,000 imperial guards, one-third of them were the old and weak; removing skewed figures including soldiers incapable of battle, the effective soldiers employed were at most 300,000. Soldiers were arrogant and corrupt and it was said that the army employs people to hold the quilt in place as others sleep, and people who don't want to carry the distributed grains hire others for them, illustrating that the soldiers were pampered. Song's cost for maintaining armies accounted for five-sixths of the total revenue. These armies were absolutely bloated and weak. Thus, the Song was doomed to misfortune.

The weak Song made China pay a heavy price. Subsequently, Mongolians and Manchus successively conquered China and entered the Central Plains, a typical manifestation of such weakness. The weakening of the Chinese martial spirit became a force of habit, and the weakness in national character became the culture, so that those brave and fierce minorities, soon after entering the Central Plains, became complacent, eroded, and weathered.

## The Opium War and a Beaten China

On October 20, 1919, Sun Yat-sen, in the preface of the *Jing Wu Ben Ji*, said, "Our nation is a peace-loving country. Initially, I didn't encourage my compatriots with militaristic and fighting spirit; but in this highly competitive era, I have realized that we cannot survive if we don't seek self-defense. From the recent wars, I realize that the causes stem from the weakness of the country. If we are a peace-loving nation and also good at defense, then the law of the jungle will not exist in the world."

As Sun Yat-sen said, due to the weakening of the martial spirit of the Chinese nation, it would not survive in a highly competitive era. For more than 100 years from the Opium War in 1840, when Western countries invaded China, to the victory of the Anti-Japanese War, the lack of fighting skill was reflected thoroughly. During this period, China could not avoid fighting, but fighting was doomed to failure, and once it failed, China had to concede territory and pay indemnities. Western countries came and fought alone or collectively. China was faced with the crisis of being divided by Western powers as well as being swallowed by Japan. China, in the global jungle, was like a big fat sheep without any defense; as a result, it was chased and hunted by a group of tigers and wolfs.

A nation without martial spirit will be a nation that has no right to existence. Before the Opium War, some missionaries had already seen that the Chinese Empire was large yet powerless, weak and ineffective, and had become a non-martial nation, unskilled in battle. They advocated the use of force to open the Chinese portal; some people collected intelligence and participated in a war of aggression against China. Karl Gutzlaff was a typical figure in this movement. Gutzlaff was a Prussian, who was sent to the Far East by the Netherlands Missionary Society; later he separated from the society and became a free preacher in 1829. From 1831, he inspected China's southeast coast ten times, collecting a great deal of information. He found that the Qing government was weak in martial spirit, lax in defense, and lagging in weapons technology. He concluded, "If we come and attack it, the resistance of China will not last for half an hour."

Later, those who invaded China won victory after victory and tasted the sweetness of fighting; in summing up the experience, they even arrogantly declared, "The way to deal with the Chinese is to beat them first and then establish a dialogue." From the Opium War in 1840 to the founding of the New China in 1949, China suffered 470 foreign invasions. Within 65 years from 1840 to 1905, China was forced to sign more than 745 unequal treaties. The one who is good at self-defense can survive. Martial spirit is a spirit of existence and survival.

## A Fighting China in the 20th Century

On November 28, 1924, Sun Yat-sen, in a speech to the Kobe business, said: "For Europeans, we cannot influence them with righteousness. Making Europeans in Asia return the rights to us peacefully is just like asking a tiger for its skin. It will be impossible. We have to resort to force if we want to fully recover our rights." China in 20th century is a fighting China that resorted to force to recover its rights. Fighting China tested the truth of theory that political power, independence, security, peace, and development stem from the barrel of a gun.

National sovereignty is a country's right to existence. Fighting China in 20th century was first and foremost a fight for the salvation of the Chinese nation. The most critical war was the Anti-Japanese War. In the eight-year war, China made huge sacrifices including 35 million casualties and huge material losses; however, it won the first complete victory in the national liberation war against imperialist aggression in the 100 years after the Opium War.

The great practices of peace growing from the barrel of the gun in the 20th century were the Korean War and the Vietnam War against the United States. These two wars were confrontations and competitions between the New China and the United States, the world's most powerful imperialist country.

The New China was founded on fighting and defended by fighting. The Korean War was a demonstration of the sword of the newly founded China, which showed that China had the courage to stand up and face the leading power in the world, and it was also a wonderful show of the Chinese martial spirit. The Korean War was the first and only head-on military conflict between China and the United States in history. The number of US fighters in the war zone was 1.789 million, among which 36,574 people died and 103,284 people were injured. In this war, China successively enlisted 25 field armies, 16 artillery divisions, 10 railway corps divisions, and 12 air divisions for combat. Together with support staff and replacements, total numbers reached over 2 million. China, a nation bullied by world powers for 100 years, was able to break even with the Sixteen-Power Allied Forces organized by the strongest global powers in just three years, and created a military miracle.

On the eve of the end of the war, Zhou Enlai profoundly pointed out that the Korean War is of special significance after the Second World War among international events. "The Korean War is local, but its significance is global." The Korean War smashed the American myth of invincibility and showed the national and military prestige of the New China. Peng Dehuai said, "It eloquently proves that the era in which, for hundreds of years, Western invaders can occupy a country as long as they had a few cannons on the Eastern coast is gone." The US military and generals joining battle had acknowledged that the Korean War was a battle with maximum cost and bloodshed and it was protracted and difficult. Mark Clark, the commander general of the "United Nations forces" who signed the Korean Armistice Agreement, later wrote in his memoirs: "I got the unenviable distinction of being the first US Army commander to sign an armistice without victory." In the commentary of the Korean War, American scholars believed that in this war, China won: "the war was constrained to the peninsula, the North Korean regime had been rescued, and the nightmare of an American military threat existing in the Yalu River disappeared." The Korean War also made China a more mature and respected country. Later, the Korean War had a very, very deep impression on policymakers of the US and it also restricted the action of the United States in the Far East. From then on, the United States and China were no longer involved in a major war. After the Korean War, countries around the world looked at China with new eyes.

China's victory in the Korean War was a great deterrent to the United States in the later Vietnam War. Bruce Palmer, then commander of US forces in Vietnam, said: "American fears for the occurrence of war with red China more reliably protect North Vietnam against invasion than any other weapon used by Hanoi on the battlefield." The Korean War deterred the United States from a direct fight with China again.

The Vietnam War began in 1961; it was an important step for the United States in implementing a global strategy to contain China. Robert McNamara, US secretary of defense, in a speech in January 1965 bluntly said America's real goal "is not to help a friend, but to contain China." This war continued until 1975, with a decade of intense fighting in the 1960s. US troops invading Vietnam had reached a peak of 543,000. At that time, the US secretary of defense also made it clear that China was the main enemy of the United States.

The Vietnam War was another sad war for the United States. Maxwell Taylor once served as commander of US forces in the invasion of Vietnam; he admitted in reviewing the war that the costs paid by the United States in the Vietnam War were unexpected and hardly for public debate. He believed that in addition to heavy casualties and astronomical military spending, because of this war America suffered from domestic division and lost its ability to solve urgent domestic and external problems, and exposed its internal weakness to the world. For Americans, the Vietnam War was a nightmare, with frustrated and disillusioned hope. More than 58,000 Americans were killed in fighting, about 150,000 people were injured, hundreds were detained in the North Vietnamese POW camps, financial expenditures reached hundreds of billions of dollars, and almost 5,000 aircraft and helicopters worth more than $5 billion were destroyed. The Vietnam War brought trauma to almost every American. Thousands of American soldiers struggled in transitioning back to life in America. The Vietnam War caused huge human, material, and financial losses to the United States. The United States sent 1.2 million soldiers to Vietnam. Casualties reached more than 200,000, among which 58,015 people were killed and 150,303 people were injured; the US military's discipline and combat capacity were seriously weakened; the war cost $200 billion, which deepened the domestic social and political crisis, and damaged America's international image. Kissinger believed that for the United States, victory of the Vietnam War was meaningless, but failure was intolerable, so America had to be released from it.

Regardless of the outcome, our country's involvement in this war invariably equates to grief; we now only hope to keep a little face in ending the war.

## A Powerful China in the 21st Century

Zheng Bijian, a renowned expert, said, "in China's development and peaceful rise, what we pursue is never to become a military power striving for hegemony in the world; instead, we should build China into a big market country, a civilized country, and a responsible country that can play a constructive role in the international community." In fact, military power does not mean a country striving for hegemony. China should be a military power that can safeguard national security and world peace, and a powerful military power that can maintain and achieve national reunification. China cannot just become a market power and a civilized power without military power. Only by becoming a military power not striving for hegemony can China effectively maintain its security as a market power and have the dignity of a civilized country, and have the power and conditions to play a constructive role in the international community and become a responsible big country.

Deng Xiaoping pointed out that China is now a strength that maintains world peace and stability, not a destructive force; the more powerful China becomes, the more reliable world peace will be. The powerfulness of China is not only in the need for China's security and development, but also the need for the world peace. China does not seek hegemony now, and will not seek hegemony even as it becomes stronger in the future. China should insist on not seeking hegemony but still achieving power.

After the founding of the United States, a debate was conducted on whether a strong army should be established or not. Alexander Hamilton, the Federalist leader, said: "If we want to become a commercial nation, or to maintain safety in the Atlantic, we must make effort to set up a Navy as soon as possible." This debate reached an agreement after the second war between the United Kingdom and the United States. In the early days of the founding, the consistent understanding of US military strategy and national security strategy was to rapidly develop the economic and military strength of the US, and to build a powerful navy and army to protect the security and commercial interests of the United States. Meanwhile, it pursued a policy of isolationism in international affairs and kept a low profile. The United States still built a strong military force even though it pursued the policy of isolationism, and the United States still built a strong navy even though it wanted to be a commercial nation.

Russia now claims that it has developed a unique strategic missile system with the capacity of orbital transfer that could break through any missile defense system. Russia also planned to build five strategic nuclear submarines in 2015. It is said that Putin said that Russia "would build a new generation of nuclear submarines even if the Kremlin has to be sold." In the 21st century, the construction of "a powerful China" is not only to build

China into a "market power," but also to make China a "military power." If a country is only strong and large in the market, but weak and small on the battlefield, it will be the prey of strong powers.

## II. A Peaceful Rise Is Contingent on a Strong Military

China's development is a process of peaceful development; its rise is a peaceful rise; its unity is a peaceful reunification; its diplomacy is a peaceful diplomacy. In fact, a powerful military force and the rapid rise of the military is the cornerstone of attaining this peace.

### "If You Want Peace, Prepare for War"

Latin author Publius Flavius Vegetius Renatus famously said: "If you want peace, prepare for war." This sentence has been regarded as wisdom by Western realists in international relations for the entire modern era. This echoes the ancient Chinese book *The Methods of the Sima*, which says that although the world is safe now, forgetting war will be dangerous. By applying these sage words, contemporary Chinese believe that to realize a peaceful rise, the military must rise. To realize peace, prepare for war.

Peace has different historical forms. The international community in the 19th century had peace under the rule of the British Empire that on colonial conquest. Peace in the latter half of the 20th century saw the emergence of the US-Soviet Cold War, a cold peace under the threat of nuclear war. World peace after the Cold War has been a peace under American hegemony. The world in the 21st century needs peace with multipolar balance, and the China in 21st century needs a peace that can protect its development and rise. Such peace cannot be obtained relying on the friendliness of other powers, nor reliance on showing weakness and keeping a low profile. Such peace can only be gained through courage and strength.

In May 2004, in a discussion of China's peaceful development plan, organized in Beijing, someone suggested Chinese love peace and uphold a peaceful rise, but if some countries curb the rise of China with the use of force, what should we do? China will not attack other countries, but what should we do if countries attack us?

China's peaceful rise depends on other countries, and especially the peaceful treatment by the United States. But will the United States maintain peace while curbing China's peaceful rise? If the United States neither supports China's peaceful rise nor is satisfied with the peaceful curbing of China—if instead it curbs China's rise with military force, or even wages war to block China's peaceful rise—then China will be forced to defend its rights though war. China cannot stop rising just for the purpose of maintaining peace or the avoidance of war. Like the Taiwan issue, China adheres to peaceful reunification, but if Taiwanese independence forces, under the support of external forces, want to split the motherland, China will not give up reunification for the purpose of peace, nor will it tolerate division for the purpose of peace. If peaceful reunification cannot be realized, and only military force can curb division and achieve unification, it will be necessary and required to end the division with war and promote reunification through military action. Of course, even if China is forced to fight for its rise, it will be different from the rise of powers through expansion or hegemony in history.

## *Understanding Safety and Power*

Theodore Roosevelt said: "Without the backing of force, diplomacy is useless; diplomacy is the servant, not the master of the military." China naturally cannot completely agree with Theodore Roosevelt's passage. However, the role of armed forces for national security cannot be denied. Diplomatic play is wisdom, but is based on power; it becomes an art in the use of force that can play an effective role if applied properly. As a rising power, to ensure national security requires great wisdom, only great strength and great wisdom will bring China to the level of global leader.

In an interview with CCTV, political science professor John Mearsheimer at the University of Chicago said: "Any American knows that it is necessary to ensure that the United States is the world's most powerful nation to maximize the safety of the United States." "The best way to ensure the survival is to become the most powerful nation in the region and concurrently the most powerful in the world . . . China has not yet owned very strong military, the Chinese are still weak in that particular area.

"I think the great competition will be economic and military. In the economic role, it is important from two angles: the first is the military reasons and for security, a nation must have economic strength to establish a strong enough military to protect themselves. The second reason is that people need property and people want to live in a prosperous country, so it always has a very high value to win the market. Strong economic power is key for survival, but without a strong military force, there are big risks incurred. In the 19th and early 20th century, when China was a very weak country militarily, Europe and Japan invaded and dominated China. China has learned that not developing a strong military power to protect themselves is foolish. Military competition is never fully eliminated, and in the future, competition between China and the United States will appear as a competition for economic and military strength." "You have to defend yourself and the only way to protect yourself is to become powerful [. . .] the United States does not want to see a strong China. Likewise, if China became the most powerful country in the future, China will not want to see other countries rise."

Though the analysis by the American experts does not completely conform to China's realities, the classic American strategic concept is that only by becoming powerful can a country attain its safety; to be safe, the country must be powerful as in this analysis it is something China needs to learn.

## China Pursues a Peaceful Rise

China's peaceful rise is based on hundreds of battles. To realize a peaceful rise, China must first realize a military rise to a level at which no formidable state in the world will dare to contain China's rise with military force.

The biggest challenge and trial met by China in its rise comes from the hegemonic powers that intend to contain its rise through wars. Carl von Clausewitz once said that an absolute state of endurance would not include making war—that is, as long as there is a country adopting the attitude and policies of absolute endurance, there will be peace. However, China's peaceful rise will in no way be a rise of absolute endurance. The peaceful rise of China does not rule out the possibility of rising through wars fought against containment. When hegemonic powers intend to contain China's rise through war, China will have to maintain and defend itself with military force.

But why does China put a great deal of effort into realizing its military rise in order to realize a peaceful rise? This is because a peaceful rise requires efforts from both parties: if the US allows China to make a peaceful rise, it will refrain from containing China's rise through Cold War, or it could implement repression through military force and wars. In "There was never a Peaceful Rise on the Earth," an article published in the *Hong Kong Economic Journal* on July 9, 2004, the author claims that, at present, China is having a difficult time maintaining its sovereignty in foreign relations. Presently, China shall make maintaining sovereignty over Hong Kong and Taiwan one of its priorities and avoid other countries taking over these territories. In the mid-term, China shall improve its relations with neighboring countries and avoid being besieged by other countries. At this critical moment, this blockage will prevent China from getting the energy required to keep its infrastructure running. All the big powers in the world wish that they could attain a peaceful rise with not a single bullet, but there was never a peaceful rise in the world. The rise of the US and the process with which it has seized and maintains hegemony is a history of wars. In today's anarchic era, we all wish for peace, but hegemony is a reality, so basically we all have to arm ourselves. Take Japan, for instance. It is very rich, but as it depends on the US for military protection, it cannot really rise. The US has already made its rise, but it is still constantly increasing military spending to build up a military force for an absolute advantage. Merely for the sake of peace and the defense of the country, China still needs the atomic bomb, the heroic spirit it expressed in the Korean War, and a powerful military force. The analysis by this author is very insightful.

Indeed, there has never been a peaceful rise in the international community. But it does not mean that there could not possibly be a peaceful rise in the future. China is to set a precedent for a peaceful rise in the world, but this requires common efforts made by both China and the US, especially in terms of the civilization and open-mindedness of the US.

After the Cold War, the US tried to counterbalance Russia through the eastern expansion of NATO and deployed a strategic encirclement of China in Asia: in the East, it established a military alliance with Japan and South Korea, and used Taiwan to pin down China; in the southwest, it supported India to expand in the South Asian subcontinent; and in the South China Sea, it also acted aggressively to promote the formation of an alliance of states to deal with China. We can see that, for the sake of a peaceful rise, China must have a military rise. The stronger China's military force is, the greater the deterrence it will pose to the hegemony, and the more contributions it will make to the peaceful rise of China.

Peaceful development and peaceful rise have become the core state interests of China in the 21st century, and its right to promote development and realize a rise in state sovereignty must be defended. Any power that attempts to block and contain China's development and rise beyond the means of peaceful containment or imposes containment through military actions, China will have to defend itself by fighting against.

## China Will Not Simply Be an Economic Force

An economic rise not supported by a military rise is very dangerous, as it may turn a people into simply an economic people. Max Weber said that a nation has to transition from an economic people into a political people to become a mature populace. The clearest manifestation of economic people is that they are comfortable with seeing problems solely from the angle of economics, and they reduce their national targets to economic targets. The obvious problems with purely economic people are as follows: first, when working out economic or foreign policy, they forget the political mission of the state; second, they simply equate economic prosperity to the power of a country, but indeed, the affluence of a country does not equate to safety and security. A country should have the resolution and the capability to turn a part of its wealth into security capabilities.

Economic people are very dangerous, as they can turn the people of a country into economic animals and drive the nation into a rich but weak and perishing state. Niccolo Machiavelli believed that the building of an army is the basis for the establishment of a state, and strengthening military force is the foundation for the government of the world. He witnessed how the Italian states like Florida and Milan, though possessing vast wealth, could not resist foreign aggression and pacification of the interior states. He believed that the excessive economic prosperity and people's excessive stress for welfare are sufficient to diminish to social morality and leave the people with no fighting spirit; in that case, the decline of the country will be inevitable.

Holland learned painful lessons from becoming an economic people. In Europe, it was not superpowers that first accepted the military philosophy of Niccolo Machiavelli but the micro-nation Holland. The Netherlands was formerly a territory of Spain. It waged a war of independence in 1568, and formally gained independence in 1648 after a period of 80 years. At the time, Spain was a world power. To fight against such a strong power, the Netherlands resorted to an extraordinary approach to improve the fighting force. It underwent a military revolution, and thus became a pioneer of European military reform. This attracted widespread attention from European countries. The young people of Europe interested in studying military science flocked to Holland to receive a military education, and studying military science in Holland become a fad. We often see the economic value created by the rise of Holland, but neglect the fact that it was also a military rise.

The rise of Holland started from fighting for national independence, and the "business is the politics" approach of the Holland government. In order to promote maritime trade, Holland placed great importance on the building of military, and possessed a powerful navy. In the first war between Britain and Holland, Holland mobilized over 200 warships in each battle, which were furnished with 600–800 cannons and 200–300 sailors. In the second war between these two countries, the Holland navy once stormed into the Thames River and directly threatened London. In terms of maritime warfare, Holland not only bested the Spanish fleet in Slark, Dunkerque, and Dans, but also held out against the allied forces of Britain, France, Sweden, and Germany without a sign of weakness. It outperformed Spain and Portugal in fighting for overseas colonies because of its military advantages. Holland also enjoyed an advantage in military technology. For example, its shipbuilding technology, especially the erection of forts in the rear compartment, set an example for the other countries of Europe. Peter I envied the shipbuilding industry of Holland very much and traveled twice to Holland to study these technologies.

Holland was an accountant's office safeguarded by fleets; however, on April 11, 1713, the Dutch signed a peace treaty with France, Spain, Britain, and Sweden and brought an end to the War of Spanish Succession. This brought an end to the role of the great Dutch Republic. After serving as Europe's leading power for over a century, the Dutch Republic voluntarily backed out of the great powers' ranks. The armies of the Republic were disarmed, fleets were left to rot in the ports, and the generals and naval marshals retired to lead a quiet life and collect their pensions. The positions of generals were taken up by the diplomats, who used their vast wealth to buy peace. Seeking peace at all costs, even through some ignominious means, became the new state policy of the republic. Holland's failure to maintain its military force in the 18th century was no different from a suicidal act. The Dutch Republic that was once was overlord of the North Atlantic now had to recruit naval officials from other countries. The weak Dutch fleet constantly took home humiliating news, and Holland's merchants and fishermen on the Atlantic were captured and driven like cattle. In the constantly declining Holland of the 18th century, people were fixated on money and economic gain. Throwing away their bullets to make more room for coins, their purses ended up in the treasure boxes of pirates.

France learned the same lesson too. The French general André Beaufre pointed out in his book *1940: the Fall of France* that right up to the eve of the Second World War, France was a relatively stable economy, and the people led a rich and happy life, but the political unity at the time was very weak. When war broke out, the French people did not serve their country in unity like they did in 1914. Having no outstanding leaders, the whole country went to war unwittingly under a chaotic political atmosphere. The people were filled with weariness, and many chose to bear humiliation rather than struggle to win the war. Prior to the war, a German writer made a vitriolic remark about this: "France is a standard dying people. It has no goal or value. Its people have lost their tradition, honor, and spirit. We should let it run its own course, without paying it any attention." The quick crumple of France in 1940 proved this to be true.

The American people have the world's leading entrepreneurial spirit and wealth, but they are not an economic people. Joseph Nye, a professor at the John F. Kennedy School of Government at Harvard University, said that a military force is very important: "I believe that the US's military bases are the center of its national strength. In the US, not all the highly educated talent works in profitable industries and fields. According to surveys, only 19% of the managerial class in the business sector has obtained a master's degree or above, while 88% of the officers at the brigadier rank have the master degree. The US, the big economic power, is truly a country that centers its national strength in its military position. The rise of China requires the building of both a rich country and a powerful military force. It shall grow into a big economic power and a strong military power, and shall never become an economic people with no spine, having the weight but not strength."

## III. There Is No War Between China and America, but There Must Be an Army in China

In the 21st century, China's army plays a crucial role in deterring war between China and America. This army is not big in size, but high in quality. China's military rise is not to beat the United States, but to not be defeated by the United States. China's military rise is not a threat to the United States forces, but rather it removes the threat posed by them. This is characteristic of China's military rise, namely the Chinese characteristic of self-defense and peace.

### There Is No War Between China and America

Why is there no war between China and America? This is primarily because the United States and China are not only large, intertwined countries, but also powerful countries with nuclear power. It will be these two countries' strategic competition that ends the trend of war between the powers. This marks an age of peace and development as a theme of our times.

As to the process of the age of great powers without great war, the United States strategy, according to Thomas Banite, is that long before the Cuban Missile Crisis, most experts believed that neither side could win a nuclear war, so the strategic confrontation between United States and the Soviet Union is far more stable than most people would imagine. After this close call, Defense Secretary Robert McNamara strode forward, promoting the concept of mutually assured destruction as a permanent cornerstone of the strategic nuclear program's status in the United States. No weapon has ever been created that was not used. To a world that had just seen nuclear weapons dropped on Hiroshima and Nagasaki, this seemed incredible. However, when multiple sides have nuclear capabilities, this concept rings true. Nuclear weapons not only constrain superpowers, they essentially terminate war between major powers. To an extent, power means the possession of nuclear weapons. Since the United States put forth the concept of mutually assured destruction, there have been no genuine nuclear weapon crises. Since the United States invented nuclear weapons in 1945, there has been no war between the two powers—this is not by chance. When we recognize and successfully export this rule to other countries, the threat of global war in human history will have come to an end.

Nuclear weapons were not being used, but were meant to ensure the demise of the Soviet Union after the first launch of nuclear weapons. We maintain conditions of a war without winners—this is the existing condition of the Cold War. Despite some people demonizing McNamara for his involvement in the Vietnam War, he left an unacknowledged legacy of ensured global peace. Of course, only the United States knowing and believing in the concept of mutually assured destruction is not enough; the Soviet Union must also accept the idea. The United States took years to educate Soviets, and Soviets eventually graduated in 1972. At the Moscow Summit between Nixon and Brezhnev, they signed the first Strategic Arms Limitation Treaty. This summit and the two following summits between these leaders greatly reduced the threat of global nuclear war and made the rules of competition somewhat fixed.

As a new view of military and war, great powers without great war has formed a consensus amongst strategic theorists and politicians in the West since the late 20th century. Through the Korean War, Americans began to study the concept of limited war. In East Asia, Americans were deeply frustrated with the costly, long-term, and vague war. Americans were accustomed to full-scale war until victories through unconditional surrender in the 20th century. In the Korean War, the United States faced conflicts of enormous political pressure from European allies rather than on the Asian continent, thus strictly limiting the scale of military operations. The United States did not use nuclear weapons. The United States did not allow Taiwan's Chiang Kai-shek army to be involved in this war. Supporters of limited war were against the notion that there is no substitute for victory in war held by

Douglas MacArthur. They believed that in the upcoming era, nuclear war must be ruled out and the purpose of war must be strictly limited, even if the result is a deadlock in the fight. British strategic thinker Lidehate pointed out, "We must guard against two of the most common delusions: seeking victory above all and that war cannot be restricted." Lidehate said in 1960 that the old concepts and old definitions of the strategy of the development of nuclear weapons is not only obsolete, but also pointless. To fight a war for the sole purpose of gaining victory is rather crazy." The forward of the 1961 edition of the book pointed out a blind spot of Clausewitz: he never recognizes the true purpose of war is peace, not victory. The fundamental ideal of policy is peace, and war is only used when attempting to achieve this ideal as a means. Eisenhower said several times at a press conference, especially in the age of nuclear weapons during the Cold War era, "Not taking account of the costs of victory would mean disaster." During the Cold War era, with the condition of nuclear weapons, fundamental changes had taken place. Victory was no longer the goal above all else; the price of victory was considered above all else. Any power can afford the initial costs of nuclear war between powers, but none can afford the costs of victory. This fundamentally determines an era without great war amongst great powers

Sino-American relations have a different set of characteristics than any other modern rivalries involving America. Different from Germany and Japan, the United States has not started a world war in the process of rising. The only big war it launched was the Cold War, The Cold War in the second half of the 20th century was a much more civilized and rational war than the two world wars in the first half of 20th century, and came at a much lower cost. When the Soviet Union developed nuclear weapons, although some argued for an immediate preventive attack, the United States government did not take action. When the Soviet Union had the ability to directly attack the United States, from the late 1950s to the early 1970s, MAD (mutual assured destruction) became the mainstream mentality in the United States. America merely attempted to deter attacks by threat of retaliation. The United States had ample opportunity to thwart the Soviet nuclear program, but flexed its civility and rational views instead.

There is no war between China and American; furthermore, Chinese personality and characteristics color this relationship to a large extent. China is a country that has no national strategic offensive agenda in thousands of years of history. It is a country that not only has not attempted to expand overseas, but also paid great attention to defense solely on land. Now the popular demand of China's rise is great. China repeatedly declares that it does not aim to dominate and that it will take a road of peaceful development—it calls for building a harmonious world. Moreover, in terms of ideology and social systems, China will not engage in expansion. Why does China sometimes call its system socialism with Chinese characteristics? The Chinese characteristics contains a profound meaning of peace—it does not popularize and promote its own patterns to the world as a commonmode, and does not engage in active cultural export. The United States and the Soviet Union both promoted their own social models as the global model to shape the world, which made contradictions and conflicts sharp. In short, when the United States and the Soviet Union were competing for supremacy in the world, confronting each other on issues from geopolitics to ideology, there was only Cold War. In the future, the United States and China, will both attempt defensive roles and not contend for hegemony but rather compete in strategy with each other. The United States will be subject to the limitations of its extant Cold War mentality. However, Sino-US relations in the 21st century could never replicate the Cold War relationship between the United States and the Soviet Union in the 20th century. The strategic competition between the United States and China in the 21st century is the competition of the post–Cold War era; the ways of Cold War competition are now outdated.

In the 21st century, there will be no war between China and the United States, because this is the trend of the times. The world is walking a path of civilization, and this is an era of strategic competition of superpowers. Europe, as the cradle of two world wars, has become a model for cooperation of great powers and is working toward integration and unity. With the trend of superpower competition becoming more civilized, the mode of China and the United States competition in the 21st century can be observed, and the fact is that neither country is pushing them toward war. Moreover, China and the United States compete with each other in terms of status, but they also have many common interests in terms of development and prosperity. In this case, even though the US will attempt to curb China, it is aware of the mutual benefits that come from cooperation. If the curbing is done exceedingly and malignantly, it will hurt China and could be detrimental to the United States.

## China Must Have an Army in the 21st Century

A Chinese army ensures there will be no US aggression. A Chinese army will not launch wars; it is actually the fundamental guarantee for preventing wars. A country needs checks and balances of political power, so that the nation can become a democracy. International society likewise needs checks and balances to be able to form a democratic world. In order to maintain peace in the world, military force helps to provide these checks and balances. The United States and the Soviet Union's arms race objectively formed a military balance. While these nations incurred the cost of an arms race, they avoided the catastrophe of a war. An arms race is not desirable, but the military checks and balances require it. China is required to have a strong army for world military balance. China's strength will be conducive to the rise of China's security and world military balance, and can help the United States maintain balance as well.

To answer US threats, China must have force. After the Cold War, the powerful United States did not slow down its pace of military development. The United States actually adopted a new military revolution to continue to boost military power. The US military revolution was actually aimed at China. United States strategic scientists Tuomasi and Banite said that after the Bush administration took office, Asia was considered a serious threat to the future of the world—and it was not looking at Southeast Asia, and certainly not Central Asia. What they are pushing ahead with the whole defense reforms is a rising competitor in the East, rather than the existing threats in the Middle East. Tuomasi and Banite also said that upon the dawn of a new century, not everyone has the same feelings in this industry. In fact, the Pentagon's entire strategic plan focus is preparation for a war with China in the distant future. We are employing many Chinese experts. We have racked our brains to reorganize our military deployment in Asia to counter China's rising influence. Both the Pentagon and Wall Street have brought China into their field of vision, but what they are considering is wedged into the different types of power in the region. The Pentagon dreams of launching long distance war with China, and pressing the button will be able to solve the problem of war. Wall Street is then affected by war anxiety in terms of long-term foreign direct investment with China. Faced with this strategic situation, the Chinese cannot, of course, just stare into the eyes of their competitor; it must also build a force in order to protects its interests.

The Chinese are a nation of great wisdom, and that is one of the important reasons why war will not happen between the US and China in the 21st century. But Chinese wisdom is a long-standing justification for abuse; it is assumed that this great wisdom means the complete avoidance of great force. In China, battles won without having been fought is a grand strategy and the highest wisdom. But subduing an army without a fight depends not only on grand wisdom and strategy but also on great force. Subduing an army without a fight is the basis and premise of the result of China's long-standing wisdom. "Without a fight" does not mean that military force does not play a role. Intelligence is the art of using force; this wisdom without force is only a castle in the sky and has no practical value. The stratagem of an empty city fooling the enemy is successful because Zhuge Liang had an army and power, and the enemy believed this force was hiding in the city. Therefore, the role of the stratagem of the empty city can be played mainly depending on force. The stratagem of the empty city could be copied for a while, but it is unable to be copied for long; it can be used once, but difficult to repeat twice. Western strategists often described the US Army as a powerful force, and the Chinese army as a strategic army, which is one-sided, because China has had unavoidable difficulties in recent historical periods. In the 21st century, to achieve Sino-US peace, China must display great wisdom and great power.

The military capabilities of China cannot remain in a weak state. The rise of China's military will fundamentally change a fundamental struggle of modern China in which it has always had to accept that it was weaker than its peers. In the 21st century, China will have riches and a strong army to protect itself. China in the 21st century will continue to promote its non-aggressive tradition while at the same time striving to build power and achieve balance. Building a strong army and bidding farewell to its inferiority is the inevitable result of China's military rise.

Today, disputes in international affairs should be resolved through peaceful means; but in international relations, the military power of a county is an effective backup force. In international relations, military force should always be an invisible hand. War is only one form of how troops play a role in their nation. Peace is the lasting embodiment of military values. Building and maintaining a large army is an indispensable security investment, development investment, and growth investment for China. China must channel part of its productive forces and part of its wealth into military capabilities.

The Chinese army's fundamental purpose is to effectively prevent and avoid war. Bonade Buluodi is recognized as the pioneer of deterrence theory. In the United States for months after the nuclear attacks on Hiroshima and Nagasaki, he passed on the thinking of a new international reality and concluded: "so far, the army's main objective has always been to win the war; from now on, the army's primary purpose must be to avert war." This idea, for a strategic and comprehensive nuclear war, is correct. He referred to bombs as an absolute weapon, arguing that any war involving the atomic bomb would be humanity's worst disaster and should be avoided at all costs. In this sense, we can conclude that building an army to avoid war is an important strategy for China's military. The fundamental objective of China's strong military is not to win the war (in the sense of world war between major powers), but to prevent war, to avoid war.

## Mutually Assured Destruction and Common Existence

China must have the ability to destroy the United States' ability in order to ensure consistency, coexistence, common security, and common development. New China's peace has always been a peace under the threat of nuclear weapons. During the Cold War, the United States repeatedly threatened to use nuclear weapons against China. After the outbreak of the Korean War in 1950, President Harry Truman declared the United States has been actively considering the use of the atomic bomb in China. In 1958, the United States military called on Congress to approve a nuclear attack on China to defend Quemoy and Matsu. In 1963, the United States learned that China had conducted a nuclear test, and planned to attack Chinese nuclear facilities. In 1994, the United States Department of Defense submitted to the president and Congress new nuclear policy proposals. China was listed as a future nuclear target. China's peace in the 21st century remains a peace under the threat of nuclear weapons.

For the United States and the Soviet Union in the Cold War, one of the most critical factors was that both nations had the ability to obliterate each other—this mutually assured destruction capability ensured the coexistence of these two countries. For the 21st century in China, with the United States in strategic competition, if China is unable to threaten the US, it would be difficult to get a decent, just peace; it would be difficult to enjoy dignified joint rights of survival and development.

National security has levels and there are differences in relative safety and absolute security. If the two rival powers have the ability to destroy each other, either would not dare to fight the other and both sides would be relatively safe. If there's a power imbalance, the strong side is absolutely safe, while the weak side is never safe. Nuclear capabilities allow for absolute safety—it is a relatively safe coexistence based on mutually assured destruction capabilities. The United States is currently in pursuit of absolute security, which is a unilateral security. The United States has developed missile defense systems as an attempt to engineer absolute safety. China is now only relatively safe; China's strong military engineering is a relatively effective project that aims to rival the United States so that it can enjoy common rights of survival and development.

The United States pursues security goals, general national security, and also tries to maintain its hegemony. The United States pursues security capabilities to allow it to be unrivaled. After the end of the Cold War, the US halted the development of its Star Wars program. In the late 1990s, it resumed preparation of a space defense program, renamed the national missile defense plan (NMD). In 2001, the Bush administration took office; despite strong international opposition, in the case that no one could compete with its powerful military, economic, scientific, and technological strength, the US moved forward with the deployment of the national missile defense system in space. This marked a graded separation between the United States and competitors in terms of military technology. A United States military scientist said that the United States NMD was deployed to cope with a nuclear-armed China. This claim, although exaggerated, holds truth of the US acknowledgment of China's rise.

US nuclear development, on the one hand, is the development of practical, operational, and tactical nuclear weapons. They are both psychological and physical deterrents to war. On the other hand it is an absolute protectorate. That is, through both a national and theater missile defense system, the United States is absolutely safe from nuclear missile attacks. The United States absolutely equates security to absolute global insecurity. World peace and security lie solely in American hands, which is tantamount to nuclear arms being stripped from all others.

Powers under the condition of nuclear war are held hostage by each other. China's chief strategic group expert, Bai Wangang, has said: "A major gap exists in Sino-US nuclear forces. China could not actually rival America, and only has minimum nuclear capabilities. US strategy regarding China will never truly consider China as its opponent or as a threat to its national interests as long as China does not have the capacity to destroy the United States, Only a small part of China's nuclear deterrence can pose a threat to United States, which is far from sufficient and could be undermined. So no matter how much progress is made in the cause of China's modernization, including the ability to win local wars under high-tech conditions, as long as the United States has a clear advantage in nuclear weapons, China's strategic initiative is in the United States' hands. Furthermore, as long as China's national security strategy and military strategy lacks the capability to maintain balanced power with the United States hegemonic power and the strong nuclear force, the national security of China will always be threatened. China's ongoing modernization is likely to be interrupted by force. The right to survival of the Chinese nation is not always guaranteed."

Bai Wangang's analysis is very insightful. The material basis of the Cold War was nuclear weapons. The nuclear balance between the United States and the Soviet Union was actually the fundamental guarantee of world peace (although it is a cold peace) in the Cold War era. Future peace, especially peace between the major powers in the world, still relies on the balance of military force, including nuclear weapons. China's military rise in the 21st century cannot and should not need equal nuclear force to the United States and cannot partake in a full-on nuclear arms race, but China must have the power to maintain mutually assured destruction with the United States. This is the strategy for China's national security, until Obama's nuclear-free world becomes a reality.

## China's Military Is Strictly Defensive

In the foreseeable future, the military of China cannot and will not surpass the United States, but China's military must ensure that it can defend itself against the United States at a minimum. Simply put, deterring the United States from attacking China is the military rise of China's strategic criteria. Because China's military goal is not victory over the United States, but only to ensure that the Chinese armed forces will not be subdued by the United States, there is not a real threat for the US. This is characteristic of China's military rise, namely China's characteristic defense, peaceful military rise, limits, necessity, importance, and urgency. There is no need for an arms race, because the goal and meaning of an arms race is to achieve strategic superiority in military strength, and the ultimate goal is defeating the enemy, not coexisting. Of course, if at some point in the 21st century, China becomes a peaceful, leading military power in the world, it will not be a bad thing, nor will it pose a threat to the United States. A leading role for China would only enhance world peace, just as Deng Xiaoping said; China is a force for maintaining peace in the world. China's martial spirit is not a threat to civilization; it is a force of justice and only a threat to thieves and criminals.

For China's military rise, there should be a powerful military force able to effectively maintain and achieve national unity, and control and crack down on separatist forces. It must be an effective force in the Taiwan Strait to counter US military intervention, which would deter the United States from supporting Taiwanese independence with force. The goal of China's military rise is to make the United States unable to afford to contain China. With this military rise, China will be able to prosper without being peacefully contained by the US, and will also be able to contain the US. China's military strength has to be more powerful than any rivals in the world to the degree and level that no nation can contain China's rise.

Doug Bandow, a senior researcher at the Cato Institute in the United States, said in an article published in the *Global Times* that the future of the 21st century depends largely on the relationship between the United States and China. United States policymakers' biggest worry is not China's economic development, but military forces. The Pentagon issues a report on China's military spending every year. However, no matter how dazzling China's national parade of 8,000 soldiers and 151 aircraft is, Beijing's military power is still far less than United States'. The United States ground army is the world's most powerful military force; they have better training, better weapons, and more military power than China's forces. Washington's nuclear arsenal is bigger and more advanced than China's. The United States' air forces are unbeatable. United States has 11 battle-class aircraft carrier groups while China has none. United States spending in 2009 was about $700 billion, seven times that of China. If war spending is subtracted, the United States military is still five times that of China's. Even if China accelerated the pace of its military modernization and the US remained stagnant, it would take decades of years to reach the United States military level. Therefore, it is nonsense that China poses a threat to the US's security. The real problem is the US's ability to attack China. Former Pentagon official Chasi Fuliman once said, "China has no intention of war with the United States on American territory, but we have drafted plans to combat China in Chinese territory." Nowadays, China is developing military forces that could stop a United States attack. Beijing need not be able to defeat the United States, nor reach US military forces. China just needs to build enough forces to prevent Washington from using its superior military power in China. In some US circles, it is outlandish that China could have a modern aircraft carrier. Military posturing in the Pacific Ocean is changing not because China might one day have aircraft carriers, but because the United States is planning how to deal with China's aircraft carriers and other conventional military forces. To prevent US intervention, China is now developing enough nuclear power to counterbalance Washington's nuclear pressure; it is also developing missile systems and submarines to counter the United States' Pacific carrier fleets. China is also developing satellites to counter the United States vast electronic monitoring systems. Once more, China's military development is not meant to fight against the United States, but to not be attached and dependent on the United States. The US is very clear in wanting to know the objective of China's strong military.

## It Is Nonsense to Revel in a China Threat Theory

In nature, animals with offensive capability are relatively safe. Although the animals with defensive capabilities often have no aggressive capabilities, but they still have a level of security. Even in the absence of offensive and defensive capabilities, animals can survive by eluding predators. As a rising great power, China is threatened by other countries without the necessary deterrent forces.

China has never threatened other countries in its history. However, along with the rise and development of China, hegemons are bound to be a deterrent, but this is not necessarily a bad thing. It is the promotion of democracy in the world that enables positive factors to restrict hegemony. In a democratic country, to halt power-hungry approaches, a balance of power is needed; this is likewise the case in a democratic world.

China's deterrent forces are the power and majesty that it must have. A country with no deterrent is not a dignified country. The rise and development of China needs not only to dispel the China threat theory, but also to intensify the construction of China's deterrent forces, and not only to strengthen itself, but also to express its will and determination. This will send a strong message to countries that are against China's national interests, especially those that covet China's core interests.

Might, deterrence, and dealing with threats are three different concepts. Might is the strength of a nation and an army. Deterrence is the psychological effect incurred by the existence of military power and influence. Dealing with threats is how the country copes with deliberately malicious aggression. In the forest, the sheep is tender and does not threaten any animals. Sheep are never a deterrent to any animals. Predators of the forest are a kind of savage beast that threaten the security of the forest. Elephants, on the other hand, are mighty beasts. The elephant is a mighty, powerful deterrent force and never threatens other animal species. China is a country that has the powerful deterrence and does not threaten other countries. China has not been a sheep in the international community since the Opium War. China has never been like the tigers and wolves that threaten small countries and hegemonic countries in the international community. China is just like the mighty elephant. Weaker animals do not feel threatened, while savage animals are deterred from attacking her.

What kind of military force China should build should be based on China's security needs, the needs of American hegemony. When China's strategic nuclear weapons can break through any missile defense system and have counterattack capacity; when China's powerful naval carriers can ride in the wind and waves in the ocean; when China's air forces and army have powerful strategic maneuvering capacity, remote delivery capacity, and fast assault capacity—then the military relationship between China and United States will be more stable and world peace will be more guaranteed.

## IV. Strong Countries Need to the Strengthen Their Armed Forces

The great rejuvenation of the Chinese nation must go hand in hand with a rich and powerful army. In order to achieve this goal, China must dare to strengthen its military force, not just its economy.

## China's Military Force Should Rank Alongside Its Economy

As for a strong military, there must be standards and goals. China's strong military standards and objectives in the new century are to build a modernized military force in accordance to China's international status, which will safeguard China's national security and development interests, respond effectively to crises, maintain peace, deter war, win wars, and realize the reunification of the motherland. China's military forces need to ensure that Taiwan cannot divide from China; the United States and other countries cannot interfere in a Taiwan Strait military conflict; and the United States cannot attempt to stop the rise and development of China.

Military development in China cannot be an arms race with developed countries, but must actively promote military reform with Chinese characteristics, make efforts to seize strategic initiative in international competition, and build a world-class military power. There is a belief that the development of China's military forces and defense modernization need to further clarify the objectives that the goal is not to catch up with the United States. China does not need to construct military forces like the United States. Primarily, security is not needed. China's military strength and national defense modernization should not set Russia's military power as the goal or role model. There is no particular interest for China. Therefore, there is no need to establish the same scale of military force.

If China's military growth with Chinese characteristics is unable to catch up with the United States and Russia, China will be a third-rate military power at the world level. Setting such a limit for China's military is a poor goal. "Rich country, strong army" is China's future direction. China's richness is more ancient than Russia's, but it still needs to catch up with the world's most developed and richest countries. China's strong military cannot be too far behind and must catch up with the world's most powerful nations. China must build first-class armies with the world-class military power.

## China's Power Shall Have No Ceiling

The right to be powerful is a kind of national sovereignty that shall have no ceiling. No country shall set a ceiling for China's power. If the US, with a population of only 300 million people, can be the leader in the world, why does China, with its population of 1.3 billion, have to be under the US in terms of military force? Why should only the US enjoy such a position? Why is there no cries of America threat to accompany the cries of a "China threat" when the military spending of China is only a tenth that of the US?

There shall be no ceiling to the power of China because the power does not necessarily mean hegemony and a powerful country can either be a hegemonic power or a non-hegemonic power. A strong hegemonic power will harm world peace while a powerful non-hegemonic country will do good for world peace. Power does not equal hegemony.

There is a belief that China's military force shall not aim to overtake the US and Russia, because China is not a superpower like the US, and it does not seek hegemony, and nor is it a country that has the capability or desire to protect its security interests all over the world. China does not have such a capability at present and even when it grows powerful in the future, it will not extend its military force to every corner of the world like the US does.

The building of a military force in China shall not repeat the path of confrontation between the US and the Soviet Union or the confrontation between the East and the West from the Cold War. On the contrary, it shall prevent and counter the same patterns from happening again. The solution to China's issue in proving that it will never seek hegemony or behave in a hegemonic manner is not that China shall be forever weaker than the US and Russia in terms of military force, but that China shall apply its powerful military force in defending its legitimate national interests, maintaining world peace, and promoting common development. It is strange to think that China does not seek hegemony, expansion, or have the desire to match the offensive capabilities of the US and Russia in terms of military force.

The fundamental measure of a big power's army is not if this army is an international force, but which kind of force it is—an aggressive one or a peaceful one. A regional military force may seek regional hegemony and invade other sovereign countries, while global military force does not necessarily mean expansion of forces, nor a force seeking to take over the world. Even if China's military force catches up with those of Russia and the US in the future, it does not mean that China is a hegemonic country. A hegemonic country must be a powerful country, but a powerful country does not have to become a hegemonic country. "Powerful but not hegemonic" is the intrinsic trait of China's military force.

It is because China does not have the capacity to protect its safety and development interests in the global scope that China has to vigorously develop its own military force. China will grow into a power that does not seek world domination, contains global hegemony, and maintains world peace. This will also require China to catch up with the US. In the future, China will not have to station its military forces all over the world like the US does now, but it must have the strategic capacity to effectively protect its national interests and maintain world peace and common development at the global level.

## China Shall Not Limit Its Own Military Development

Some people once came up with the idea of limiting our own military force development to address foreign powers' cries of a China threat. This idea is as follows: "as long as we disarm ourselves of nuclear arms, the US will not dare to attack us, because in that case, the whole world will jointly send a punitive expedition against it, and the American people will stand up to overthrow its government." Others advocate that China should show its goodwill to the US by cutting military spending and whittling the military force. In fact, this policy of exchanging disarmament for safety and security is inadvisable.

The determination of China's military force development shall not be based on other countries' feelings toward China's threat, but rather China's own feeling of being threated. There is not a single country in this world that will take the international community's assessment and feelings toward its military force as a hindrance to development. Instead they decide targets on the basis of national interests and conditions. China shall, in particular, not take Western countries' anxieties and doubts about China as the basis for its military development goals.

To break the Western countries' containment of China's development of a strong army, China must strengthen its voice in terms of military matters and intent. The goal of China in developing military forces, catching up with the state-of-the-art military forces of the world, and building a first-class military force is not to threaten other people but to ensure necessary deterrence of aggression and containment. The powerful military force of socialist China will impose just deterrence on the power politics, hegemonic behaviors, and the strategic attempts to split and contain China or even to invade China by external forces, which is required for China's safety, unity, and peaceful development as well as the world's peace and common prosperity.

## A Powerful Army Boosts a Rich Country

A powerful military can boost an already wealthy country. The key to this relation is how to combine these two things. The root cause of the Soviet Union's failure in the arms race against the US did not lie in participating in the race but in taking the wrong approach to it. Its separated civil-military mechanism under the planned economy system confronting the US's civil-military integration mechanism under a market economy resulted in Russia's fatigue and the US's further prosperity. After the Cold War ended, the US continued to spend money on its military and maintain high economic growth. The key to the US's success is civil-military integration and mutual promotion. After World Wwar II, the US launched a large military program that drove the development of its civil industry. This included the atomic bomb project in the first ten years, the Apollo moon landing project in the second ten years, the space shuttle project in the third ten years, the Star Wars project in the fourth ten years, the "information superhighway project" in the fifth ten years, and most recently its missile defense project. The Apollo moon landing project drove the development of aerospace business, costing $24 billion and creating an output of $2 trillion—an economic benefit of one hundred fold.

The "two bombs and one satellite" and "Shengzhou V and VII" projects of China drove the development of high-tech industries and attained very good effect. The manned space flight project of China cost RMB 18 billion, and by now has created an industrial gain of over RMB 100 billion. China must free its mind concerning participation in military competition. China used to have to choose between cannons and butter, but now under the new national defense model, China can have both at the same time. China used to say "build a rich country and then a powerful army," stressing the sequential order of realizing both things, but now China insists on the unification of both goals. A powerful army can not only effectively push but also strongly drive the building of a rich country.

## China Cannot Engage in an Arms Race

At present there are over 40 countries engaging in military reform in the world, forming a new round of military competition on the international military stage. The military spending of the US is about $700 billion, over one-half of the world's military spending. For an army, there are only two periods. The first is the period is permeated with the smoke of potential war, and the second is the period of competition and the flame of war. The so-called peaceful period is only the period in which preparation for war is made from the angle of military, that is, military competition. When the world's military reform takes on an accelerated momentum, the US is always leading it, and Russia also achieves remarkable military reform by greatly speeding up its pace of military building.

China is presented with a strategic opportunity to build both a rich country and a strong army. We can say that the building of national defenses and military has the best strategic opportunity since the establishment of the state. Since the New China has been established, China has witnessed three different stages concerning the relations of building a rich country and a strong army: In the 20 years after the establishment of new China, it faced serious military threats from hostile forces. In order to safeguard its independence and sovereignty, though it had a very poor economic basis, it had to input a great deal into military building. In this period, China was forced to build a strong army while sacrificing other development. In the second stage—nearly 20 years after the reform and opening up—for the sake of national economic building, China implemented an endurance policy, and built a rich country on the basis of long-term endurance in the building of national defenses and military. In this period, building a rich country was accelerated, but the progress of building a powerful army lagged far behind, resulting in a standstill of China's army and seriously backward weaponry. The gaps between modernized world powers widened. In the third stage, the new stage since 2000, on the basis of the high-speed development of national economy and great enhancement of the comprehensive national strength, China has returned to developing its military while also further growing its economy and comprehensive national strength.

We can say that since the establishment of New China, China has mostly attempted to build a powerful army on the basis of a poor country. The Western countries say that China tightened its belt to build national defenses, and made an atomic bomb even when it had no money to buy trousers. Now China has finally got the conditions to build a strong army while also building a rich country under the basis of its sustained high-speed development of the national economy. In the new stage of scientific development of national defenses and army building, China must seize the strategic opportunity to build a strong army.

# CHAPTER 8

# A CALL FOR THE COMING

# COLLAPSE OF CHINA

The national anthem of New China was written when the Chinese people were at their most vulnerable time. The idea of being prepared for unexpected development is expressed in the most thrilling words of the anthem: "The Chinese people have arrived at their most dangerous time." At this most dangerous time, facing the possibility of national subjugation and genocide, the people needed to save their own country from subjugation and ensure survival. An even more dangerous time comes when a nation grows day by day and meets successive victories, at which time the dangers are often ignored. The China of the 21st century has a bright future in rising to be a great power, but on the other hand, it also has the possibility to decline as a power and faces the serious danger of collapsing. The spirit of the national anthem warns us to be aware of the risks inherent in rising as a big power.

## I. The Thin Line Between Rising and Declining

Nothing is so certain as the unexpected. There is never a formidably wide gap between the rise and fall of a nation. The numerous cases in both China and abroad from the ancient times to present give us deep insight into this.

## *The Fate of a Nation Can Change in One Night*

On July 14, 1789, the Parisians conquered the Bastille castle, and the French Revolution began. On the evening of that day, a duke responsible for managing the clothes for King Louis XVI told him about everything happening in Paris. The king asked with surprise, "Is this a riot?" "No, your majesty, this is a revolution," answered the duke. The king wrote two words in his diary: "Nothing happened." This is a classic case of a king's lack of preparation for unexpected developments.

George Kennan, the American diplomat who came up with the "containment" theory for the Cold War, pointed out in his article "The Sources of Soviet Conduct" that if anything were ever to occur to disrupt the unity and efficacy of the Soviet party as a political instrument, Soviet Russia might be changed overnight from one of the strongest to one of the weakest and most pitiable societies. The collapse of the powerful Soviet Union indeed ultimately occurred in one night.

## *China Will Become an Increasing Threat*

On September 24, 1956, Mao Zedong said that "it may take 50 to 100 years' time for China to become a rich and strong country" and "what China will look like depends on how it develops. China may err and become corrupted." "China may make the error of corruption, bureaucratize, it might become chauvinist, arrogant, and so on." "At present, the Chinese people are very humble, and are glad to learn from other people [. . .] But we shall prevent such mistakes from happening in the future, which will be a risk in 10 or 20 years, and even more so 40 or 50 years later." He said this in his talk with the delegation of the Socialist Federal Republic of Yugoslavia while attending the Eighth National Congress of the Chinese Communist Party. This was a warning given to the Chinese people by the founding father Mao Zedong after New China was first established. China is now in this period that he spoke of.

## *A Developed Economy Has Many Problems*

On September 16, 1993, in a talk with his brother Deng Ken, Deng Xiaoping said: "How could a population of 1.2 billion people get rich? How should the wealth be distributed? It's even harder to solve these problems than it was to develop in the first place. We have to prevent the polarization of the rich and the poor. In fact, the problem of the polarization will occur spontaneously, and we have to solve this problem with all kinds of means, methods, and schemes. Despite the capabilities of the Chinese people, there will be increasing problems of increasing complicity. New problems may occur at any time. For example, as a minority of people acquires a large portion of wealth and a majority of people have nothing, sooner or later, the unjust distribution will cause serious polarization, and this problem will be highlighted at a certain time and have to be solved. We used to say that we should get the economy developed. Now it seems there will be even more problems when the economy is developed."

China is developing, but China's problems are also developing. While China is rising, the conflicts of China are also rising. In the 30 years after the Opening Up and Reform of China, the building of socialism with Chinese characteristics has made great achievements. However, if the problems of polarization and corruption are not solved, socialism with Chinese characteristics is very likely to transform into capitalism with Chinese characteristics through peaceful evolution. In recent years, Mr. Wu Jinglian repeatedly stressed the importance of preventing China from stepping on the path of crony market economies—that is, crony capitalism. This is a manifestation of the political conscience of an economist concerned with his country and people.

## China Can Only Rise After Overcoming Its Decline

Tang Dynasty poet Du Mu summed up the lessons learned from the demise of the six states existing before the First Emperor of Qin established the Qin Dynasty, as well as the failures of the Qin Dynasty, in his writing *The Ode to Epang Palace*, and pointed out that it is not Qin that unified the six states, but the six states themselves; it was not the whole people that destroyed the Qin but Qin itself. He believed that the root cause for the destruction of the six states and Qin was not external factors, but internal factors. In our time, the two big powers, the US and Russia, had a Cold War that lasted half a century. America cannot extricate itself from the collapse of the Soviet Union, but the root causes for the failure of the Soviet Union were internal factors.

A country, no matter how developed it is, is always a contradictory force that unifies opposites, consisting of both flourishing factors and declining factors. To realize a rise, a country must first overcome its own decline. Amid the rising of China, there are still some factors that may cause its decline. The rapidly increasing social wealth is the material basis for the rise of China. But the growing gap between the rich and the poor is a factor that will cause a decline. The Chinese Communist Party started by solving the allocation of wealth, arousing tens of millions of people with its policy of overthrowing the local tyrants and division of lands, and finally becoming the party in power. In the 21st century, China once again is faced with a wealth distribution problem. The CCP has the full capacity to turn China from an impoverished country into a rich and just country. According to experts, Japan's crime rate is the lowest among the Western countries. There was no polarization in Japanese society since World War II, and it gradually eliminated the difference between the rural and urban areas. Most Japanese people think that Japan is an equal, non-hierarchical, and homogeneous society. Japan has established a rather equal salary system, which narrows the gap between management and ordinary employees in a company, and collects pretty low income taxes from farmers, self-employed, and the medium and small private enterprises. Only 3 in 10 of Japan's yen are reallocated. The wealth distribution system of Japan allows it to have a beautiful rise at good times and maintain in times of decline.

While boosting rapid economic development, the socialist market economy also causes corruption to extend and develop, which is a factor that causes a country to decline. China could never make a rise without a fight against corruption, but if the fight is not proper, it will also affect the rise of China. China once conducted utopian socialism in economic building, but took a detour in the Great Leap Forward. China will not attempt utopian democracy in the political building or be trapped in the pit of a great democratic myth. It will set out on democratic road with Chinese characteristics, adapting to the realities and rules of China, and effectively curb corruption's damages to the rise of China.

The factors that cause China to decline are developing along with factors that cause China to rise. The problems of getting old before getting rich, spending beyond means, and fast consumption of resources have attracted serious attention. The Chinese people control their own destiny. The realization of China's rise will not be impaired by the Westernization and policy implemented by the US, but by its own corruption and rigidity. Only by overcoming these factors causing decline can China really realize a great rejuvenation.

## II. China Needs to Be More Vigilant than Ever

In regards to China's achievements, the Chinese people feel accomplished, the American people feel anxious, and the whole world's people are often surprised. The development of China has become a world wonder. The rise of China will continue to write a new legend of the century. At the moment, China is singing a song of triumph for the rejuvenation of the Chinese people; humility, reasonableness, and calmness are especially precious at this juncture. The awareness of unexpected development of a great people can be reflected by their alertness.

### America's Demise

According to experts, preaching of America's decline started in the 1950s and has never faded out to. Such preaching has reached eight peaks, which are respectively after the Korean War, after the man-made satellite of the Soviet Union was successfully launched, after the Vietnam War, after the economic stagnation in the 1970s, after expansion of the Soviet Union and the rise of Japan, after the Cold War, after the 9/11 attacks, and after the financial crisis.

It was the American people who came up with theory of America's decline. For example, in the 1960s and 1970s, when the US was deeply engulfed in the Vietnam War, calls of

America's decline went way up. A representative of such an argument is Samuel Huntington, a professor of Harvard University, and Arnold Toynbee, the famous British historian. Mr. Huntington predicted that the US would meet its decline in 2000. In 1987, after Paul Kennedy's masterpiece *The Rise and Fall of the Great Powers*, the theory of America's decline once again gained support. Every time the US runs into a periodic crisis in internal and foreign matters, there will be a debate on whether the US has begun its decline. In the 21st century, the famous American scholar Immanuel Wallerstein once again stirred another round of prophecy about America's decline; his masterpiece *The Decline of American Power* called 9/11 a landmark of the US's decline.

The US has maintained its supremacy for over 60 years. After almost every frenzy, the US has supposedly undergone a change, transformation, or enhancement. Such preaching has become the alarm bell and trumpet for the American people. The US goes into decline as indicated by such preaching, but ultimately these prophecies bring motivation, coercion, new excitement, and enthusiasm to the American people. This is a reflection of the American people's awareness of unexpected development and their art of applying such awareness.

## *The Sinking of Japan*

In the 1970s, when Japan shocked the world with its soaring economy, the film *Sinking of Japan* became a hit in Japan. Though it was just a sci-fi disaster film, the Japanese people's awareness of being prepared for danger in times of safety and China's intoxication in peace formed a powerful contrast. What the Chinese people are prepared for is not the future rise but unexpected decline, for perhaps in 20 years, the likeliness of decline will be higher. While it is not easy to rein in its rise, it will be even harder to deal with a decline. A lack of preparation will leave China unprepared and throw the whole country into severe crisis.

Xue Yong, a Chinese scholar studying in the US, pointed out that it's not easy for Japan to attain a stately decline. In the 1970s and 1980s, it had become an undisputable fact that Japan's economy had risen and would exceed that of the US. *The Rise and Fall of the Great Powers* and *Japan as Number One* and other similar titles became bestsellers in the US. Paul Kennedy, a historian at Yale University predicted that what the US would face is not whether it would go into decline but how to make a stately decline, as the British Empire did. In the 1980s, the per capita income of Japan exceeded that of the US, and later scooped up American assets with a strong Japanese yen in such a way that rumors circulated in the media that Japan was buying America. But in the 1990s, Japan's economy stopped growing and even showed negative growth, and the Japanese people's living standards dropped under that of the American people. But Japan handled the decline well. Despite the economic recession, the society is still in a rich and stable state and stays in order. The real challenge facing China right now is not how to realize a rise but whether it can decline in a stately manner like Japan did in the Heisei Recession. Japan is one of the wealthiest societies in Asia, and most of its citizens have the skills and resources required to participate in competition under a market economy. With such competition, Japan has formed an especially innovative society, which can achieve a well-regulated decline. With the wide gap between the rich and the poor in China, a lack of well-trained citizens, and lagging innovation, China will be in a very unfavorable position in the future. This lack of innovation, high added value, and protection, once decline begins, will face severe challenges in maintaining basic social order. Xue Yong also said that from now on, China shall make preparation for a stately decline.

Chinese leaders have repeatedly demanded that the Chinese people enhance their awareness of unplanned developments. Being prepared for danger in times of safety and for decline in times of prosperity is a cultural tradition of the Chinese people. The viewpoint of Xue Yong is consistent with the national tradition and the national leaders' scientific development thinking.

Japanese people made the cry of a "sinking of Japan" when their economy was bullish and the rise of the country was at its climax. This was the Japanese people's warning and it reflected strong sensitivity toward danger. The so-called preparation for danger is the American people's preparation for decline and the Japanese people's preparation for sinking.

## China Lacks Preparation for Its Collapse

Beginning in the 1990s, the West's focus on China mainly had four aspects: the rise of China, coming collapse of China, China's threat, and China's responsibilities. Among these four aspects, the Chinese people like to hear about the rise of China and do not like to hear about the coming collapse. The thinking is that this argument is not simply a smear of China, but a curse. How could the rising great China collapse? In fact, among the four aspects, the theory of coming collapse holds the biggest value for China. As in the so-called awareness of unexpected development, what the Chinese people worry most about is collapse. When we say dealing with issues before they occur is important, this means China should deal with the issue of collapse. Only with such full preparation can China truly get prepared for any conditions that might occur.

In August 2009, America's *Foreign Policy* magazine named the ten most dangerous countries and areas in the world, and listed the US and China respectively in the first and second position. The reason for such a ranking is that the stronger a country is, the more danger it will trigger. The US was listed as the most dangerous country because there is no a country stronger than the US, and at this time, this means the error or inaction of the US will also do the biggest harm; America's economic missteps may send the world into economic crisis. People will ask: which one does more harm to humanity, terrorist atrocities or Wall Street atrocities? Let's not go into the question of whether it is reasonable to list China as the second most dangerous country in the world. Some experts have different opinions about this. But the American people's listing of the US as the most dangerous country undoubtedly shows an American awareness of unexpected development, which merits attention.

China is in a period of strategic opportunity, and has the greatest opportunities and risks in the world. What decides a country's fate is usually its own weakest links. The American people often preach about the American decline to prevent the real decline; during the rise of the Chinese people, listening to the cries about the coming collapse of China will help to prevent the collapse and achieve the rise.

## No Nightmares, No Sweet Dreams

The *Global Times* on February 12, 2009, published an article titled "The Human Being Can Not Live Without Nightmares." According to the report of a British newspaper *The Sun* on February 10, 2009, a study showed that human being's nightmares could be the memories passed down from ancestors, and they can warn us to be alert to dangers from time to time. A study by Finland researcher Andy Lifonso shows that three-fourths of dreams human beings have are nightmares. He believes that these dreams are the experiences of our ancestors, passed down to us through genes. These dreams can help people to address a dangerous living environment. Though we are afraid of nightmares, nightmares help to get us prepared for tomorrow. Therefore, we should thank those frightening dreams; they are good for us in the end. Without these dreams, humans may not have survived till now.

The ancient Chinese classic *The Book of Changes* says that the superior man, when resting in safety, does not forget that danger may come. When in a state of security he does not forget the possibility of ruin. When all is orderly, he does not forget that disorder may come. This is a demonstration of the Chinese people's awareness of unexpected development.

Sima Xiangru said that smart people can see things that have not happened, and wise men prevent dangers before they emerge. This is the ancient Chinese people's foresight and sagacity in addressing dangers.

For a China that is realizing the great rejuvenation, in the strategic opportunities of rise, it's very important to not forget the prospect of decline in times of prosperity. A people without dreams has no future, but it is very hard for a people that has only sweet dreams to be sober. The nightmare of the decline of the American people is well known, for their American dreams keep them enjoying the position of world leader, and will help them keep a sober mind. The Chinese dream shall consist of sweet Chinese dreams and Chinese nightmares. The nightmares of coming collapse of China will prevent the Chinese people from growing too intoxicated in prosperity and help them achieve the sweet dreams of China's rise.

## How Many Negative Ways Does China Lead the World?

Issue No. 10 of the *People's Liberation Army Daily* in 2009 reprinted an article titled "Look at Our 'World No. 1' with Cold Detachment," written by Le Peng. The article points out that China has achieved a lot of global superlatives in its long history, and with its soaring economy it tops the charts in many ways. However, China holds the number-one spot for a number of negative reasons as well.

The number of corrupt officials in China is probably the highest in the world. Though there is no precise data, this prediction seems accurate to many. The amount of bureaucracy in China tops the charts. The number of civil servants, 40 million, equates to the population of a small country. The administrative costs of China are also the world's highest. In recent decades, the fiscal revenue has increased 28 times, while administrative costs have expanded from less than RMB 5 billion to nearly 1 trillion, nearly 200-fold.

Public spending in China is definitely a world high. According to statistics of the State Information Center, in 2004, RMB 370 billion of public funds was spent in recreational activities, RMB 398.6 billion in the purchase of government vehicles, and RMB 240 billion in outbound tourism. The total of these three items have exceeded over 1 trillion yuan, accounting for 40% of the year's fiscal revenue. The number of accidents and deaths in China is also the world's highest. China is also the world's leader in fraud and producing knock-offs. China shall maintain its leading position in the world in good aspects, but it should also increase its output and production capacity. And in addition, China shall face these bad aspects directly and set out to solve these problems. Only after solving the bad aspects can China fully achieve the position of world leader.

## III. The Elite Crisis Is the Most Deadly Crisis

Among the many crises that might cause the decline and collapse of a country and its people, the most dangerous is the elite crisis, and the most deadly is the political elite crisis. Only with the rise of elites can China realize the rise to power. However, a degraded elite group would not be able to lead and support the rise of a big power. This is a lesson we learned from the rise and fall of the Soviet Union.

A key to the rise of a big power is the rise of elites. Elites are a country's core competitiveness. Arnold Toynbee said that the growth of a civilization relies on the creative minority. These elites must have both the ability to successfully address the challenges they meet in society and the strength to unite the non-creative majority to their side. Henry Kissinger pointed out that during the development of the US, President Woodrow Wilson played a very special role. The appearance of President Wilson was a turning point in the history of the US, and is one of the cases in which a rare leader completely changed the historical direction of a country.

The rise and fall of big powers has a lot to do with the rise and fall of elites. In the 18th century, great people seemed to fade away from Holland. In this period, you cannot find one man of extraordinary capacity in the realm of international politics in Holland. After producing outstanding generals and politicians for five generations, the House of Orange-Nassau's lineage became extinct and its title and rank and honor were succeeded by the collateral Stadholder of Friesland Province. But these two princes that should have played their parts in the 18th century. William IV and William V had very mediocre abilities and second-rate qualities. Though they had very good intentions, they did not have the strength, courage, and the enterprising spirit of their ancestors. The long list of great statesmen seemed to suddenly break here. Their positions were replaced by politicians—some of them smart but shameless, and others just shameless; there was not one politician that seemed to see a larger picture than their hometowns. In 1814, a very small amphibious troop stormed the capital of US. When one squadron passed the cemetery of George Washington, it fired a courtesy 21-gun salute. This is the effect of a legendary elite class: it gains the respect of even the enemy.

In the study of the history concerning the rise of great powers, the statesmen, as the elites that lead and command other elites, play a special strategic role. A people without great statesmen cannot rise up. All the great powers have their great statesmen. Their design and establishment of the country, their wisdom, capabilities, struggles and sacrifices, and connection and contact with the public enable them to stand in the vanguard of the era and at the strategic helm to guide and boost the country and its people toward prosperity. The rise of the Soviet Union is inseparable from Lenin and Stalin. The rise of China is also closely related to the great leaders such as Sun Yat-sen, Mao Zedong, Deng Xiaoping, and Jiang Zemin.

## The Political Elite Must Be Talented

For a large Socialist Party and large country, knowledge structure, thought and theory, political level, and the ability of party and senior national cadres to rule the country and the party are directly related to fate of the party and future of the country. An important reason for the collapse of the Soviet Communist Party was a mediocre elite class and the degraded capability of party leaders. Watts Boldin, who served as assistant to Gorbachev, argued in *The Rise and Fall of Gorbachev* that it is unbelievable that one important reason is degradation of cultural enrichment from its leaders.[7] Lenin was a theorist with outstanding ability, a strategist and tactician in politics, a passionate orator, and a person who had high cultural enrichment. His successor Stalin was a not-so-excellent and accomplished political leader, and despite Stalin not being a great orator, he was still knowledgeable and had very good theoretical training and strong organizational skills. After the death of Stalin, Khrushchev was promoted. While he was very talented, he was weaker in theory, ideology, and

cultural enrichment. I have seen Stalin's handwritten letters, articles, resolutions, and mod-
ifications, his corrections on documents were very accurate, we can see that he was a keen
political activist and master of rhetoric, his endorsements in hundreds of books indicated
that he read a lot of things, and he not only understood the writings of Marxist scholars,
but also writings of those philosophers, economists, and historians against him. I have seen
Khrushchev's instructions, and unfortunately they gave an impression that he was less lit-
erate and engaged in other works. Indeed, it should be admitted that something he dictated
to a stenographer was very interesting, the words were very vivid, but many parts were not
suitable for publication; I have modified his stenographic transcripts for publication in the
newspapers, it is really a very grueling job. Brezhnev came to power, but he did not change
people's impression on party and state leaders due to low cultural accomplishments. He had
not written anything; his comrades, members, and probably the whole community knew
this was the case. Because he was tolerant at last and sincerely hoped that the people could
gain happiness from socialism, people forgave him in many aspects. Andropov came to
power, bringing a bright light across a dark sky, he was very talented and highly educated
and full of knowledge, but the time he served as general secretary was too short, and it
was difficult for him to make conclusions. Chernenko, who succeeded him could neither
show his own merits nor contribute to the party's cultural makeup. Finally, Gorbachev was
elected, he was undoubtedly a learned man and had two diplomas at least, his culture was
broader than Brezhnev's and Chernenko's, but like almost all representatives of the first
generation of intellectuals, he was a successor of the traditional rural lifestyle with various
advantages and disadvantages. Reform and New Thinking was his highest achievement in
theory written by him—there may be something else, even though I know he never wrote
anything personally from start to finish. Of course, the cultural quality of several general
secretaries was degraded because the overall level of the party's supreme body was not so
high that Gorbachev was fully in line with the level of leadership, even though many people
were more talented, more principled, more enterprising, and of course more sincere than
the new general secretary. There were undoubtedly social elites amongst the Members of
the Political Bureau and the leaders' community of the party, but unfortunately, they had
not become mature. Maintaining the ruling status of the Communist Party requires strong
political advantages, and also strong talent advantages; without talent advantages, it is difficult to maintain political advantages.

## The Political Elite Cannot Become a Privileged Class of Interests

Soviet cadres rose out of the masses and became a special interest group. The Soviet
Union began to show signs of specialized adverse cadres in the 1930s. Then the approach
was applied in which they paid additional wages to leadership, from a few hundred to several thousand rubles more, depending on the level of the post, issued in secret in an envelope.

In 1935, in response to an invitation to visit Moscow, French progressive writer Romain wrote: "Soviet dignitaries lived a privileged upper class life, even Gorky also (although he rarely touches his food) wasted a lot of food, enough for many families. They unknowingly lived like feudal lords yet did not feel any enjoyment." In 1976, Brezhnev's 70th birthday created a gift-sending climax; the head of the Republic of Azerbaijan sent a gold bust of Brezhnev to him. Gorbachev's corruption outdid his predecessor; he spent 850 million rubles to build his villa in Foros (located on the Crimean peninsula's south coast). Brezhnev's villa was very luxurious, but compared with Gorbachev's Foros house, it was just a broken shed.

During the Soviet upheaval, some scholars conducted a social survey with the title of representatives of the Soviet Communist Party. The results reported that the CPSU accounted for 7% of the total workforce in the country; social workers accounted for 4% of that workforce; bureaucratic cadres accounted for 11%; and party government workers accounted for 85%.

Since the CCP took on the ruling position, it has stuck together with the masses to a greater extent. In the 1950s, learning lessons from the affairs of Poland and Austria, Liu Shaoqi pointed out that a serious problem with the Eastern European countries was that they deviated from the masses; he warned that if China was not careful, a new noble class could emerge in the country. China must prevent the emergence of such a noble class. He believed this would be the most serious test faced by China's ruling party. Mao agreed with Liu's idea: if we are not careful, and don't live a hard life like many of our comrades, we will be thrown off.

## Reform Is More Difficult than Revolution

The political elite shall realize the transformation from a revolutionary to a reformer. To rejuvenate China, two kinds of statesmen are needed: revolutionary statesmen and reformers. Basically all the so-called great statesmen fall into these two categories. Revolutionaries are always trying to accumulate division while the reformers must strive to disperse and eliminate division. Revolutionaries push for the ossified politics, while the reformers advocate flexibility and adaptability; revolutionaries must divide the various social forces into two parts, and the reformers must learn to rein them all in. Therefore, the reformers must have greater political skills than the revolutionaries.

In fact, another important difference between revolutionaries and reformers is that revolutionaries are the motive force of revolution but never the target of revolution; reformers are both the motive and target of reform. This is because the reformer is trying to solve internal problems. The reformer changes his own rights and interests and limits special interest groups.

Socialist reformers have to stand the test of the socialist market economy. The market's test of reform is severer than the battlefield's test of revolutionaries. In wartime, most leaders set an example and take the lead in fighting, and are not afraid of death. But nowadays it is hard to promote even a system as simple as the declaration and disclosure of government officials' property. According to a survey, 97% of the officials are against the disclosure of private property, and some provincial officials asked the question: why do civilians need not disclose their properties? More than twenty years have passed since senior government officials started to discuss the possibility of promoting a property disclosure system in November 1987. So far, China's government official's property declaration system is still in its pilot stage. Implementing such a system is the most effective and cheapest corruption fighting method, and is often referred to as the sunshine act. From President Obama, to the Russian president and premier, all the top officials have to declare their property. Chinese officials will go through this procedure as this is required by the advancement of the CCP and global trends.

## IV. Ensuring the Long-Term Safety and Security of China

Three conflicts might impede the rise of China. Innovation must be made to address the conflicts.

**1. Conflicts Between Humans and Nature:** Western nations say that the excessive consumption of resources, such as energy, land, forests, water, and petroleum, causes the destruction of over half of the forests, making China a country with some of the lowest forest coverage. China is growing increasingly dependent on the world's resources and raw materials. It is now the largest buyer of iron, copper, and petroleum. It is projected that China will reach the US's consumption level in 2031, and will have more houses and cars per capita as well. This will not only hollow out China but the whole world, and cause global environment disaster. These views seem sensational, but they are not fully lies.

**2. Conflicts Among People:** Because of polarization of interests, widening of gaps in wealth allocation, and corruption, at present China is very tense in two aspects: political relations between the people and the CCP and for the political relations between the government and the citizens since the establishment of the new China. China is now experiencing the largest number of mass incidents of unrest.

**3. Conflicts Between China and the World:** China threat, balancing China, and counterweighing China are frequently proposed by many people. The rise of China is still a new thing to the world, and a new subject for the Chinese people, which can only be effectively dealt with in innovative ways. Innovation shall be made not only in science and technology but also politics.

## Creating the Chinese Democracy Better than the American Democracy

The US does not acknowledge that China has a market economy and that China is a democratic country. What China is trying to build is a democratic country and a democratic society with Chinese characteristics. To create a Chinese democracy better than the American democracy, it has to enhance the nation's cohesion, creatively adapt to strategic requirements, and enhance socialism's competitive strength.

We have to eradicate the blind admiration of American democracy. There are all kinds of forms of democracy in the world. American democracy is not the supreme form or the ultimate form of democracy, nor the only form. It is not the benchmark and model of global democracy, nor does it have the right to decide and judge which form of democracy is good or bad. American democracy did not stop Wall Street's greed, America's hegemony in the world, and the US's decline. Chinese democracy has ensured high-speed development and a rapid rise in the past three decades. Of course, Chinese democracy still needs further reform, innovation, and improvement.

Some experts in Western countries have seen that the recognition of Chinese democracy shall not be totally based on the Western countries' traditional ways of thinking. The Chinese political system will be more like a hybrid of traditional culture (especially Confucianism), communism, and Western culture. They believe that the future political system with Chinese characteristics will be an inheritance of China's excellent tradition and a mirroring of the world's various excellent systems combined with the new inventions of the 21st century. The US's political model is only one of those looked at by China in the innovation of political systems. The former chancellor of Germany, Helmut Schmidt, said, "Quite a few people in Western countries believe that China shall take the Western road of democracy. But I think, as the Chinese culture has its particularities, China shall not be measured on the scale of Western countries. European culture is a tree, and Chinese culture is another tree. The West often reads China wrong. China's democratic development must follow its own path, and the Westerner should not think of themselves too highly."

The American writer John Naisbitt said in his book *China's Megatrends* that Western countries have no right to dictate the political party and government of a nation of 1.3 billion people. The West rarely talks about the ruling art of the CCP, but its political achievements have explained everything. Naisbitt also thinks that China is creating a democracy model that is in line with its history and way of thinking, which can be referred to as a vertical democracy. This democracy's main advantage is that the leadership is able to make long-term plans, rather than having to address short-term electoral pressures. The defining characteristics of the Chinese vertical democracy are the combination of the top-down and bottom-up forces. Under such a democratic environment, the country's political operations do not rely on opposite parties or political campaigns and disputes. In this system, the executive level takes in the needs and ideas from bottom up and formulates a political guideline, the masses participate in administration and discussion of state affairs, and there is vertical exchange and unification of ideas from the bottom up. If China establishes a Western horizontal democratic system, much time will be spent in campaigns, and a great deal of candidates will come up with countless solutions to solve the problems of China, finally resulting in confusion, which will affect stability and harmony. China understands that there is no one who can replace the CCP, and the CCP shall not challenge the patience of the people. Western democracy was not built in one generation but gradually matured over several hundred years of development.

Western countries wish that China would implement democracy in the same way it implemented the Great Leap Forward, which would also be the fastest and cheapest way to undermine China. The reform of the Chinese political system shall incorporate the CCP's leadership, the people being masters of the country, and management of state affairs according to law. When China creates a Chinese democracy better than American democracy, the American democracy will lose its ability to contain China politically.

## Creating Wealth Distribution Fairer than the Welfare States

The West created the welfare country, which effectively eases up the fragmentation of society and class conflicts. Some Westerners highlight widening wealth allocation problems in China, concluding that China is more capitalistic than the US. To build a harmonious society, China needs to create a wealth distribution system to follow the creation of wealth production and growth.

Some foreign and domestic experts predict that China's current economic growth model is not sustainable in the long run. China must adjust the overheated liberal model to a more harmonious, traditional, balanced direction that focuses on social security. China has turned from a highly equal society to one of the most imbalanced countries in the world with the largest wealth gap of any nation. This is a very serious problem and should be a priority. The differences between the coastal and inland areas, the rural and urban areas, and the formal and nonformal are creating increasingly serious social tensions, contradictions, and conflicts. They have become an important factor undermining social stability and negating reform and opening up. The measures taken presently have very little effect. The government has made excessive investments in construction to the degree that it cannot finance a new social security plan. Education and medical access for the general public are seriously lacking. The government can now only shoulder 16% of medical expenditures, a figure that is 44% in the US and 70% in Europe. Most people have no medical insurance and a low sense of security.

The Livelihood Project is a very important foundation for the rise and rejuvenation of China. It focuses on the health and well-being of the general populace. China must quickly improve its weak links in the Livelihood Project during its rapid development, and consolidate general welfare, the cornerstone that stabilizes society. The economic aggregate of China has reached the world's forefront, but a number of its welfare indicators still lag behind global averages. According to some foreign and domestic institutions' assessments, at present, the human development index of China ranks No. 81, remaining in the development stage of a moderately developing society; its environmental sustainability ranks No. 129; its health-care level ranks No. 144, and its medical equity ranks fourth from the bottom; industrial production safety ranks significantly lower than that of developed countries. The largest bottleneck of the development of China is the livelihood plight at the grass-roots level. Due to lagging welfare levels, some of the general population live with anxiety and uncertainty about life. If the difficulties involving basic bottom-line and basic livelihood security can not be effectively solved in the long run, they will certainly impact the rise of China.

President Hu Jintao pointed out in the 17th CPC National Congress in 2007 that the deeper the reform of income distribution system, the greater the increase in the income of rural and urban residents so all our people will enjoy their rights to education, employment, medical and old-age care, and housing, and build a harmonious society. The Chinese government proposes to basically eliminate absolute poverty and establish a social security system that covers the urban and rural residents by 2020. The social security system that covers one-fifth of the world's population will be the largest system in the world. China will become the largest welfare nation in the world. The new health-care reform will ensure that the medical insurance system covers 90% of the population, and the government will bear a large part of the medical expenses of the people by 2011.

## Creating Long-Term Stability and Integrity

The leaders of the governing party at all levels have two hands, one of which serves the people, while the other may extort bribes and seek personal gains. The construction of a clean government is a worldwide problem. Since reform and opening up, China has made great achievements in the fight against corruption, but is still facing serious situations. According to a 2010 report by the watchdog group Transparency International, New Zealand, Denmark, Sweden, and Singapore rank as the least corrupt governments, while China scored a 3.6, lower than the passing score of 5.

Western countries produce a traditional view popular in the world that says only multiparty systems can effectively prevent corruption, and the one-party state is a source of corruption. Is the one-party state bound to give birth to a privileged class? Is it true that the party that is in office for the longterm cannot prevent its own corruption? Hu Angang once conducted a survey, from the land reform to the death of Mao Zedong (1950–1976), when some 60 monumental political activities unfolded in China. Mao Zedong tried to restrain those plundering hands through constant and periodical political purges. These corruption-fighting campaigns failed to solved the issue of corruption in the party, and the

present plundering within the party and the government organizations are on an even larger scale. China must find a path for the construction of a clean government with Chinese
characteristics, to build a clean state, and clean society with Chinese characteristics. The
rich and powerful China must be a clean China.

A clean government with Chinese characteristics must be a system that sticks to the
guidelines of a multiparty cooperative party system under the leadership of the Chinese
Communist Party and can effectively eliminate corruption. This requires creation. How
can China build a clean government system with Chinese characteristics? This is a problem
the Chinese government is trying to find a solution for. If the CCP cannot fundamentally
eradicate corruption in the long term, its ruling position will be a challenge, and the multiparty system will become a political option. The fight against corruption shall be a priority
in the strict disciplining of the party, and the construction of a clean government shall be a
priority in the ruling of the country according to the law.

## The US Should Not Hold Any Illusions About China.

In the duel of the century between China and the US, neither party shall have any
illusion about each other, nor make the error of political immaturity. The British scholar
Martin Jacques argues that Western countries should expect the violent change of Soviet
Union and Eastern Europe to happen in China. This is a strategic illusion Western countries
will not give up easily. In fact, this is not the only strategic illusion of the Western countries
about China. The strategic intelligence disclosed by the peaceful rise of China to the US is
that it should not hold the following illusions about China.

1. The US cannot change China. It should not hold the strategic illusion that it can implement political revolution or political transplant in China. China would not copy the US's
political system, which would not work in China. It should not have any illusion on this
point.

2. The US cannot expect to create a crisis on the Taiwan Strait. China will not shrink back
from the idea of taking back Taiwan. The US should not gamble its own fate on the Taiwan
independence issue.

3. The US cannot expect China to be the second collapse of the former Soviet Union. The
Chinese Communist Party will have a long political life and socialism with Chinese characteristics is filled with vitality, vigor, and competitiveness.

## *Three American Political Laws That Will Not Work in China*

For a long time, the US applied three American political laws to conduct the political containment of China. These laws are deliberately used in attempts to overthrow the CCP:

**American political law 1:** A one-party system is the source of corruption, and only multi-party competition can cure corruption. This has led a few Chinese policy makers to believe in multiparty competition, thinking that elections can control corruption.

**American political law 2:** The source of Soviet Union's collapse was its one-party system. As China sticks to the same system, it will certainly follow suit.

**American political law 3:** Only a country that abolishes the one-party system and carries out multiparty competition is a democratic country. To become a democratic country, China must carry out "great democracy" in the same way China carried out the Great Leap Forward campaign, as per the US's requirements, or China will be considered a non-democratic country, totalitarian state, and autarchy.

The facts and achievements in the CCP's long-term ruling will dispel these American political laws set by the US, especially for China. Jacques said that China is successfully re-alizing rapid economic development, and in the next 20 years, the CCP will still be China's domestic political system, but by that time, the CCP will not be what it is now, and the pol-icies it implements will not completely conform to the classic theory of Marxism-Leninism. China is a continental state. Comprehensively speaking, it has more advantages than the US and India in terms of area and population. The multiparty democratic system preached about by Western countries has never really worked properly or taken root in such a large area. China will realize democracy in its own way. China's political system is very unique. The government rarely shares the power with other forces and always maintains concen-trated power. Its policy rarely has rigidity, and when facing crises and dramatic changes, it can quickly adjust the development direction. The political system of China has excellent historical continuity and excellent innovative ability. Since 1949, while continuing with the political tradition, China has experienced two major self-transformations: the first was the birth of the new country created by the CCP and led by Mao Zedong; after the reform and opening up, and when China experienced a new birth and rejuvenation. In the future, the heavy burden of reform will still be shouldered by the CCP. A long time from now, China will still be ruled by the CCP, and China will be different from the Soviet Union on the basis of continuous innovation of traditional culture. No second collapse will happen in China.

# NOTES

**Foreword**

1.   Paul Starobin, "After America: Chinese Century," *National Journal* (2009).

**Chapter 1: China's Dream for a Century**

1.   Mao Zedong, "In Commemoration of Dr. Sun Yat-sen" (Nov. 21, 1956), in *Dr. Sun Yat-sen: Commemoration Articles and Speeches* (Beijing: Foreign Language Press, 1957).

2.   Mao Zedong, "Talk at an Enlarged Working Conference Convened by the Central Committee of the Communist Party of China" (Jan. 30 1962), *Peking Review*, no. 27, July 7, 1978.

3.   Mao Zedong, "China Will Take a Great Leap Forward" (Dec. 13, 1964), *Peking Review*, no. 52, December 1977.

4.   Deng Xiaoping, "Respect Knowledge, Respect Trained Personnel" (May 24, 1977), in *Selected Works of Deng Xiaoping*, vol. 3 (Beijing: Foreign Language Press, 1994).

5.   Deng Xiaoping, "We Shall Expand Political Democracy and Carry Out Economic Reform" (April 15, 1985), in *Selected Works of Deng Xiaoping*, vol. 3 (Beijing: Foreign Language Press, 1994).

6.   Deng Xiaoping, "Two Kinds of Comments About China's Reform" (Aug. 21, 1985), in *Selected Works of Deng Xiaoping*, vol. 3 (Beijing: Foreign Language Press, 1994).

7.   Deng Xiaoping, "Revitalizing the Chinese People" (April 7, 1990), *Selected Works of Deng Xiaoping*, vol. 3 (Beijing: Foreign Language Press, 1994).

8.   Ibid.

9.   Donald H. Straszheim, "China Rising," *World Policy Journal* 25, no. 3 (2008): 157.

10.  Sun Yat-sen and L. T. Chen, *San Min Zhu Yi: The Three Principles of the People* (Chung king: Ministry of Information of the Republic of China, 1943), p. 110.

## Chapter 2: The Fight for the Century

1.   Henry Kissinger, *Diplomacy* (New York: Simon & Schuster, 1994), p. 1.

2.   George Modelski, *Long Cycles in World Politics* (Seattle: University of Washington Press, 1987).

3.   Walter LaFeber, *The Cambridge History of American Foreign*, vol. 2 (Cambridge: Cambridge University Press, 1993), p. 237.

4.   Stephen G. Brooks and William C. Wohlforth, "American Primacy in Perspective," *Foreign Affairs* 81, no. 4 (2002): 24–25.

5.   George Kennan, "The Long Telegram," Feb. 22, 1946.

## Chapter 3: The Chinese Century

1.   Zalmay Khalilzad, "From Containment to Global Leadership: America and the World After the Cold War," RAND Corporation, 1995.

2.   Samuel T. Huntington, "The Lonely Superpower," *Foreign Affairs* 78, no. 2 (1999).

3.   Warren I. Cohen, *The Cambridge History of American Foreign Relations*, vol. 4 (Cambridge: Cambridge University Press, 2008).

4.   Yu Fengzhi, *Wo yu Hanqing de yi sheng: Zhang Xueliang jie fa fu ren Zhang Yu Fengzhi hui yi lu* (The memoirs of Mrs. Feng Tze Chang, Di 1 ban. ed.) (Beijing Shi: Tuan jie chu ban she, 2007).

## Chapter 4: Building a Benevolent China

1.   Matteo Ricci, Nicolas Trigault, Horace Cardon, Jean Julliéron, and Jacques de Fornazeris, *De Christiana expeditione apud Sinas suscepta ab Societate Iesu. Editio recens ab eodem auctore multis in locis aucta & recognita,* ed. Lugduni (Lyon: Sumptibus Horatii Cardon, 1616).

2.   Lester Thurow, *The Zero-Sum Solution* (New York: Simon & Schuster, 1985), p. 67; "Is America a Global Power in Decline?" *Boston Globe*, March 20, 1988.

3.   Zbigniew Brzezinski, *Second Chance: Three Presidents and the Crisis of American Superpower* (New York: Basic Books, 2007).

4.   Mao Zedong, "Talk at an Enlarged Working Conference Convened by the Central

Committee of the Communist Party of China" (Jan. 30 1962), *Peking Review*, no. 27, July 7, 1978.

5.   Deng Xiaoping, "Keeping to Socialism and the Policy of Peace" (April 4, 1986), *Selected Works of Deng Xiaoping*, vol. 3 (Beijing: Foreign Language Press, 1994).

6.   Sun Yat-sen and L. T. Chen, *San Min Zhu Yi: The Three Principles of the People* (Chung king: Ministry of Information of the Republic of China, 1943), p. 33.

7.   Deng Xiaoping, "Four Modernizations, Do Not Seek Hegemony" (April 4, 1986), *Selected Works of Deng Xiaoping*, vol. 3 (Beijing: Foreign Language Press, 1994).

**Chapter 5: A Great Strategy Requires Great Thinking**

1.   Alexis de Tocqueville, *De la démocratie en Amérique*, 17th ed. (Paris: C. Lévy, 1888).

**Chapter 6: Learning from Mistakes Made Abroad**

1.   Nicholas John Spykman, *America's Strategy in World Politics: The United States and the Balance of Power* (New York: Harcourt, Brace, 1942).

2.   Ross H. Munro, "Awakening Dragon: The Real Danger in Asia Is Coming from China," *Policy Review* 62 (1992).

3.   Dmitrii Mikheev, *The Rise and Fall of Gorbachev* (Indianapolis: Hudson Institute, 1992).

4.   Mao Zedong, "'Friendship' or Aggression?" (Aug. 30, 1949).

5.   Thomas P. M. Barnett, *The Pentagon's New Map: War and Peace in the Twenty-First Century* (New York: G. P. Putnam's Sons, 2004), pp. 100-101.

6.   Ibid., p. 59.

# INDEX

## A

## B

Russell, Bertrand, 86
Russian Dream, 140

# S
safety
    and absolute security, 216
    China's security and, 88–89
    and power, 206–207
    as strategic goal, 25
Santayana, George, 161
Schlesinger, Arthur, Jr., 126, 182
Schmidt, Helmut, 237
*Second Chance: Three Presidents and the Crisis of American Superpower* (Brzezinski), 105
*Seven Military Classics*, 200
Shirong, Qi, 154
Sima Xiangru, 231
Singapore model, 74–75
*Sinking of Japan* (film), 229
Sino-US relations
    and China's rise, 174, 176
    Cold War, competition and, 50–52, 176–177
    and deterrence of war, 212
    establishment of Sino-US alliance, 186–188
    and fantasies of America, 140
    readjusting, 35–43
    US imperialism and, 179–181
slavery
    Atlantic slave trade, 64–65, 92
    in the US, 191–193
Social Darwinism, 146
socialism, 8–9, 56, 74–75, 143–144, 168, 212, 228, 233
"Sources of Soviet Conduct, The" (Kennan), 226
Soviet Union
    cadres, 164, 234
    in champion nations conflicts, and containment, 37–38, 48
    in Cold War, 157–170, 212–213, 215
    as Cold War enemy, 182, 184–185, 189–190
    and Cold War mentality, 48, 49
    collapse of, 189–190